VEGAN WITCHCRAFT

Vegan Witchcraft is the first book to blend theories of animal rights, feminism, and modern witchcraft in pursuit of total liberation.

Perhaps the most foundational of all ethics in modern witchcraft is the creed "Do no harm." Despite this, multispecies suffering persists in nonvegan witchcraft. *Vegan Witchcraft* examines this intriguing conflict, unpacking the role of Nonhuman Animals in modern witchcraft from a vegan feminist perspective to illuminate inequalities that persist in alternative spiritual practices in the West. Recognizing Nonhuman Animals as comrades instead of consumables, vegan witchcraft confronts the harm imposed on nature, humans, and other animals, and identifies witchery as a powerful conduit for social change that draws its energy from plant-based foods, multispecies solidarity, and feminine power. The book critically analyzes popular witchcraft pathways in Britain and America to interrogate the many ways in which Nonhuman Animals are overlooked, objectified, or exploited, highlighting theological inconsistencies and missed opportunities that might be overcome to create a stronger practice for women and their communities. It reimagines witchcraft practice and lore to manifest justice and compassion for fellow humans, Nonhuman Animals, and nature. Veganism is advanced as a magical practice of self-care, community responsibility, conscious consumption, societal transformation, and environmental protection. The book calls for the redirection of the modern witch's path toward a just world and away from the systematic symbolic and material exploitation of Nonhuman Animals that permeates witchcraft today.

This book will be essential reading for those interested in critical animal studies, animal rights, ecofeminism, vegan religious studies, environmental philosophy, and witchcraft.

Corey Lee Wrenn is Senior Lecturer of Sociology in the School of Social Sciences at the University of Kent, UK, and co-director of the Centre for the Study of Social and Political Movements. She is the co-founder of the International Association of Vegan Sociologists, a member of The Vegan Society's Research Advisory Committee, and the founder of the Vegan Feminist Network, an academic-activist project engaging intersectional social justice praxis. She is the author of *A Rational Approach to Animal Rights: Extensions in Abolitionist Theory* (2016), *Piecemeal Protest: Animal Rights in the Age of Nonprofits* (2019), and *Animals in Irish Society* (2021).

ROUTLEDGE STUDIES IN ANIMALS, SOCIETY AND THE ENVIRONMENT

Vegan Witchcraft
Contemporary Magical Practice and Multispecies Social Change
Corey Lee Wrenn

For more information about this series, please visit: www.routledge.com/Routledge-Studies-in-Animals-Society-and-the-Environment/book-series/RSASE

VEGAN WITCHCRAFT

Contemporary Magical Practice and Multispecies Social Change

Corey Lee Wrenn

Routledge
Taylor & Francis Group
LONDON AND NEW YORK

earthscan
from Routledge

Designed cover image: Getty Images

First published 2026
by Routledge
4 Park Square, Milton Park, Abingdon, Oxon OX14 4RN

and by Routledge
605 Third Avenue, New York, NY 10158

Routledge is an imprint of the Taylor & Francis Group, an informa business

© 2026 Corey Lee Wrenn

British Library Cataloguing-in-Publication Data
A catalogue record for this book is available from the British Library

ISBN: 978-1-032-64974-0 (hbk)
ISBN: 978-1-032-64971-9 (pbk)
ISBN: 978-1-032-64980-1 (ebk)

DOI: 10.4324/9781032649801

Typeset in Sabon
by Taylor & Francis Books

To all the magical animals who have shared my life and all those still waiting for liberation.

CONTENTS

Preface   *viii*
Acknowledgments   *xvi*

1   Introduction to Vegan Witchcraft   1

2   Animal Familiars   28

3   Green Witchcraft   59

4   Kitchen Witchery   95

5   Sabbats and Speciesism   123

6   Spellwork for a Vegan World   151

7   Conclusion   180

Further Reading   *200*
Index   *201*

PREFACE

Corey Lee Wrenn

I am a Vegan Witch: Author Reflexivity Statement

Upon publication of this book, I will effectively have proclaimed myself to be a witch, an admission that would have, only a few decades ago, rendered me on the wrong end of the law or at the very least unemployable. But witchcraft in the 21st century is now comfortably part of pop culture. As I more openly embraced my interest in witchcraft in my adulthood, I noted that quite a few folks around me were doing the same. And not just friends. The more I discussed my research for this book, the more *vegan scholars* in my academic circle excitedly shared with me their own pagan, Wiccan, and witchy leanings. Maybe I shouldn't be surprised. The work we do in this field is not easy; it can be psychologically devastating and many of us suffer from or must actively work to resist anxiety, depression, or post-traumatic stress disorder as a result. Compounding this, there is considerable stigma associated with veganism and Nonhuman Animal rights activism. For the distress this can cause, there is very little support from our nonvegan social networks or even from the vegan movement itself, with its masculinized emphasis on rationality and the suppression of emotion. Working witchcraft, I think, can be empowering and sustaining. It grounds us by drawing attention to our inner world as well as the natural world around us. Merging a rational approach to advocacy with a more emotional, intuitive compassion for other animals and the wider environment can be important for preventing burnout but also for finding some joy in a world that is so saturated in sorrow.

As I will cover in this book, ecofeminism has been arguing this case since before I was born. Yet, raised an atheist and having trained as a scientist, ecofeminism's spiritual teachings, as it were, did not especially resonate with me in the way witchcraft has. I wonder if it could do with some repackaging as a new generation of activists strive to merge mind, body, and universe in a new frontier of activism increasingly removed from the countercultural wave of the late 20th century that inspired the ecofeminists. Many vegans, whether secular or spiritual, still long for these deeper, more emotional, caring connections with nature, other animals, and their own selves. But culture has changed, as have the frameworks that today's vegans use to organize and enact their advocacy and self-care. I subsequently introduce vegan witchcraft as an ecologically-minded spiritual practice of vegan feminism that sees magic in nature and multispecies possibilities. It is a social movement strategy of self-empowerment and self-care, but also a measure of solidarity with marginalized humans and more-than-humans. It is a theory that finds the shared persecution of marginalized groups, women, and other animals, in particular, bound by notions of what is considered natural, civilized, good, and sacred. Finally, it is a critique of anthropocentric witchcraft. This book argues that witchcraft holds considerable relevance for current social justice movements—environmentalism and feminism, in particular—though its commitment to anti-speciesism wavers considerably.

Witchcraft today has moved quite dramatically to the forefront of inclusive, nature-based spiritual practice since its popularity began to coalesce in the 1970s. By the turn of the 21st century, it was suddenly socially permissible, perhaps even cool, to be a witch. I can be included in the phenomenon of "teenage witch" that was popularized with the help of positive representations in popular media in the millennial years (Berger and Ezzy 2007). At the age of 13, I discovered Fleetwood Mac, spinning my parents' vinyl records in my room late into the night. I became (and still am) a massive fan of Stevie Nicks. *The Craft* (Fleming 1996), which was released on VHS that same year, mesmerized me. *Sabrina the Teenage Witch* (Hart 1996–2003) had just launched in 1996, making its weekly run on Friday primetime television. It was not long before my friends and I were collecting candles and swapping spell books. At the same time, I was stepping into my power as a young woman and finding my determination to use that power in service of other animals. At the age of 13, I also became a vegetarian. I have been asked many times in interviews what brought me to a career in vegan studies; what predisposed me to waking up to these realities. I have always thought it relevant that, as a child, our family owned only two child-friendly VHS tapes, *Honey I Shrunk the Kids* (Johnston 1989) and *Charlotte's Web* (Nichols and Takamoto 1973), both of which lend personhood to objectified, invisibilized animals and invite compassionate resistance to violence. Feminist Mary Daly[1] (1978) picks up on the undertones of goddess creationism and protectionism in the archetype of the spider that Charlotte represents, a story that she advises "deserves the serious attention of Spinsters" (397). Any remaining innocence to the realities of slaughter and butchering would come to an end following my exposure to graphic imagery on a PBS cooking show, when I finally acknowledged that "meat" derived from unconsenting sentient beings. As the internet was still inaccessible to me in the mid-1990s, I wrote to People for the Ethical Treatment of Animals (PETA), receiving literature on anti-speciesism and veganism in return. I knew then that I had to go vegan, but, living in a very low-income household in Appalachia, it did not seem practical. Instead, I decided to go vegan as soon as I was able to live independently as a university student, which I did on my first day on campus at Virginia Tech, mid-August 2001. Although I may not have recognized it at the time, all of these countercultural, rebellious identities—vegan, feminist, witch—emerged concurrently, entangled together in fundamental values of compassion, equality, and empowerment.

These personal identities matter because they inform the work I do. Feminist methodology encourages scholars to share, as appropriate, their biography and any political and personal alignments because, whether the scientific community wishes to admit it or not, everyone's research is shaped by who they are, what they believe in, what interests them, and what motivates them. I am incredibly privileged to identify as a professional vegan because it not only encapsulates my identity, beliefs, interests, and motivations, but it also pays the bills. I have been publishing on the politics of veganism as a social movement and a subculture throughout my career, with a particular interest in the role of identity politics in shaping campaigns, strategies, and efficacy. I currently teach and research in social movements, environmental politics, and Critical Animal Studies at the University of Kent in Canterbury, England. Moving to England from the United States has not only been an incredible boon to my career as a vegan, but England's relative esteem for paganism has also revitalized my interest in witchcraft. It is significantly easier to practice both veganism and witchcraft in the British Isles. For me, witchcraft embodies much of what draws me to my academic practice—it is ecofeminist, it encourages each of us to take responsibility for ourselves and others, it embeds within us the possibility of both personal and societal change, and it reminds us to be skeptical of established institutions that have historically controlled the many for the benefit of a few. My own interpretation of witchcraft has always been informed by my compassion for Nonhuman Animals and a sense of responsibility for the natural world. It also aligns with my deeply rooted feminist identity. As an atheist and a sociologist specializing in the politics of social movements, however, my personal and professional interest in veganism and witchcraft are secular and solution oriented. I see strategic value in acknowledging the role of empathy, nature, and feminism in achieving lasting social change. In particular, I am drawn to vegan feminist theory as most useful for examining the gendered nature of speciesism and environmental destruction and the intersections of oppression experienced by marginalized human and nonhuman groups.

Methodology

Vegan Witchcraft develops a nature-oriented, intersectional, explicitly feminist, and explicitly anti-speciesist secular *or* spiritual theory of total liberation for the benefit of all life on Earth. To do so, it relies upon a critical literature review of contemporary publications on the modern practice of witchcraft. This analysis is primarily based on books. As I have examined elsewhere (Wrenn 2022), writings are important conduits for the making and sharing of cultural movements, particularly those that are associated with deviant subcultures with dispersed populations. Clifton's (2006) analysis of American Wicca and paganism has observed the continued importance of books for spreading witchcraft, even surpassing internet resources and peer influence. "Witchcraft is bookish," they comment, with more books available per practitioner than other new religious movements (Clifton 2006: 121). A tangible book in hand, furthermore, helps connect the practitioner to a wider collective. The secrecy with which witchcraft has tended to operate also means that the written word is a primary introduction for practitioners (McColman 2002). Putting histories, interests, values, goals, and aims into writing helps make it "real," so to speak. For practices like witchcraft which rely on the transmission of wisdom from elders and ancestors in a society that has greatly marginalized or even penalized alternative ways of knowing, thinking, and worshipping, books are central to the manufacture and maintenance of tradition. This creative aspect is all the more important for cultural movements that are in a state of emergence or transition, as is the case for witchcraft, which was moving from the shadowy world of the occult into mainstream new age spirituality in mid-20th century. It is thought that the proliferation of these books on witchcraft has been at least partly responsible for the growth of witchcraft (McColman 2002). Of course, there is also something romantic and enticing about physically leafing through a book on the mysteries of magic, and books play an important role in the witch community as part of daily study and practice. Many witches even maintain their own, known as a "book of shadows." These are grimoires that include their personally tailored and curated, often handwritten, collection of knowledge, lore, and rituals. Bookstores, too, speak to the importance of the written word in witchcraft. London's Atlantis Bookshop has served as more than a place to acquire hard to find books on witchcraft; it also offers a communal space for practitioners to meet, practice, and find community in the years before witchcraft was legalized.

As witchcraft as a contemporary practice grew in popularity, so did the availability of books for the practitioner. Entire publishing houses have emerged to volley this subfield, meaning that a comprehensive analysis of witchcraft books could not be possible. Instead, my sampling technique involves a blend of convenience and purposiveness. First, I examined books (primarily academic on historical interpretations of witchcraft) from my university library. These books were primarily academic and historical, with only Scott Cunningham's (1995) *Wicca* available in the collection as a representative of the type of books used by actual practitioners, offering pagan thealogy, ritual guidelines, and crafting suggestions. Cunningham (who passed in 1993) is considered one of the most influential leaders in modern witchcraft, publishing many books that defined, introduced, and developed the practice. The end matter of *Wicca* contains a very useful annotated bibliography that I used to identify seminal publications. I also consulted Carl McColman's (2002) *The Well-Read Witch: Essential Books for Your Magickal Library*, an annotated bibliography that highlights fundamental as well as topical texts. There was considerable overlap between Cunningham and Colman with regard to "required reading"[2] in modern witchcraft, but Colman's book having been published a decade after Cunningham's offered some newer texts and also provided quite a few references in kitchen witchcraft that I pursued. *The Well-Read Witch* was also useful in documenting the historical progression of witchcraft literature and its impact on both the community and wider public. I procured books identified through Cunningham and Colman's bibliographies, where available, through my library's document delivery service. Some older, out of print publications, could be found digitally archived online. A handful of books central to this book's theme were not available through my university's library, document delivery, or online archive. I purchased some books myself using online bookstores and occult bookshops in Kent or London (including the famous Atlantis Bookshop). Books sampled in this study were for two purposes: to identify the key values of contemporary witchcraft and to identify the main ways that Nonhuman Animals feature (or could feature) in that witchcraft.

Second, I intentionally sought contemporary witchcraft books that prominently featured Nonhuman Animals, books that were not mentioned by the bibliographies discussed above. Many of these were impossible to source through my university's document delivery service as they were primarily published by non-academic metaphysical and occult publishing houses. This necessitated purchasing these myself for my personal collection. Due to my limited funding and limited shelf space, I could only afford to select books that appeared to be generally relevant. Books that discuss a variety of Nonhuman Animals as familiars or offer more generalized theory about familiars, for instance, were chosen over very specialized books (quite a few publications explore cat and owl magic, for instance). Lastly, I revisited my existing collection of books on witchcraft that I had acquired over the years based on personal interest. While not all were relevant to veganism and Nonhuman Animal welfare, quite a few did include some discussion of plant magic, power animals, nonhuman folklore, animal-based rituals and celebrations, spellwork for Nonhuman Animals, implicit speciesism, and anti-speciesism in recommendations for tools, ingredients, and recipes. Indeed, these themes represent the primary ways that Nonhuman Animals feature in contemporary witchcraft, not only in my personal collection, but in most witchcraft books.

There are limitations to this methodology that warrant mention. First, a convenience and purposive qualitative content analysis will be subject to bias— that is, the sample relies on the researcher's interpretation of what should be relevant and the resources available to them. To this point, several key texts that have been identified as being influential in shaping modern witchcraft were out of print and difficult to source, including one of the first anthropological studies of modern witches, *Witches U.S.A.* (Roberts 1971). I did find significant saturation in my sample, however, with many researchers repeating similar themes with regard to human relationships with other animals such that I am confident this analysis is reasonably representative. Second, although books are particularly popular in the witchcraft community, there are other mediums that might also have been analyzed. Witchcraft communities of the 20th century also produced and consumed a wide variety of periodicals and zines. The difficulty of locating some of these materials prohibited my exploration of them, as did the sheer magnitude of publications. However, I suspect the discourse sampled herein is relatively generalizable. For instance, a precursory browse through *Woman-Spirit*, [3] the first feminist spirituality periodical in the United States, makes only occasional mention of Nonhuman Animals, while veganism, vegetarianism, and liberatory anti-speciesism are only *very* sparsely mentioned. Likewise, *Reclaiming Quarterly* (1997–2011), the witchcraft magazine spearheaded by a leading founder of American Wicca, Starhawk, showed characteristic engagement with social justice politics, but no significant mention of Nonhuman Animal rights, veganism, or solidarity with other animals (indeed, these topics primarily surfaced only in the "Kitchen Witch" column with regard to the use of animal-based ingredients and the occasional plant-based substitution). Its predecessor, the *Reclaiming Newsletter*, consisted primarily of workshop announcements and classified ads for the Bay area witchcraft community, which was of little use to this study.

There is truly an array of research opportunities. While many of these are potentially fruitful, they lie beyond the scope of this book. Today's digital mediascape complicates the creation of a representative sample as well. Social media platforms such as YouTube, Instagram, and TikTok are, as of this writing, highly influential in spreading trends and shaping witch culture. Social media is much more difficult to analyze systematically but would be a worthy endeavor for a more nuanced understanding of species politics in witchcraft. There are other cultural artefacts that might be researched, such as tarot cards and oracle cards. These cards are rather ubiquitous in popular witchcraft (many books cited herein include discussions of how to use and interpret them). Tarot and oracle cards utilize complex symbolic imagery for the purposes of meditation, intention-setting, decision-making, and divination. Nonhuman Animals are regularly featured in decks. In fact, some decks are based completely on Nonhuman Animal imagery. To overcome the bias of researcher interpretation, furthermore, interviews with actual practitioners would be informative, as would participant or non-participant observation of witches' moots, sabbats, and other gatherings. Lastly, I had hoped to visit the Museum of Witchcraft and Magic, which houses archives and collections relating to both traditional and modern, including a display on animality. Unfortunately, it is located in a remote area of Cornwall that proved too difficult to access.

Final Considerations

Language in this study abides by standard editorial rules in Critical Animal Studies. As vegan sociologist Hanh Nguyen (2019) has examined, everyday language tends to strip other-than-human animals of their personhood, agency, and power. As a vegan sociologist myself, I take seriously the role language plays in upholding systems of violence and actively protest them in my writing. I have placed euphemistic terms, such as "meat" and "hunting" in quotation marks to denote them as contested and to flag their ability to normalize human violence against other animals. I also alter some terms to resist human domination, respect nonhuman autonomy, and clarify origin or ownership. For instance, I will refer to "milk" as *cows'* milk and "honey" instead as *bees'* honey. I avoid using the term "animals" on its own as doing so can uphold the human-nonhuman binary, falsely depicting humans as something other than animal. Instead, I may refer to them as "other animals" or Nonhuman Animals. Because these phrases still grammatically center the human, I intentionally capitalize Nonhuman Animals to delineate them as an oppressed group and, hopefully, offer some element of dignity. This editorial leeway is common practice in Critical Animal Studies, but witchcraft, too, sees the manipulation of language as vital for the creation of a just society. Feminist witch Kristen Sollée (2017), for instance, encourages the community to acknowledge the importance of language for normalizing violence and oppression. Reclaiming is paramount, as "reappropriating language with a dedicated ethic can create change" (85). Daly, too, emphasizes the power of language, even composing a new dictionary for witches, what she calls a "wickedary," for "freeing words from the cages and prisons of patriarchal patterns" (1987: 1).

Readers may also have questions about the implications of this research. Do you have to be vegan to read this book or go vegan after reading it? Although the feminist in me deeply desires that everyone who is in a position to do so (which is most of us) would go vegan out of respect for Nonhuman Animals and the Earth that we all call home, the scientist and the witch in me brings with it some temperance. No one will go vegan and stay vegan because they are simply told or "made" to. The social science on vegan transitioning is quite complex; most people go vegan and remain so because they are within a supportive social network or they enjoy structural incentives (such as the availability of whole foods, fruits, vegetables, and occasional treats or convenience items in grocery stores and restaurants) (Wrenn 2016). For that matter, one of the more fundamental aspects of witchcraft is to avoid the active manipulation of others.

However, I draw a distinction between the selfish manipulation of others and the selfless encouragement of others to live in line with their ethical convictions. I also draw a distinction between selfish manipulation and a genuine, selfless plea for others to pay attention to those suffering out of sight in the margins. Free will should be protected, but that freedom must be checked when it impedes upon the freedom of someone else. As humans, we have (for the most part) the privilege of choosing what we eat and wear, but the Nonhuman Animals who suffer and die to create nonvegan consumables have no choice in that matter. Even ethically-minded magical workings that avoid the manipulation of others in their intention will still involve manipulation if they use Nonhuman

Animals as ingredients, tools, or conduits. Vegan witchcraft encourages equality in theory *and* in practice, bringing other animals to mind in all our interactions. It is my genuine intention that readers consider this new theory of vegan witchcraft with an open mind and critically examine the myths, stories, and romances we have been taught by thousands of years of patriarchal rule and anthropocentric conditioning. We liberate other animals when we liberate our own selves from institutions and ideologies of domination.

So mote it be.

Notes

1 Some of Daly's radical feminist theory does not age well, offering offensive and inaccurate claims about the transsexual and transgender community, specifically those who have transitioned from male to female.
2 Included in "Part One: Discovering Wicca" (Colman 2002: 43–78).
3 Full texts are available on JSTOR.

References

Berger, H. and D. Ezzy. 2007. *Teenage Witches*. New Brunswick: Rutgers University Press.

Clifton, C. 2006. *Her Hidden Children*. Lanham: AltaMira Press.

Cunningham, S. 1995. *Wicca*. St. Paul: Llewellyn.

Daly, M. 1978. *Gyn/Ecology*. London: The Women's Press.

Daly, M. 1987. *Webster's First New Intergalactic Wickedary of the English Language*. London: The Women's Press.

Fleming, A. 1996. *The Craft*. Columbia Pictures.

Hart, P. 1996–2003. *Sabrina the Teenage Witch*. ABC.

Johnston, J. 1989. *Honey I Shrunk the Kids*. The Walt Disney Company.

McColman, C. 2002. *The Well-Read Witch*. Franklin Lakes: New Page Books.

Nguyen, H. 2019. *Tongue Tied*. New York: Lantern Books.

Nichols, C.A. and I. Takamoto. 1973. *Charlotte's Web*. Paramount Pictures.

Roberts, S. 1971. *Witches U.S.A.* New York: Dell.

Sollée, K. 2017. *Witches, Sluts, Feminists*. Berkeley: ThreeL Media.

Wrenn, C. 2016. *A Rational Approach to Animal Rights*. London: Palgrave.

Wrenn, C. 2022. "Society Writings." pp. 333–348, in *The Edinburgh Companion to Vegan Studies*, L. Wright and E. Quinn (Eds.). Edinburgh: Edinburgh University Press.

ACKNOWLEDGMENTS

This book owes much to the research contributions of several friends and colleagues. Carol Adams graciously provided some insight into feminist spirituality from the 1970s, including some materials from her personal archives. My divisional librarian Emma Mires-Richards at the University of Kent went above and beyond to help me source some of the more obscure and older texts analyzed in this book. My dear friend and expert linguist Sam Thomas contributed some etymological insight that I found helpful. I'm also grateful to fellow witch and late-night debater Ciarán Barata-Hynes for posting me a number of books from the more esoteric side of magical philosophy. A special thanks also to the fellow vegan witches who have shared many chats with me on the topics raised in this book. As always, I must thank my nonhuman cohabitators, Mishka my little disabled, deaf, and intersex dog rescued from Bulgaria and my sweet as can be cat of the house, Keeley Jr. Both kept me company as I poured through stack after stack of books in researching for this project.

Finally, I would also like to acknowledge all those who have come before me to make it possible to even write on the radical ideas of feminism, witchcraft, and veganism. I am grateful for their perseverance in the face of extreme repression.

1

INTRODUCTION TO VEGAN WITCHCRAFT

Introduction

Readers might be surprised by this book's co-mingling of veganism and witch-craft—what could they possibly have in common? Veganism is a political resistance to speciesism (institutionalized discrimination based on species) that entails eating plant-based foods and eschewing animal exploitation. Witchcraft, by contrast, is a pagan practice, a spirituality, and sometimes a religion that links individuals and communities to the rhythms of nature for purposes of healing, empowerment, and, for some, metaphysical influence. Witchcraft escapes consensus in definition given its prioritization of individualism, crea-tivity, and flexibility (Stevens 2024), but, for the purposes of this book, will be understood as "a mystery religion, based on ritual, on consciously structured collective experiences that allow us to encounter the immeasurable" (Starhawk 1987: 7). The stereotypical Broom Hilda is most often associated with stewing cauldrons of toads and newts, not chickpeas and tofu. Witches are thought to live in spooky shacks in the woods with hopes of roasting tasty little children, not advocating for social justice. Witchcraft as it is actually theorized and practiced in real life, however, is indeed very much aligned with plants and peace. As leading American feminist witch Starhawk explains, the "ultimate interest" of making magic should be "restoring value to our own lives and to the community of beings—human, plant, and animal—that share life with us" (1997: 219). Indeed, many modern-day witches agree with this sentiment, prioritizing a connection to nature and other animals and interpreting this connection as encouraging responsibility for restoring what has been lost fol-lowing thousands of years of sexist, speciesist and ecocidal oppression.

In this book, I will argue that both veganism and witchcraft interrogate humanity's domination over nature, rejecting the prevailing anthropocentrism

DOI: 10.4324/9781032649801-1

of modern life and developing empowerment and liberation through the manifestation of more equitable, deep ecological, and caring relationships between humans and other animals. I also argue they offer something more, something "magical" to everyday politics. Although both veganism and witchcraft can be practiced secularly, I argue they are also spiritually relevant for several reasons. First, veganism and witchcraft are profoundly experienced and embodied by many practitioners. Second, they contemplate the purpose of life, the qualities of what would constitute a *good* life, morality and responsibilities to one another, and the role of humanity in nature (often to the extent to which they directly challenge prevailing religious belief systems on these matters). Third, veganism and witchcraft shape the very identity of practitioners in such a way as to link them from an individual level to wider societal, natural, and universal processes. There seems ample room for exploring vegan ethics in the modern witchcraft community, as there is a liberatory spirit to both. Indeed, Jone Salomonsen (2002) summarizes in her feminist survey of American and British practice that, "The goal of Witchcraft is eventually to liberate people, sanctify the world, and unify the spirit and politics. This means to unite the values inherent in divine reality and values circulating in social reality" (152). For the purposes of this book, it is precisely witchcraft's intentional reimagining of humanity's relationship to nature and other animals, its challenge to hierarchical thinking and processes of domination, and its nurturing of personal and community agency that indicate parallels worth investigating. In other words, veganism is more than eating plant-based, and witchcraft is more than lighting candles and reciting spells. They are ways of knowing and being that radically investigate connections between individuals, communities, the Earth, and beyond.

In the UK, the Office for National Statistics (2021) reports that, in 2021, 56,610 Brits identified as pagan and an additional 11,766 identified as Wiccan.[1] The U.S. Census Bureau report (2011), meanwhile, has noted a doubling of Wiccans from 134,000 in 2001 to 342,000 in 2008. Presumably, this number has only increased. Recent academic research (Aloi and Johnston 2007, Miller 2022) and news coverage (Bosker 2020, Kopf and Singh-Kurtz 2018), for instance, has noted the resurgence in witchcraft made possible with the assistance of social media. Veganism, meanwhile, has also witnessed considerable growth in recent years. According to The Vegan Society (2024), approximately 600,000 Brits identified as vegan in 2019, an increase by a factor of four since 2014. Similar numbers can be found in other Western countries, and this total grows substantially when accounting for vegetarians as well. Flexitarianism, furthermore, has become the norm. Almost half of Brits in a 2022 study reported that they were considering a reduction in animal product consumption (Chiarelli 2022). Veganuary registrations also indicate the rapid growth of veganism in the West; the 2023 campaign witnessed 700,000 registrants, up from 600,000 the year before (Vernelli 2023). It is not known how many witches are vegan, nor how many vegans are witches, but it is clear that both groups comprise a substantial minority of American and British populations and that this minority is on the increase.

This book does not only examine intersections between veganism and witchcraft but also missed connections and distinctions. The parallel rise of both nature-based countercultures has seen them cross paths in many ways, but there are unique qualities that warrant exploration and possible assimilation. The ritual aspects of witchcraft with its mindful observance of Earth's natural rhythms and that of the universe beyond may prove especially useful to the vegan community, as would its attention to intention-setting and collaborative manifestation. The Western Nonhuman Animal rights movement is deeply secularized, with about three-fourths of vegans identifying as atheist or agnostic (Wrenn 2019a). The prominence of atheism in the vegan community might suggest little interest in witchcraft. I suggest, however, as an atheist myself who has previously advocated a secular approach to anti-speciesist activism (Wrenn 2016), that the seeming incongruence of the two paths relates to semantics. Whether or not witchcraft involves supernatural belief is up to the practitioner, and whether rooted in the physical or metaphysical world, it can offer positive psychological effects. For spiritual and nonspiritual vegans alike, "magical" practice may prove beneficial. Doing veganism is psychologically difficult; it requires the adoption of a highly stigmatized identity and a conscious and deliberate acknowledgment of nonhuman suffering in a world that is largely ignorant of that suffering, uncaring in the face of that knowledge, and hostile to those who would challenge it (Greenebaum 2016). Indeed, anti-speciesist work tends to take a considerable emotional toll on participants, and rates of burnout are high (Wrenn 2023). Finding connection with other animals and the Earth as witchcraft encourages is a profoundly radical act with the potential to counter the considerable emotional burden that anti-speciesism entails, but for all its rational emphasis, the modern vegan discourse tends to leave the more supportive and nurturing elements of that connection untapped. Witchcraft, often practiced as nature-based ritualism or spirituality, prioritizes self-care, wellness, and kinship, all of which are important elements for resilience and wellbeing that may be strategic in social movement spaces. These characteristics are also compatible with secularity. Witchcraft is frequently defined as a religion but actually requires no belief in a supernatural higher power, only that practitioners tune in and pay attention to the cyclical movements of nature and humanity's place in those movements. Anyone can be a witch, be they Christian, Jewish, Wiccan, atheist, or any other religion or lack thereof. Indeed, even astrophysicist and agnostic Neil DeGrasse Tyson (2017) (often claimed by the new atheist movement) describes a "cosmic perspective" (like that adopted by most witches) as "spiritual—even redemptive—but not religious" (206), one that "embraces our genetic kinship with all life on Earth [...] as well as our atomic kinship with the universe itself" (207). Whether religiously or secularly practiced, witchcraft aligns with many core aspects of veganism. For that matter, veganism's commitment to environmental sustainability and solidarity with other animals expressed materially through dietary changes, consumer boycott, adoption and rescue, and other political measures may offer modern witchcraft a more tangible means of realizing principles of feminist, nature-based power and responsibility for the Earth and other animals.

In this book, I argue that the parallel paths that veganism and witchcraft have followed are unnecessarily disconnected and would benefit from some theoretical and practical entanglement. In doing so, I explore popular witchcraft discourse as it circulates in foundational books, paying particular attention to how Nonhuman Animals and multispecies liberation are accounted for. I employ a vegan feminist perspective to demonstrate the interconnectedness of nature, Nonhuman Animals, and feminized human groups. I also use it to critique witchcraft's failure to acknowledge this interconnectedness, despite modern witchcraft having emerged to theorize and resist this multifaceted oppression of nature and those living in its margins. As a spiritual practice that seeks to re-embed the human species in nature, it still has much to learn from the historical (and contemporary) treatment of Nonhuman Animals. Humanity's relationships with other animals have ideological and material consequences for Nonhuman Animals, and these consequences reach beyond the nonhuman to impact humans in return, witches included.

Witchcraft, then, is not unlike other institutionalized religions in this inattention to more-than-human animals. Vegan activists have been reluctant to embrace the spiritual for just this reason: despite claims for compassion, peace, and togetherness, religions tend to uphold human dominion—either in theology, practice, or both—failing to substantially extend these lofty values to other animals. The onus is on witchcraft, so to speak, to prove itself distinct in this regard, but I also see a responsibility for vegans to consider the ways in which alternative, feminist spiritualities might offer something useful for Nonhuman Animal liberation in return, if only in helping activists to navigate the personal and collective challenges of anti-speciesist work. This chapter subsequently explores the return to religion in multispecies studies. The Nonhuman Animal rights movement and especially veganism in the West rely primarily on secular philosophical discourse to advance Nonhuman Animals, but scholars are increasingly reinterpreting Christianity (Covey 2024), Judaism (Gross 2024), Islam, and other mainstream religions (Goossaert 2024). Feminist religious practice as it relates to veganism and anti-speciesism, however, remains largely unexamined outside of ecofeminist discourses. Witchcraft, I argue, is one such ecofeminist spiritual practice that holds particular relevance to vegan studies, vegan *feminist* thought in particular.

Theorizing Veganism

Veganism and modern witchcraft share a common history; in the late 1960s and 1970s both rode the sticky transition from modernity to postmodernity in the West. The back to the land movement, the natural foods movement, environmentalism, and other counterculture initiatives challenged the power of state and industry, critiquing and resisting unequal social structures. It is perhaps no coincidence that veganism, having formally organized under The Vegan Society in Britain in 1944 and the American Vegan Society in the United States in 1960, was gaining momentum just as the modern witch movement began to flourish with the repeal of Britain's 1735 Witchcraft Act in 1951 and the rising popularity of ecofeminist spirituality and witchcraft in the United States in the 1960s and 1970s. In the heady post-war years, the UK and US emerged as firmly democratic societies with expanding wealth, widening citizenship rights, and keener attention to the ramifications of modernity on human life and the environment. World wars, pandemics, environmental and urban decline, and industrializing speciesism were some of the many trends of the late 19th and early 20th centuries that upset the expectation that humanity was on a trajectory of progress. Vegans, witches, and other contrarians looked back on the past with scrutiny and began to consider a means of returning to an idealized past in a forward-thinking manner, resurrecting a more harmonious existence with nature and other animals and challenging prevailing institutions of power that normalized violence and monopolized truth.

The anthropocentric rationalism that had dominated Western knowledge systems was coming under scrutiny as well. Mid-century veganism as a philosophy, ethic, and politic had represented the culmination of many decades of internal debate in the British vegetarian movement. By the late 19th century, the religious and hygienic elements of vegetarianism in the West had given way to ethical claims of anti-speciesism. Plant-based consumption had become more than a matter of spiritual purity or optimal health; it had also come to resist humanity's unnecessary imposition of violence on other animals. Although many vegetarian activists in these early years agreed with a vegan approach, they were afraid of presenting an overly difficult diet to their constituents, ultimately encouraging vegans to go their separate way. This split was relatively amicable, but the new vegans were keen to differentiate themselves both ethically and strategically from their vegetarian progenitors. Of course, vegans wanted to make clear their rejection of dairy, eggs, "leather," and other animal products, but perhaps less predictably, they also chose to align themselves with the rising hegemony of science. In addition to utilizing a scientific framework in their claimsmaking, activists invested heavily into researching vegan nutrition and alternatives to dairy, "leather," and other animal products (Cole 2014, Wrenn 2019b).

This secular approach was not universal. Because Nonhuman Animals have been useful for teaching religious morality, some activists hoped to extend these lessons beyond the anthropocentric to also include nonhuman welfare. Anti-speciesist activists have subsequently relied on appeals to religion since the inception of animal liberation in the 18th century (Kean 1998). Earlier incarnations of plant-based eating imbrued with religiosity—as consuming only simple, unstimulating and animal-free food—was believed to be purer, cleaner, and pious, but many anti-speciesists, furthermore, were deeply skeptical of science, a trend that re-emerged in mid-20th century activities and publications of The

Vegan Society (Wrenn 2019b). Throughout the 1950s, 1960s, and 1970s, the society actively collaborated with Christians, Jews, and Hindus. The American Vegan Society, having been founded by a Jain who aligned veganism with the principles of ahimsa, arguably *never* operated outside of this religious framework (although today the Philadelphia-based society prioritizes frameworks of food justice for Black communities). The shift to modernity likely informed this religious response. Science and rational thought hailed by the Enlightenment increasingly came to inform knowledge production and social organization in the early 18th and 19th centuries, displacing religion as the primary shaper of moral practice (Kean 1998). The rise of science itself brought new affronts to vegan morality. Vivisection, for instance, became such a common feature of scientific inquiry that many anti-speciesists extended their opposition to Non-human Animal testing to reject science itself. By the 20th century, both the United States and United Kingdom had become considerably more secularized, presenting a cultural context altogether different from that faced by 19th century activists. Whereas religion and spirituality had been central to Victorian activism, modern activism was more likely to identify religion as a domineering institution responsible for considerable speciesist violence.

As veganism came into its own, the religious legacy of anti-speciesism and its distrust for science was a sore point for a modern movement hoping to prioritize rational philosophy, research, and technological development. There may be merit to this approach. While religion is a major ideological framework within which individuals and communities engage moral decision-making, social psychological research finds that those ascribing to more conservative religiosity tend also to ascribe to human supremacist values and, on average, consume more animal flesh (Dhont and Hodson 2014). It may prove difficult to use a belief system to challenge entrenched hierarchies *within* that belief system (Mika 2006). Indeed, my previous research into the history of the Nonhuman Animal rights movement has found several organizations taking explicitly secular positions to improve resonance (Wrenn 2016). Yet, the growth of witchcraft and ecofeminism in the latter half of the 20th century demonstrates alternative, more transgressive and liberatory spiritual practices are possible. Might veganism lock on to these movements to inform a more persuasive and equitable belief system and political practice?

Vegan Religious Studies

Despite its current atheistic tendencies, religion has been a foundational element of veganism. Sociology, historically, has overlooked the role of Nonhuman Animals in religious practice, but this exclusion is increasingly criticized as diminishing human-nonhuman relationships and being insufficiently representative of social life (Beaman and Strumos 2023). Religious studies scholars Aaron Gross, Dave Aftandilian, and Barbara Ambros (2024) have argued that this disconnect persists precisely because of religion's function in differentiating humans from other animals. Reinterpreting religion for a multispecies society, they argue, is not only ethically important for the wellbeing of other animals but for enriching religious studies as well. "Thinking about animals and religion," they summarize, "helps us *rethink what religion itself is*" (2024: 10). Indeed, as veganism has proved itself a cultural mainstay, academia has responded with increasing attention to the individual, social, political, and ethical examination of veganism in society. Vegan studies have been more or less in scholarly practice since the turn of the 21st century, but only in the mid-2010s did the field begin to gather momentum, with dedicated vegan studies networks and textbooks not emerging until the 2020s. An interdisciplinary pursuit, vegan studies scholars examine all facets of veganism in society, including how veganism impacts the lives of animals and the human experience. Vegan religious studies, by extension, pushes this discourse to consider the many ways in which organized religion has informed multispecies awareness and theologizes Nonhuman Animal liberation.

To date, the majority of this research has centered Christianity (Covey 2024), Judaism (Gross 2024), and, to a lesser extent, Islam and religions native to South and East Asia (Goossaert 2024), with exceedingly few attempts to apply a critical animal approach to pagan religions on the margins. Most leading religions have used animality to differentiate humans as morally and spiritually superior, but pagan practices, which are overwhelmingly animist and deeply ecological, could disrupt this pattern. The only institutionalized religion to mandate plant-based living is Jainism, but Jains are few, and most lean toward vegetarianism despite the clearer affiliation its theology has with veganism. Otherwise, most vegans and vegetarians who also identify as Christian, Jewish, Muslim, Buddhist, or Hindu do so *despite* the dictates of their religion (Savvas 2024).

Religiosity thus sits uneasily within the vegan discourse, and this may explain why most vegans practice no religion, identifying as agnostic or, more prevalently, as atheist (Wrenn 2019a). To that end, Kim Socha (2014) has argued that an atheistic approach is crucial given that religious arguments "merely hack away at or stretch the parameters of religion to make animal liberation fit what is essentially an anthropocentric, speciesist, hierarchical belief system" (2). Religion, Socha concludes, is essentially oppressive, and this, for her, includes Wicca. Although Wicca does acknowledge and purport to care for other animals, it fails to promote veganism and defaults to predator-prey relationships in nature for moral guidance. Likewise, the doctrine of Sybil Leek, a seminal leader in the reclaiming of modern witchcraft, emphasizes that humans are "apart from living things" given their unique capacity for reason and decision-making (1975: 31).

Nonetheless, feminist and some Eastern religions disrupt this hierarchical ideology in suggesting a multispecies comradery. Others have argued that religion is well situated to accommodate animal ethics. Editors of a special issue of *Religion* have championed the "lived and believed multispecies relationality" of human religiosity as an important new frontier in religious studies (Pribac and Johnston 2023). One contributor suggests even that the "basic feature of religious discourses is the active organisation of human entanglements with the more-than-human world" (Stuckrad 2023: 631). Nonhuman Animals, for these scholars, are useful for examining the human condition. They teach and challenge humans, too, thereby defining the roles of humans in the natural world. Indeed, Nonhuman Animals are quite prominent in religious storytelling the world over. Although religions frequently frame the human role as supremacist in some way, they *do* engage with Nonhuman Animals, who are used in stories and scripture to teach appropriate values, beliefs, knowledges, and behaviors. Stuckrad is clear, however, that religious study need not always work to validate human supremacy; it can also "open up to the many voices of the planet" (632) for a more equitable interpretation that supports multispecies coexistence.

Religiosity and spirituality are distinct qualities, however. While the former is involved in ritualized worship of a supernatural external "god" or higher being, spirituality refers to an internal relationship one has with life, the universe, and the *personal* being. Given these nuances, some have questioned whether veganism might serve as more than a philosophy and represent a secular, spiritual, or religious practice (Abbate 2023, Krone 2024). Likewise, Savvas (2024) has observed that modern vegan writing tends to position anti-speciesism as a "moral way of being in the world" (105). A spiritual approach to Nonhuman Animal rights is not unknown in vegan spaces. Carol Adams' (2004) *Prayers for Animals* sees species-inclusive spiritual practice as an act of self-care and supernatural assistance to other animals. Barbara Darling (2024) describes rescuing Nonhuman Animals from speciesist institutions and sanctuary work as spiritual. These practices, she reflects, frequently entail a contemplation of universal oneness between humans and other animals, the healing properties of care and love, and the mysteries of death, all of which transpire in daily sanctuary life. Anti-speciesism thus demonstrates considerable potential for aligning with spiritual practice, but it also demonstrates a clear feminist undertone.

Vegan Feminism

These qualities of care, love, radical intervention, and regeneration are well established in feminist spiritualities, suggesting an easy congruence with liberatory veganism. Indeed, the rise of ecofeminism—which contains elements of a very robust multispecies, sometimes vegan thealogy—has countered traditional patriarchal religions as well as the highly rationalist, androcentric environmental theory that predominated academic thought in the 20th century. Alloun (2015) notes that ecofeminism's applicability to Nonhuman Animal advocacy (and a variety of other oppressions for that matter) is made possible by its emphasis on otherization. Here, nature has served as the ultimate "other," but, by association, all that is categorized as "wild," "primitive," or "nonhuman" may also be otherized, marked as inferior, and denied equal consideration. This has been ubiquitously applied to human and nonhuman animals alike, with a history reaching back many thousands of years.

Vegan feminism would coalesce on this shared oppression at the turn of the 21st century, sprouting from both ecofeminism and Critical Animal Studies as a critical theory that prioritized the understanding and dismantling of human violence against other animals. The history of ecofeminism will be examined in further detail in a forthcoming chapter, but for now, it is important to recognize vegan feminism as a 21st-century theory of multispecies liberation that—while today is largely secular in its analysis—owes its existence to the spiritually imbrued efforts of 20th-century ecofeminists. Vegan feminist theory draws on the shared oppression and possibility for resistance experienced by women, Nonhuman Animals, and other feminized and systematically oppressed groups such as trans and nonbinary persons, lower class persons, children and older persons, persons with disabilities, and people of color. Vegan feminist theory draws heavily on the work of Carol Adams (2000), Josephine Donovan (1990), Marti Kheel (2007), and so many others who have identified the many ways that women and other animals are similarly treated, both symbolically and physically, in a male-dominated, anthropocentric society. A number of vegan feminist scholars, Adams included, pushed the ecofeminist discourse to consider the inclusion of Nonhuman Animals as subjects in their own right, also clarifying the major role that speciesism plays in environmental destruction and the ideological normalcy of dominance and exploitation in society (Adams and Gruen 2014). More than a critique of social inequality, it is also a theory of social justice, particularly as it is informed by environmental and anti-speciesist scholar-activist thought. Vegan feminism explores past and present systems of domination, arguing for a radical multispecies solidarity that rejects hierarchy, celebrates difference, and acknowledges the potential for agency and resistance in the margins. These aspects, as I will demonstrate, echo many of those found in witchcraft today.

Based in vegan feminist theory and drawing on a legacy of ecofeminist spirituality, vegan witchcraft aims to identify the ways in which feminized groups, especially women and other animals, have historically shared oppressions that are usually based on the vilification of their association with nature and their defiance—whether real or perceived—of patriarchal, often religious, control to disrupt solidarity. To that end, vegan witchcraft also theorizes how this shared marginality might create opportunities for alliance, and, equally, how that alliance could invite institutional measures of control. History is key here, as a long legacy of persecution of witches and other animals in the West continues to inform contemporary witchcraft and vegan movements. This often means looking backwards to look forward. Critical Animal Studies scholars (Nibert 2002) have argued that early humans had a more equitable relationship with nature and nonhuman species which informed widespread animism across most human cultures. Before the rise of "hunting," early humans were primarily plant-based in diet. Human violence against other animals was minimal and, for most societies, hardly systematic. Nonhuman Animals were respected across a variety of spiritual and cultural practices as community members, friends, familiars, relatives, rivals, and sometimes as gods. It would be more recent geological and cultural changes that encouraged the shift to killing other animals for food, such that humanity's relationship to other animals became less equitable.

This shift to speciesism has also been linked to the creation of gender roles and the devaluation of women (Mason 1993). As many human cultures moved from a "hunting" economy to an agricultural one, the status of Nonhuman Animals *and* women plummeted. With domestication came the demystification of reproduction and the incentive to control reproduction to ascertain lineage. The need to delineate property also emerged to sustain an agricultural economy as growing and harvesting required communities to remain more stationary. Thus, control over women's bodies to protect lineage and inheritance to grow patriarchal power replaced the sacred respect for femininity that had predominated in so many ancient cultures. The domination of nature, in other words, is heavily entangled with the domination of women. The mystical unknown of female power and women's connection to the environment was no longer a matter of reverence. Subsequently, the mysteries of the natural and feminine worlds gradually dissipated as rationalized ideologies and systems of predictability and control normalized under male rule (Sjöö and Mor 1991).

By the Middle Ages, this devaluation was amplified with an element of fear and an urgent effort to fully extinguish the remaining vestiges of feminine power. As Horkheimer and Adorno (2002) have argued, the ideals of the Enlightenment settled across Europe, signaling an early modern era with its own superstitions and myths, namely those of intense rationalization, institutionalized capitalism, manufactured culture, and heavy consumerism. A humanistic, "enlightened" ruling class would manufacture a new system of domination, one comparable in many ways to the oppression models that preceded it. More intense ideological conditioning and institutional controls were introduced, with disastrous impacts for women and other animals. Horkheimer and Adorno add that this shift, based on the cleansing of paganism, supernatural beliefs, and the mythical is "paid for with the estrangement of human beings" from nature, one another, and their own selves: "Animism has endowed things with souls," they explain, but as capitalism comes to commodify the life world, "industrialism makes souls into things" (2002: 21). Horkheimer and Adorno warn that, as a consequence of this widespread commodification, social injustice becomes "justified in the guise of brutal facts as something eternally immune to intervention" (2002: 21). What constitutes truth, valid knowledge, fact, evidence, and even reality, then, is no less a social construction in the "enlightened" age. Witchcraft and veganism alike tap into this contested truth in a commodified world, emphasizing that the environment and human and nonhuman people have inherent worth and are not commodifiable.

What is Witchcraft? A Review of the Literature

Witchcraft in Medieval and Early Modern Europe and America

Because witchcraft is as much a cultural practice as it is a religion, its meaning has shifted considerably over the centuries. Although today's witches have some commonalities with those persecuted hundreds of years ago, the craft has been reinterpreted for an alternative, often resistance-based, and usually nature-based style of living and thinking in a highly civilized, capitalist, and often alienating society. Johannes Dillenger, editor of the *Routledge History of Witchcraft*, has rightfully advised caution in drawing comparisons between witches of history to those today, as the distinctions are so many and profound. A number of tropes based on vague historical memories, for better or for worse, continue to inform contemporary understandings of witchcraft, particularly those related to their presumed allegiance with demons, devils, and all things evil. Despite popular misconceptions, misunderstandings, and mystery in general about witches, Dillenger quips, "most people would claim that they know what a witch is" (2020: x). Explanations for the belief in witchcraft, the practice of witchcraft, and efforts to control witchcraft are as varied as the multitude of cultures in which witchcraft surfaces. This book focuses on witchcraft in the West— Great Britain and the United States in particular[2]—as it dominates the mainstream imaginary. Witchcraft, however, has been and continues to be practiced by people the world over (Gershman 2022), including Indigenous persons of the Americas, who have been marginalized by European colonization (Monteagut 2021). Indeed, even Western variations of witchcraft incorporate traditions from across the world (Moura 2020), and further variations exist within Europe itself, including the magical folkways of Celtic, German, Italian, Nordic, Slavic, Spanish, travelling communities, and more.

Misogyny must be acknowledged as a fundamental reason for the persecution of witches. "In essence, the Spinster is a witch," muses Daly, "derided because she is free and therefore feared" and "since derision is not powerful enough to stop her spinning, she is the object of attack" (1978: 394). Women, of course, have been pitted as representatives of all that is fallible and potentially evil in humanity including, in the Christian tradition, humanity's banishment from Eden. Women who eschewed patriarchal institutions such as marriage were particularly vulnerable, as were women who exuded any sort of power, such as those who owned land, those who were able to heal with herbs and plant medicine (Gardner 1970), or those who simply spoke their opinion too confidently. Indeed, many authors emphasize that persecution most frequently resulted from women's supposed disreputable behavior or community-level feuds (Davies 2002, Gentilcore 2002, Levack 2002). Given the extreme stigma, bodily harm, and financial penalization associated with being labelled a witch, the threat of accusation could be enough to return women to their subservient feminine role.

With the Industrial Revolution and increased urbanization, persecutions abated. Hughes (1965) notes that changes in Nonhuman Animal agriculture were specifically responsible, as Britain moved from the reliance on a cattle economy to that of sheep and "wool" production. This shift required a mass removal of people from the countryside to make way for millions of exploited sheeps, but it also forced many into the city to undertake the hard labor of transforming sheeps' hair into woolen fabric. Women, in particular, were enlisted into spinning, a form of drudgery that allowed "unproductive" women to accrue capital within the confines of the domestic space or the factory. This observation is predictable in vegan feminist thought, whereby economic relations with other animals are understood to shape other systems of exploitation, including sexism (Ducey 2018, Nibert 2002, Wrenn 2017). In this case, women's lowered status was linked to the lowered status of other animals, both justifying their intense economic exploitation for the dominant anthroparchal class.

With land clearances and privatization requiring the displacement of humans to make way for more sheeps, organized witchcraft persecution at the level of local and regional government may have been a means of swift removal. Starhawk (1997) has pointed to this shift as endemic of the encroachment of capitalism, whereby new attitudes surfaced to equate productiveness with social worth. This shift would further imperil women, especially those who were older and disabled. Animal-based agriculture and domestication debased the personhood of both women and other animals as property to be controlled on land that was increasingly privatized by powerful men.

In the premodern era, life for most in the British Isles and its colonies revolved around agricultural cycles. Any disruptions to this control could be attributed to the evil doing of these very victims of anthroparchy. A recurrent element of witchcraft accusations related to perceived responsibility for the loss of productive "livestock" (Briggs 2002). Nonhuman Animal agriculture has a notoriously deleterious effect on the wellbeing of Nonhuman Animals even in the best of conditions, but medieval husbandry techniques were likely to have been much cruder such that the death and suffering of enslaved animals would have been greater, creating many more opportunities for frustrated farmers to turn on local women as culpable. More animals, for that matter, would also have been lost to predators before wolves, bears, and other such species were eradicated in the early modern era. Witches became symbolically useful for explaining these regular disruptions to anthroparchal rule. They could also be blamed for any unusual weather events, which would have impacted Nonhuman Animal welfare. Behringer (2002) has noted this connection between witchcraft persecution, "livestock" disruption, and food insecurity, pointing to several extreme weather events that took place in the medieval era, including the Little Ice Age, as responsible for increased persecution.[3] Superstitions, folklore, and rituals abounded regarding the protection of crops and farmed animals from evil. Nonhuman Animals kept as "livestock" seem to be particularly in danger of witchery, perhaps due to their immense value as agricultural producers. As their livelihoods were tied to the wellbeing of the Nonhuman Animals they owned and exploited, farmers were understandably anxious about their wellbeing. By way of an example, until the turn of the 20th century in Ireland there persisted a widespread belief that "butter witches" would steal into pastures and bewitch cows, leaving them "elf-shot." The witches were thought to either steal the milk and butter, spoil the lot, or render the cows unproductive (Saunderson 1961).

Thus, witches of the early modern era were symbolic identities (imposed on real people) that the patriarchal dominant class could wield to maintain control, and they were tightly bound to systems of speciesism. These cultural creations were codified in law, creating legal edifices to bureaucratize and normalize the persecution of those who challenged this control, including property forfeiture, imprisonment, or execution. Daly (1978) has pointed to the power of patriarchal mythmaking in controlling public discourse—silencing women's dissention or alternative perspectives. The history of witchcraft persecution is subsequently a political construction. Indeed, the personal accounts of those accused of witchcraft (or those believing themselves to be witches) are scant, such that the account of the persecutors have come to dominate the discourse. The horrific details of women's torment are generally obscured as a result, and the significant economic and cultural differences between then and now further obfuscate. Notably, the popular witchcraft imagination does not acknowledge that the persecution of "witches" was tied to agricultural interests such as property rights, "livestock" health, and harvest quality.

Witchcraft in 20th- and 21st-Century Britain and America

Belief in witchcraft began to decline in the wake of advancements in free thinking, science, and other harbingers of modernity, which, "largely replaced what the witch had to give" (Gardner 1970: 84). Yet, the belief never fully dispersed. Its persistence in the 21st century is sociologically interesting given that Western countries with high levels of technological, scientific, and economic development would theoretically have long since abandoned pagan practices and beliefs. Sociologist Max Weber (1958) identifies the Reformation period as hastening the disenchantment of society, displacing superstitions and belief in magic with a belief in productive, obedient, piousness to achieve salvation. These characteristics were, as it turned out, also conducive to the rise of capitalism. Rationalization as it surfaced in religious ideology would become deeply informative to the organization of modern society. That said, it is difficult to clearly demarcate an "enlightened" contemporary society from its supposedly irrational past, given that belief in immanence and the supernatural persists today in a number of social institutions, namely organized religion (Walsham 2008). Furthermore, intellectual investigations of all things magical continued throughout the Enlightenment era (and beyond), irrespective of increased secularization, rationalization, and scientific hegemony (Davies 2021). Conservatism, with its disenchanting effects, actually helped to sustain cultural interest in mysticism (Russel 1985). Astrology, divination, spiritualism, and séances found considerable following in the 19th century, the era in which scientific rationality is supposed to have prevailed, and are still entertained by much of the public today.

The reclaiming of witchcraft, too, was a resistance to the encroaching rationalization of modernity, with its demystifying insistence on separating humanity from the natural world. Witchcraft, Greenwood (2000a) notes, responds to the fracturing of society and self in a postmodern society, and aids women and other practitioners in grappling with associated anxieties. In modern witchcraft, magic remains a part of everyday life and can be wielded by anyone with sufficient intent,[4] although some of those who identify as witches allege to have descended from those who survived persecution. For these reasons, Paige Vanderbeck (2020) frames witchcraft as a spiritual mind set, one that maintains a path to explore the unknown and the unknowable in active resistance to the epistemological mastery and universality that the Enlightenment has claimed. As such, many women inspired by second wave feminism would embrace it as a means of empowerment and resistance (Eller 1991), although many witches in the West come to the craft having been inspired by Indigenous practices, Eastern religions, or occultism (Hughes 1965).

The variations of witchcraft are too numerous to explore here but can be broadly divided into British neo-paganism and American feminist spirituality. In Britain, Gerald Gardner is largely credited for spearheading witchcraft (what he termed Wicca) as a new religion based upon his interests in occultism and goddess worship. Gardner's Wicca pulled from a wide variety of sources and was strategically boosted by the repeal of Britain's Witchcraft Act in 1951 (Adler 2006, Davies 2021, Russel 1985). Gardner would later work closely with Doreen Valiente, who contributed significantly to the historical understanding of witchcraft and modern incarnations. She authored many of the first Wiccan books and rituals, later splitting from Gardner as a collaborator, citing concerns with his excessive efforts to publicize Wicca and his inaccurate and liberal appropriation of a wide variety of European folkways (Valiente 1978). Gardnerian Wicca is typically associated with naturism, goddess worship, and folk traditions of Europe, but there is also Alexandrian Wicca, which is based on the work of Alex and Maxine Sanders, who rose to prominence after Gardner's death in 1960s England. Alexandrian Wicca is similarly eclectic but perhaps more ceremonial than Gardnerian.

The murky anthropology on which modern witchcraft rests is not necessarily a detriment, as creativity and mythology have been openly embraced for building the practice and maintaining its cultural relevance (Adler 2006). Although British witchcraft has drawn heavily on a huge variety of regional pagan practices of the common people in the British Isles and Europe, the 20th-century incarnation was very much so an intentional creation pulled from a variety of sources, not all indigenous to Britain or even global antiquity.

Prior to this, Chas Clifton (2006) credits major religious movements in the 19th century for laying the groundwork for American paganism. The personal responsibility for redemption that religious revivalism established in American culture, incidentally, would also influence early American vegetarian and anti-speciesist traditions (Shprintzen 2013). British emigrants Raymond Buckland and Sybil Leek did much to popularize witchcraft in 1960s America as well. It would be the feminists, however, who truly brought American witchcraft to fruition, especially in California. Clifton notes the influence of Berkeley humanities studies as key to this development, and, indeed, American witchcraft would take on a much more symbolic and poetic nature compared to the archaic and somber tone of its British counterpart. Pockets of witchcraft emerged in more conservative communities of the Midwest as well, while Jewish- and Eastern European-influenced witchcraft formed in the New York City region. Recognizing these variations and diverse influences, the American witchcraft scene by the end of the 1970s had nonetheless taken on a predominantly West Coast feminist flair. The efforts of several American women in the 1970s saw witchcraft reinterpreted as a means to reclaim women's power and challenge the domineering and hierarchical structure of a patriarchal society and its institutionalized religions (Salomonsen 2002). Goddess worship would become central to witchcraft for many, including Starhawk, who explains that "to be a witch is to make a commitment to the Goddess, to the protection, nurturing, and fostering of the great powers of life as they emerge in every being" (1987: 8). The feminist inclinations of American witchcraft would go on to influence British witchcraft in return (Clifton 2006). Not all American witchcraft, of course, is linked to the feminist movement. American witchcraft also has roots in African, Latin, Ozark, Appalachian, and Indigenous traditions, but these traditions of minoritized communities have not garnered as much attention in mainstream witchcraft discourse. Lastly, Western witchcraft has also been influenced by environmentalism and several subcultures including hippies and goths. With this incredible diversity, identifying shared characteristics can be troublesome, but some loose commonalities might be offered. Witches today tend to prioritize personal experience and encourage personalized practice rather than adhere to dogma as is typical in institutionalized religions (Gottschall 2000). Likewise, as it is in many ways in response to or in rebellion against institutionalized religion, modern witchcraft is fiercely anti-institutional and individualist. All participants are encouraged to be actively involved in leadership and decision making, as witches characteristically reject enacting "power over" others (Berger 2000: 109, Starhawk 1987).

What is *Vegan* Witchcraft?

Vegan Entanglements

To reiterate, it is difficult to identify a comprehensive, agreed-upon definition of witchcraft, but its respect for personal autonomy, prioritization of harmonious relations between humans and nature, and concern with women's resistance to domination all mark it as especially conducive to a species-inclusive, plant-based, and social justice-informed spiritual practice. As will be explored, there is a deep entanglement of the experiences of women, nonhumans, and nature, an entanglement that has been examined by both the modern witchcraft movement and the Nonhuman Animal rights movement, given their shared roots in ecofeminism. Vegan witchcraft seeks to realign these traditions, explicitly recognizing that the interconnections between humans and other animals shape social relations and ideologies with real-world consequences for life outcomes. Where vegan feminism sees women and other animals, for instance, as experiencing similar forms of oppression such as objectification, sexualization, fragmentation, and consumption (Adams 2000), vegan witchcraft also explores the ways in which women and other animals have been stereotyped as evil and persecuted, vilified, and slain for the benefit of the dominant class.

Vegan witchcraft *as a theory* analyzes systemic violence as it happens in the context of religion, patriarchy, modernity, and capitalism. The marginalized people burned at the stake in Medieval Europe, for instance, are not so physically or symbolically removed from the Nonhuman Animals who are baked, broiled, boiled, and barbequed today. Both may be rendered "scapegoats" and killed in the name of social order. Both must be rendered less-than-human to justify domination, including killing to obtain the land they live on, killing to obtain the wealth their bodies might provide, or killing to reinforce and reproduce systems of inequality. It speaks back to white male patriarchal Judeo-Christian institutions that have historically oppressed women and other marginalized genders, gay, lesbian, and queer-identified persons, Black, Brown, Indigenous, and Nonhuman persons. Vegan witchcraft *as a practice* advocates for an alternative, life-affirming and liberatory spirituality that sees magic in multispecies life on Earth. This spirituality serves as solace, inspiration, and resistance in a society dominated by anthroparchal religion. Vegan witchcraft, then, is a vegan feminist perspective and eco-practice, one predicated on a meaningful spiritual or psychological connection to and solidarity with other animals.

Vegan witchcraft may seem somewhat superfluous given that witchcraft already claims to embrace other animals as familiars and guides. In the following chapter, this dominant framework in Western witchcraft will be critiqued as otherizing and objectifying, but it should be noted that more serious intersectional failures flourish in practice. For instance, Aleister Crowley, perhaps England's most famous occultist, who greatly informed Gardner's Wicca, is reported to have sacrificed Nonhuman Animals and used their corpses to sexually penetrate women in his ritual sex (Jencson 1998). The sexualized entanglement of domination against women and other animals is a theme that is well documented in vegan feminism (Adams 2015, MacKinnon 2004). Women and other animals, both objects, are disproportionately degraded by men through ritualized parallel acts of violence on their bodies. They are used as conduits for men's sexual pleasure, with that pleasure deriving from their complete submission, usually with an element of humiliation. These rituals are largely confined to the turn of the 20th century, but even today the legacy of this intersectional violence serves as means to reinforce the lower status of women and other animals in paganism (Jencson 1998).[5] Crowley's example may be an extreme case, but his lasting popularity demonstrates a need for conscious reckoning. Importantly, this is not just a matter of male violence. Later chapters will demonstrate how this legacy of pleasure-seeking entitlement and general callousness toward nonhuman suffering surfaces in even the most feminist branches of the craft.

Autonomy, Agency, and Individualism

The role of independence and freedom from dogma, furthermore, will be unpacked as a serious detriment to consistent animal ethics. Personal autonomy takes a sacred quality in witchcraft, a direct response to the centuries of Christian and patriarchal domination. According to the author and priestess Deborah Blake, modern witchcraft is "a spiritual practice that is based on personal responsibility" (2015: 3). "Witches," she continues, "believe we are all responsible for our own actions and the consequences that follow them." This contrasts with institutionalized religions, which typically attribute power to the supernatural as embodied by men, hierarchically, from the elite rulers to the head of the family household. As vegan scholars have pressed, this is not only a patriarchal manifestation of power, but also a human supremacist one. These hierarchical religious structures are part of what sociologist Erika Cudworth identifies as a system of *anthroparchy*, "a complex and relatively stable set of hierarchical relationships in which 'nature' is dominated through formations of social organization which privilege the human" (2011: 67). For Cudworth, this system is also deeply patriarchal in its function and ideology. In finding power through human agency attuned to natural processes, it could be said that witchcraft fundamentally challenges anthroparchy and, as such, it expands beyond the personal realm of spiritual practice to also align with broader social justice efforts of the 20th and 21st centuries.

In her seminal text *Positive Magic*, Marion Weinstein (2020) distinguishes between supplication magic and affirmation magic (211). Supplication magic entails bargaining and deal-making with higher powers, often based out of fear and perceived powerlessness and vulnerability as is typical in mainstream religions. Affirmation magic, by contrast, is premised on the idea that power resides within the practitioner, not in an external god or goddess. This also positions witchcraft as especially poised to benefit other animals and the goal of a nonviolent vegan world, as it does not rely on scripture, external coercion, or threat of punishment but rather personal responsibility and capability. The magnitude of nonhuman suffering can be so overwhelming that it can disempower human allies; researchers have found that those working in Nonhuman Animal care and protection efforts experience high rates of compassion fatigue and burnout (Stevenson and Morales 2022). Suffering and inequality, however, are not believed to reflect some divine order that must be endured for spiritual purity and atonement for humanity's sins. Witches see these conditions instead to be products of human enterprise or naturally occurring happenstance. As such, they can be manipulated for a more pleasurable and equitable life on Earth. By this interpretation, witchcraft makes the personal political, and it demands the practitioner recognize how their actions are linked to the wider wellbeing of society. It is not only the agential value of witchcraft that lends itself to veganism but also its specific responsibility to the Earth and all its inhabitants. It serves as a regenerative energy, the protection and improvement of the self and others.

Vegan witchcraft reinterprets the historic relationship between women and other animals as a cosmic endowment, rather than, as anthroparchal religions would suggest, a shameful relationship of evil that must be suppressed. As the next chapter will examine, for instance, the shared marginalization of women and other animals has encouraged multispecies cohabitation as a measure of material and psychological security. Today, modern witches consciously confront the animalized woman-close-to-nature trope to reimagine a special connection with other animals. By encouraging self-confidence, self-efficacy, agency, consciousness-raising, and other elements of self-actualization, witchcraft rallies women and other feminized groups as a potent force of social change. *Vegan* witchcraft, then, empowers practitioners to actively engage with the very worst historical oppressions with the aim of raising consciousness, motivating, mobilizing, and finding strength in that which has been vilified. The philosophy, rituals, and spells that make up the actual practice of witchcraft are manifestations and strategies for healing and revolution.

Of course, not all vegans take interest in intersectional oppression. Not all vegans recognize gendered relationships with food or other animals or even veganism's ecological connotations. Nor do all witches place import on the legacy of misogyny, environmental contempt, and anthropocentric control that fueled the burning times. For that matter, not all witches see a place for diversity, leftist politics, or social justice campaigns in their practice. But many *do*, as is evident in the popular writings of both fields. Marian Green, for instance, has noted in the bestselling *A Witch Alone* (2002) that many witches, far from embodying the horrible trope of the animal-sacrificing Satan worshiper that is imposed upon them, instead "keep pets, are vegetarian or even vegan" (60). Preliminary work has already begun on this connection between the occult and anti-speciesism. Daly incorporated Wicca into her ecofeminist theory, for example, and Patricia MacCormack has specifically employed secular occultism for the purposes of multispecies abolition. The latter's *Ahuman Manifesto* (2020) argues that humans might adopt ahumanism—eschew the structural privileges that the Anthropocene affords human beings. MacCormack also identifies consumerism as a root issue in the assault on the nonhuman, advocating a fierce resistance to the tendency for activism to remain in the philosophical realm, effectively "transforming the verb to the noun" (2020: 32). While

MacCormack does not specifically engage witchcraft, she does acknowledge the role of "occulture" as a replacement for traditional institutions and systems that maintain societal inequality. This occulture is defined as a "bricolage of historical, fictional, religious and spiritual trajectories" (2020: 95) and is useful for acknowledging the wide variety of witchcrafts and associated practices. Occulture "queers the tools available" to activists and, she explains, "taps into new paradigms of value that resist phallocratic capitalist hierarchies" (2020: 97).

MacCormack is clear that this approach must involve an acknowledgment that the death of nonhumans is morally equal to that of humans. This is a sort of death activism, she adds, that requires the death of human ego. Indeed, witches may purport to absorb humans into the wider tapestry of nature, but conventional witchcraft nonetheless protects human superiority in granting power to the individual as the ultimate arbiter of morality, justice, and decision-making. As such, it would be disingenuous to assume that witchcraft, paganism, or any other variant of the "occulture" is inherently any less dangerous to the nonhuman. Consider also that witchcraft is, in many ways, an attempt to return magic into the mundanity of a heavily rationalized, complicated, and often isolated modern life. The comparative closeness that humans once enjoyed with other animals may be alluded to in these historical imaginaries. The "good old days," however, were not so good for everyone, and the witch imagination too often traps Nonhuman Animals in anthroparchal times, protecting them from modern anti-speciesist values.

Reclaiming a Multispecies History

Modern ideas about historical relationships between humans and other animals tend to be rooted in ideologies and structures of domination and fail to critique the inherent violence of these societies. Recall that domestication, in particular, has been central to humanity's disconnect from nature and the cultural development of species-based violence but also sex-, gender-, and class-based violence. Vegan sociologist David Nibert (2013) theorizes that the subjugation of human communities across the globe has been motivated by the desire to either spread Nonhuman Animal agriculture into new regions or to obtain resources to sustain that agriculture. These resources needed to sustain Nonhuman Animal agriculture are extensive, including water, land for grazing and growing feed, and energy to operate farms and transport Nonhuman Animals and products extracted from their bodies. The new colonies were also important for establishing additional markets for these animal products. The desecration of nature, in other words, is very much an extension of the baser oppression of Nonhuman Animals, a process Nibert describes as "domesecration." As Nonhuman Animals were domesticated to allow for full reproductive control and material exploitation of their bodies, the same processes would be applied to female-bodied humans. Vegan feminist Jim Mason argues that the anthroparchal worldview with its support for hierarchy, domination, and exploitation is grounded in agrarian culture, "which is the manipulation of plants and animals for human wants and needs" (1993: 210). The domesecration of Nonhuman Animals and women, in other words, transpired along similar anthroparchal mechanisms. Agriculture, he explains, is based on both harnessing and subduing plants, animals, and nature, and this system is thousands of years old in the history of human culture. Vegan witchcraft, then, would caution against the uncritical celebration of early agrarian society that is ubiquitous in Western witchcraft today.

Mason also sees the anthroparchal agrarian worldview as responsible for a wide array of historical injustices, including the burning times. In the years of Western persecution of witchcraft, women and other animals alike would be punished for resisting this forced domestication with physical and psychological domination. Thus, in order for 21st-century witchcraft to confront its traumatic history and reclaim it for liberatory aims, it must contend with the historical entanglement of sexism and speciesism. Starhawk, a leading feminist witch of the reclaiming tradition, underscores the deeply political nature of historical events and remembrance: "the past is still alive in the present" (1997: 185). Witches remember and reflect upon the burning times out of respect for the dead but also to conceptualize and confront present power relations. The early witchcraft persecutions resulted in large-scale expropriation of land, knowledge, and other resources. They were also an ideological manipulation that eradicated women's power, self-worth, and sacredness, even the very memory of these strengths to the present day. For Starhawk, it was nothing short of a "war against the consciousness of immanence" (1997: 189). Witchcraft persecution, then, continues to feed a legacy of material and symbolic devaluation of women as a class. A critical historicity becomes foundational to modern witchcraft and, ultimately, total liberation. Summarizes Barbara Mor, "Knowledge of our truly *revolutionary* past can resolve our present dilemmas" (Sjöö and Mor 1990: xvi). Veganism joins this conversation, noting that it is also the systematic devaluation of Nonhuman Animals that informs societal inequalities, including that experienced by women. And, although the ramifications of speciesism for women's status are certainly important, it must also be acknowledged that the burning times for other animals never ended. In fact, more animals are killed now for the benefit of those in power than in any time in the history of humanity. If the status of Nonhuman Animals does inform the status of women and other marginalized groups, as vegan feminism argues, then witchcraft's challenge to the domesecration of women must also include a challenge to the domesecration of other animals.

Capitalism, Consumption, and Body Politics

Postmodernism has also informed anti-speciesism and witchcraft in challenging what constitutes "truth" and allowing for more pluralistic systems of knowledge. Relative to rationality's heavy focus on the mind, however, the body has become another shared site of contestation, surveillance, and control. For Nonhuman Animals and women, in particular, their bodies are systematically manipulated, bought, sold, and consumed. It is unsurprising then, that witches in their rebelliousness to anthroparchal power find resilience in the body and work to reclaim corporeal power for the purposes of personal healing, community regeneration, and the broader uplift of women and nature (Greenwood 2000b). Adams (2000) has observed this same phenomenon of alienation with regard to Nonhuman Animals, who are symbolically and physically butchered for identity-based consumerism in 20th- and 21st-century society. Indeed, for Adams, it is not possible to properly conceptualize the alienation of women without also considering the entangled experience of Nonhuman Animals, whose oppression not only stems from but directly informs the degradation of women and nature. Nibert's sociological approach is also relevant here in highlighting the capitalist undertones of entangled oppression. Veganism, on its surface, challenges everyday consumer habits, eschewing Nonhuman Animal products as much as possible. However, it reaches beyond individual consumer choices to challenge the capitalist system itself, as capitalism is critiqued as a system that necessitates and encourages exploitation to produce surplus value and maximize profit, well exceeding the oppression of the agrarian economy that proceeded it. As such, it is a system that normalizes inequality, encourages competition, alienates individuals from one another, erodes communal bonds, and turns persons into things. Ideologically, it disenchants the natural world, prioritizes quantity over quality, invests in growth over sustainability, and concentrates wealth and power into the hands of a small percentage of the population. All of these consequences have negatively impacted Nonhuman Animals, who are fully and completely objectified as exploitable resources or valueless impediments to capitalist growth that must be eradicated. For this reason, vegan witchcraft is also concerned with consumption. Witchcraft, after all, is a practice that engages with natural "resources" but in doing so has championed working *with* nature, rather than viewing it as something to be owned, exploited, bought, or sold.

Conclusion

This book examines the role of Nonhuman Animals and veganism in modern witchcraft from a vegan feminist perspective, with the aim of illuminating inequalities that persist in alternative spiritual practices in the West and identifying possibilities for cross pollination and multispecies solidarity. Witchcraft today is, in some respects, a response to the broken promises of modernity, presenting a postmodern challenge to seemingly universal conceptions of knowledge and reality. It resists conformity, challenges the notion of an absolute truth, and resists clear boundaries and categories imparted by the Enlightenment project. That which is "matter of fact" has become matter of conflicting interpretation. Ecofeminism and feminist spiritualties more broadly have embraced this fracturing to create new ways of knowing, being, and relating to the self, others, nature, and the cosmos. Vegan feminist theory, borne of both ecofeminism and Critical Animal Studies, has contributed to this reflexive discourse in championing intersectionality as a lens for understanding the shared mechanisms that oppress marginalized humans and nonhumans alike. Vegan feminism, I have argued, is well positioned to advance analyses of Western witchcraft, past and present, in championing the acknowledgment of, and reclaiming this common oppression as necessary to achieve total liberation. It is deliberately multispecies in perspective and interrogates prevailing anthropocentric theories of oppression and change, namely in identifying Nonhuman Animals as persons in their own right and confronting the harm that nonvegan social institutions impose on nature, humans, and other animals.

Given these fundamental similarities in values and goals between veganism and witchcraft, I introduce the concept of vegan witchcraft with hopes of marrying the strengths of both paths for the mutual benefit of all. Vegan witchcraft sees witchery as a powerful conduit for social change that draws its energy from plant-based foods, multispecies solidarity, and feminine power. It charges that the witch's path could and should be directed toward a just world, and that world can be manifested without the symbolic or material exploitation of Nonhuman Animals. Vegan witchcraft recalls entrenched anthroparchal myths that disparage women's connection to other animals to disrupt exploitation of both.

Vegan witchcraft is, in many ways, a long time coming. As this book will recount, the seeds for this flowering can be found in some pockets of feminist, vegan, and pagan histories, but missed opportunities are omnipresent. By way of an example, the Dianic collective Pomegranate Productions organized "Through the Looking Glass" in 1976, a feminist conference held in Boston featuring a variety of talks and workshops on the goddess worship, paganism, witchcraft, feminist resistance, and women's spirituality. Zsuzsanna Budapest, a deeply popular leader of the Southern Californian feminist witchcraft movement, was present to give a talk on the "Politics of Spirituality and Herstory of Goddess Worship." The aforementioned Carol J. Adams, an equally influential founding scholar in vegan feminist thought, was also presenting at this gathering on the topic of "The Oedible Complex: Feminism and Vegetarianism." Conference organizers had originally prepared to center vegetarianism, even flagging the connection between gender and species on the commemorative T-shirts, but an anthropocentric feminism would ultimately win the day.[6] Adams recounts:

> While at first Gloria and the Pomegranate Women were going to make vegetarianism central to the event, including a keynote by me, the issue got demoted; those T-shirts were never made. On the day of my workshop, I found the room was full with women. PACKED. They were listening to Z. Budapest. When she realized that she had to abandon the room, she invited whomever wanted to, to go with her, and I watched as the entire room emptied. I was heartbroken.[7]

Vegan witchcraft attempts to reverse this demotion, bringing Nonhuman Animals front and center to the witch's attention. Witchcraft scholars and practitioners alike stand to benefit from a more critical acknowledgment of the nonhuman condition and the ramifications that speciesism holds not only for Nonhuman Animals, but also for environmental integrity, women's liberation, and so much more. Vegan witchcraft also aims to expand the small but growing field of vegan religious studies to include feminist paths beyond the traditional anthroparchal establishment. Feminist spiritualities, as ecofeminists began to argue in the mid-20th century, have far more potential to advance an egalitarian, life-affirming worldview. Vegan studies scholars who fail to explore beyond the hegemonic religious institutions unnecessarily limit theoretical and activist possibilities. The same may be said of vegans overly committed to secular ideologies and tactical approaches. Embracing magical potentials and the enchantment of nature, even from a secular position, might offer activists valuable support and comfort in the face of so much suffering. It might also encourage confidence and solidarity in a capitalistic anthroparchal society that actively diminishes these strengths. Most importantly, vegan witchcraft can offer even the most atheistic vegan a creative imagination for what is possible. Imagination and creativity are, as witchcraft asserts, the building blocks of social change.

Notes

1 Witchcraft is somewhat distinct from Wicca. Wicca is a religion that was developed by Gerald Gardner in the early 20th century based on goddess (and sometimes god) worship, shamanism, and other pagan interests, and it overlaps quite a bit with the aims of witchcraft (Cunningham 1995). However, witchcraft, on its own, is a secular practice that aims to connect the practitioner with the natural world, serving as a ritualistic means to set intentions and realize goals.
2 Likely due to preexisting indigenous beliefs in magic and faeries that had already normalized the concept of witchcraft, Ireland largely avoided the trials (Sneddon 2012).
3 Witches could even be blamed for interfering with "livestock" exploited for transportation. Valiente (1962) notes that witches were, in her home county of Sussex, reported to have stopped horses and disrupted carts.
4 Wiccan leader Scott Cunningham's definition of magic is also helpful, explained as "the projection of natural energies to produce needed effects" (1995: 19) that might be drawn from oneself, the natural world, or as is sometimes the case in Wicca, the divine. For some, the idea is that magic is "real," in that it can harness the supernatural and create change through the casting of spells. For others, witchcraft is only real in its ability to influence the witch psychologically, allowing them to focus on particular desires and align their behaviors accordingly. The definitions and distinctions are many. Within witchcraft and Wicca, there is further variation in practice and belief, and as is the case with any cultural movement, a number of internal schisms as well. See Appendix A on Wiccan denominations in Raymond Buckland's (2002) *Complete Book of Witchcraft*.
5 Jencson (1998) notes that Crowley's reported sexual encounters with goats (the stereotypical sacrificial animal) are incorporated into sexist jokes in the pagan community that interweave heroic tales of his sexual conquests with women. Humor of this kind becomes a means of protecting the gender hierarchy by implicitly suggesting the

lowered status of women, who serve as the butt of the joke: "Women who object to the implication that they have a purpose similar to that of goats, and who wish to assert their personhood, are commonly silenced by the 'no sense of humor' charge" (1998: 259–60). This says nothing, of course, of the even lower status of goats, who have no one to object on their behalf. Jencson (1998) has also observed the practice of polygamy in late 20th-century witchcraft, whereby men take on multiple wives (but rarely the reverse).

6 The final program does not even mention Adams.

7 Conference organizational materials mentioned were provided by Carol Adams from her personal collection (Personal correspondence, 2023).

References

Abbate, C. 2023. "*The Philosophy of Animal Rights: A Way of Life or Religion?*" Paper presented at the annual Tom Regan Memorial Lecture, Harvard University, October 4.

Adams, C. 2000. *The Sexual Politics of Meat*. London: Continuum.

Adams, C. 2004. *Prayers for Animals*. London: Continuum.

Adams, C. 2015. *The Pornography of Meat*. New York: Lantern Books.

Adams, C. and L. Gruen. 2014. "Groundwork." pp. 7–36, in *Ecofeminism*, C. Adams and L. Gruen (Eds.). London: Bloomsbury.

Adler, M. 2006. *Drawing Down the Moon*. London: Penguin.

Alloun, E. 2015. "Ecofeminism and Animal Advocacy in Australia." *Animal Studies Journal* 4 (1): 148–173.

Aloi, P. and H. Johnston (Eds.). 2007. *The New Generation Witches*. London: Routledge.

Beaman, L. and L. Strumos. 2023. "Including Non-human Animals in Studies of Lived Religion and Non-Religion." *Social Compass* 71 (3): 406–424.

Behringer, W. 2002. "Weather, Hunger and Fear: Origins of the European Witch-Hunts in Climate, Society and Mentality." pp. 69–86, in *The Witchcraft Reader*, D. Oldridge (Ed.). London: Routledge.

Berger, H. 2000. "High Priestess: Mother, Leader, Teacher." pp. 103–118, in *Daughters of the Goddess*, W. Griffin (Ed.). Oxford: AltaMira Press.

Blake, D. 2015. *Everyday Witchcraft*. Woodbury: Llewellyn.

Bosker, B. 2020. "Why Witchcraft is On the Rise." Retrieved April 25, 2024, from: http s://www.theatlantic.com/magazine/archive/2020/03/witchcraft-juliet-diaz/605518/.

Briggs, R. 2002. "The Experience of Bewitchment." pp. 57–68, in *The Witchcraft Reader*, D. Oldridge (Ed.). London: Routledge.

Buckland, R. 2002. *Complete Book of Witchcraft*. Woodbury: Llewellyn.

Chiarelli, N. 2022. "Almost Half of UK Adults Set to Cut Intake of Animal Products." Retrieved April 25, 2024, from: https://www.ipsos.com/en-uk/almost-half-uk-adults-set-cut-intake-animal-products.

Clifton, C. 2006. *Her Hidden Children*. Oxford: AltaMira Press.

Cole, M. 2014. "'The Greatest Cause on Earth': The Historical Formation of Veganism as an Ethical Practice." pp. 203–224, in *The Rise of Critical Animal Studies*, N. Taylor and R. Twine (Eds.). London: Routledge.

Covey, A. 2024. "Animal Theology." pp. 117–121, in *Animals and Religion*, D. Aftandilian, B. Ambros, and A. Gross (Eds.). London: Routledge.

Cudworth, E. 2011. *Social Lives with Other Animals*. London: Palgrave.

Cunningham, S. 1995. *Wicca*. St. Paul: Llewellyn.

Daly, M. 1978. *Gyn/Ecology*. London: The Women's Press.

Darling, B. 2024. "The Spiritual Practice of Providing Sanctuary for Animals." pp. 169–178, in *Animals and Religion*, D. Aftandilian, B. Ambros, and A. Gross (Eds.). London: Routledge.

Davies, O. 2002. "Urbanization and the Decline of Witchcraft." pp. 399–412, in *The Witchcraft Reader*, D. Oldridge (Ed.). London: Routledge.

Davies, O. 2021. "The Rise of Modern Magic." pp. 195–226, in *The Oxford Illustrated History of Witchcraft and Magic*, O. Davies (Ed.). Oxford: Oxford University Press.

DeGrasse Tyson, N. 2017. *Astrophysics for People in a Hurry*. New York: W. W. Norton.

Dhont, K. and G. Hodson. 2014. "Why Do Right-Wing Adherents Engage in More Animal Exploitation and Meat Consumption." *Personality and Individual Differences* 64: 12–17.

Dillenger, J. 2020. "Editor's Preface." pp. x, in *The Routledge History of Witchcraft*, J. Dillenger (Ed.). London: Routledge.

Donovan, J. 1990. "Animal Rights and Feminist Theory." *Signs* 15 (2): 350–375.

Ducey, K. 2018. "The Chicken-Industrial Complex and Elite White Men." pp. 1–17, in *Animal Oppression and Capitalism*, D. Nibert (Ed.). Santa Barbara, CA: Praeger.

Eller, C. 1991. "Relativizing the Patriarchy." *History of Religions* 30 (3): 279–295.

Franklin, A. 1999. *Animals & Modern Cultures*. London: SAGE.

Gardner, G. 1970. *Witchcraft Today*. London: Citadel Press.

Gentilcore, D. 2002. "Witchcraft Narratives and Folklore Motifs in Southern Italy." pp. 97–108, in *The Witchcraft Reader*, D. Oldridge (Ed.). London: Routledge.

Gershman, B. 2022. "Witchcraft Beliefs around the World." *PLOSOne* 17 (11): e0276872.

Goossaert, V. 2024. "Vegetarianism, Prohibited Meats, and Caring for Animals in Chinese Religious History." pp. 154–157, in *Animals and Religion*, D. Aftandilian, B. Ambros, and A. Gross (Eds.). London: Routledge.

Gottschall, M. 2000. "The Mutable Goddess: Particularity and Eclecticism within the Goddess Public." pp. 59–72, in *Daughters of the Goddess*, W. Griffin (Ed.). Oxford: AltaMira Press.

Green, M. 2002. *A Witch Alone*. London: HarperCollins.

Greenebaum, J. 2016. "Questioning the Concept of Vegan Privilege." *Humanity & Society* 41 (3): 355–372.

Greenwood, S. 2000a. *Magic, Witchcraft, and the Otherworld*. Oxford: Berg.

Greenwood, S. 2000b. "Feminist Witchcraft: A Transformatory Politics." pp. 136–150, in *Daughters of the Goddess*, W. Griffin (Ed.). Oxford: AltaMira Press.

Gross, A. 2024. "The Ethics of Eating Animals: Jewish Responses." pp. 234–242, in *Animals and Religion*, D. Aftandilian, B. Ambros, and A. Gross (Eds.). London: Routledge.

Gross, A., D. Aftandilian, and B. Ambros. 2024. "Introduction to Animals and Religion." pp. 8–22, in *Animals and Religion*, D. Aftandilian, B. Ambros, and A. Gross (Eds.). London: Routledge.

Horkheimer, M. and T. Adorno. 2002. *Dialectic of Enlightenment*. Stanford: Stanford University Press.

Hughes, P. 1965. *Witchcraft*. London: Penguin.

Jencson, L. 1998. "In Whose Image? Misogynist Trends in the Construction of Goddess and Woman." pp. 247–267, in *Spellbound*, E. Reis (Ed.). Wilmington: Scholarly Resources.

Kean, H. 1998. *Animal Rights*. London: Reaktion Books.

Kheel, M. 2007. *Nature Ethics*. Lanham: Rowman & Littlefield.

Kopf, D. and S. Singh-Kurtz. 2018. "The US Witch Population has Seen an Astronomical Rise." Retrieved April 25, 2024, from: https://qz.com/quartzy/1411909/the-explosive-growth-of-witches-wiccans-and-pagans-in-the-us.

Krone, A. 2024. "Veganism as a Spiritual Practice." pp. 164–168, in *Animals and Religion*, D. Aftandilian, B. Ambros, and A. Gross (Eds.). London: Routledge.

Leek, S. 1975. *The Complete Art of Witchcraft*. London: Leslie Frewin.

Levack, B. 2002. "State-Building and Witch Hunting in Early Modern Europe." pp. 213–225, in *The Witchcraft Reader*, D. Oldridge (Ed.). London: Routledge.

MacCormack, P. 2020. *The Ahuman Manifesto*. London: Bloomsbury.

MacKinnon, C. 2004. "Of Mice and Men: A Feminist Fragment on Animal Rights." pp. 263–276, in *Animal Rights*, C. Sunstein and M. Nussbaum (Eds.). New York: Oxford University Press.

Mason, J. 1993. *An Unnatural Order*. New York: Simon & Schuster.

Mika, M. 2006. "Framing the Issue: Religion, Secular Ethics and the Case of Animal Rights Mobilization." *Social Forces* 85 (2): 915–941.

Miller, C. 2022. "How Modern Witches Enchant Tiktok: Intersections of Digital, Consumer, and Material Culture(s) on #WitchTok." *Religions* 13 (2): 118.

Monteagut, L. 2021. *Brujas*. Chicago: Chicago Review Press.

Moura, A. 2020. *Green Witchcraft*. Woodbury: Llewellyn.

Nibert, D. 2002. *Animal Rights, Human Rights*. New York: Rowman & Littlefield.

Nibert, D. 2013. *Animal Oppression and Human Violence*. New York: Colombia University Press.

Office for National Statistics. 2021. "Number of People Who Identified as Wiccan and Pagan in the 2021 Census." Retrieved April 25, 2024, from: https://www.ons.gov.uk/aboutus/transparencyandgovernance/freedomofinformationfoi/numberofpeoplewhoidentifiedaswiccanandpaganinthe2021census.

Personal correspondence. 2023. Carol Adams, October 20.

Pribac, T. and J. Johnston. 2023. "Animal Spirit: Other Bodies in Relation." *Religion* 53 (4): 611–615.

Russel, J. 1985. *A History of Witchcraft*. London: Thames and Hudson.

Salomonsen, J. 2002. *Enchanted Feminism*. London: New York.

Saunderson, G. 1961. "Butterwitches and Cow Doctors." *Ulster Folklife* 7: 72–73.

Savvas, T. 2024. *Vegetarianism and Veganism in Literature from the Ancients to the Twenty-First Century*. Cambridge: Cambridge University Press.

Shprintzen, A. 2013. *The Vegetarian Crusade*. Chapel Hill: University of North Carolina Press.

Sjöö, M. and B. Mor. 1991. *The Great Cosmic Mother*. San Francisco: HarperSanFrancisco.

Sneddon, A. 2012. "Witchcraft Belief and Trials in Early Modern Ireland." *Irish Economic and Social History* 39 (1): 1–25.

Socha, K. 2014. *Animal Liberation and Atheism*. Minneapolis: Freethought House.

Starhawk. 1987. *Truth or Dare*. New York: HarperCollins.

Starhawk. 1997. *Dreaming the Dark*. Boston: Beacon Press.

Stevens, P. 2024. *Rethinking the Anthropology of Magic and Witchcraft*. London: Routledge.

Stevenson, R. and C. Morales. 2022. "Trauma in Animal Protection and Welfare Work." *Animals* 12 (7), article 852.

Stuckrad, K. 2023. "Undisciplining the Study of Religion: Critical Posthumanities and More-than-Human Ways of Knowing." *Religion* 53 (4): 616–635.

The Vegan Society. 2024. "Worldwide Growth of Veganism." Retrieved April 25, 2024, from: https://www.vegansociety.com/news/media/statistics/worldwide.

U.S. Census Bureau. 2011. "Statistical Abstract of the United States, Population." Retrieved April 25, 2024, from: http://www2.census.gov/library/publications/2010/compendia/statb/130ed/tables/11s0075.pdf.

Valiente, D. 1962. *Where Witchcraft Lives*. London: The Aquarian Press.

Valiente, D. 1978. *Witchcraft for Tomorrow*. London: Robert Hale Limited.

Vanderbeck, P. 2020. *Green Witchcraft*. Emeryville: Rockridge Press.

Vernelli, T. 2003. Veganuary 2023 Breaks All Records in Campaign's 10th Year. Retrieved April 24, 2024, from: http://veganuary.com/veganuary-2023-breaks-all-records.

Walsham, A. 2008. "The Reformation and 'The Disenchantment of the World' Reassessed." *The Historical Journal* 51 (2): 497–528.

Weber, M. 1958. *The Protestant Ethic and the Spirit of Capitalism*. New York: Scribner.

Weinstein, M. 2020. *Positive Magic*. Newburyport: Weiser Books.

Wrenn, C. 2016. *A Rational Approach to Animal Rights*. London: Palgrave.

Wrenn, C. 2017. "Toward a Vegan Feminist Theory of the State." pp. 201–230, in *Animal Oppression and Capitalism*, edited by D. Nibert. Santa Barbara, CA: Praeger.

Wrenn, C. 2019a. "Atheism in the American Animal Rights Movement: An Invisible Majority." *Environmental Values* 28 (6): 715–739.

Wrenn, C. 2019b. "The Vegan Society and Social Movement Professionalization, 1944–2017." *Food and Foodways* 27 (3): 190–210.

Wrenn, C. 2023. "Shocked or Satiated? Managing Moral Shocks Beyond the Recruitment Stage." *Emotions* 7 (2): 298–321.

2

ANIMAL FAMILIARS

Introduction

The stereotypical witch is accompanied by a nonhuman helper of some species, usually a black cat, sometimes a toad and, in the case of Oz, even flying monkeys. Vegan feminist theory, which understands the oppression of women and other animals to be intertwined both symbolically and materially, would see this deprecative witchy human-nonhuman companionship as a predictable effort to render both groups as marginal, untrustworthy, dangerous, and even sinful. This stigmatizing trope, however, is also based on anthroparchal hierarchical ranking. The belief that witches were capable of species transfiguration was key to their villainization; they became transgressors of human supremacy and destabilized the boundary between humans and other animals. Although comparable shamanic themes can be found in folklores of the world, the concept of the nonhuman "familiar" is a British one (Parish 2019).[1] Nonhuman Animals were sometimes brought to trial and executed, having been feminized as human witches in magical form (Franklin 1997). Consorting with other animals, then, was dangerous business for both parties. Although popular belief in witchcraft has largely waned in the West, the connection between women and other animals as dangerous others remains. Modern witches have largely attempted to reclaim this association, turning it from a reason for suspicion to a measure of strength. As this chapter will argue, multispecies relationships have posed a threat to the anthroparchal social order, undermining human supremacy and male control over women and other animals. As such, allegiance between women and other animals, or even the perception of an allegiance, has been stigmatized. Historically, this stigmatization may have had fatal consequences, but even today as witches adopt it as a source of empowerment, the legacy of anthroparchal control, entitlement, and objectification continues in the witch's epistemology, undermining this solidarity.

DOI: 10.4324/9781032649801-2

This chapter examines several popular texts on witchcraft[2] which explore the concept of familiars as historic phenomena as well as their contemporary reincarnation in modern witchcraft. Employing vegan feminist theory, this analysis finds that familiars are an important representation of the symbolic entanglement of women, other animals, and nature. However, the underlying patriarchal, anthropocentric, and ecocidal objectification and exploitation of Nonhuman Animals categorized as "familiars" remains unproblematized. Familiars—be they physically or metaphysically envisioned—are predominantly categorized as vessels, servants, or symbolic resources for the witch's personal gain. Vegan witchcraft is thus presented as a means for celebrating the familiar as a point of potential comradery rather than another point of anthroparchal exploitation. As a multispecies practice, it becomes a means of connecting the civilized human world to undomesticated wild spaces of both the physical and psychological kind. To accomplish this, it must disrupt the oppressive historical influence that domestication has had on both women and other animals. This chapter subsequently explores some areas of liberatory familiar work. It also examines the Wiccan thealogy of reincarnation as well as its ritual incorporation of nude practice as points at which the species hierarchy might be collapsed.

Familiars and the Human-Nonhuman Boundary in Early Modern Witchcraft

Familiars were primarily nondescript, but during the English witch trials of the 1500s and 1600s many familiars appeared in reports more specifically as commonplace animals, usually smaller species. Larger domesticates were less likely to be suspected as familiars, perhaps because of their ubiquitousness in early British farm life (Serpell 2002). Sometimes also mentioned were birds (wild and domesticate), cats, ferrets, flies, moles, mice, rabbits, rats, snails, and toads. Horne (2019) suggests that animals categorized as pests or associated with the underground were even more likely to be seen as familiars, and presumably this provided further evidence to the evil of their witch accomplices. For persecutors, familiars served as intermediaries between humans and the supernatural or demonic realm. In medieval and early modern eras, Satan was often depicted as an animal or at least with the ability to take on an animal form as disguise. The *Malleus Maleficarum* (the most famous handbook for witch-hunting that survives from the 15th century) also suggests that these evil entities frequently manifest in the form of Nonhuman Animals. Of course, witches themselves were also thought to transfigure, often recorded as taking the form of Nonhuman Animals as part of their devil worship (Hughes 1965).

Historical Context of Familiars

The belief in familiars was not just a concoction of persecutors; it derived also from popular folk beliefs, and these beliefs were targeted for eradication by the church to protect its supremacy in the face of conflicting supernatural beliefs. Indeed, European conceptions of witchcraft contained "at least vestigial traces of shamanism" (Serpell 2002: 184). While historian Boria Sax (2009) supposes that the lack of fairy tales indigenous to England can be explained by the appropriation of popular folklore during the witch trials. Fairy tales that survive from other countries often include familiar relationships between humans and other animals, with Nonhuman Animals frequently depicted as receiving gratitude for the service done to them and offering service to the witch in return. Under English persecution, this folklore had been marked as a demonic threat to Church power and was largely suppressed. Familiars, then, were important symbolically to the construction of the witch but also the construction of human and male supremacy. Whether completely imaginary or an adulteration of real relationships between women and other animals, the concept of the familiar makes clear the entangled marginal status both women and other animals occupied. Particularly in the centuries beyond systemic domestication and the many social, political, economic, and even weather-related upheavals of the medieval and early modern eras, the control of women and other animals through witchcraft narratives and persecution was likely key to the maintenance of newly established social hierarchies. Rendering women, Nonhuman Animals, and any other feminized groups subservient was an anthroparchal priority.

England makes for an interesting case study in the entanglement of women and other animals in its great attempt to separate humans from nature. Humanism, supported by a number of social institutions including but not limited to those of a religious nature, became a direct enemy of animism, chipping away at pagan belief systems (Thomas 1983). Women, representing the uncomfortable mediator between human civilization and uncivilized nature, were subject to heavy policing. Midelfort (2002) has described the era of witch persecution as a "burst of misogyny without parallel in western history" (115), but more-than-human animals, too, were vulnerable in this regard, given their perceived closeness to nature, sentience, capacity for agency, and tendency to cohabit human-inhabited spaces. Yet, familiars were not always assumed to exist in the material plane or even in animal form. They were also thought to do bidding in some other spiritual or metaphysical configuration, but the Nonhuman Animal form was by far the most common in the days of persecution (Serpell 2002). The connection between women and other animals that had been celebrated in pagan times became a point of suspicion and a threat to establishing Judeo-Christian anthroparchal orders. Any alliance between women and other animals could be interpreted as an attempt to exercise power in a society that had stripped their access to it. Of course, until only recently in Western society, women were the property of men with little to no legal rights. Extreme social stigma against spinsterhood ensured that many women (and their families) willingly participated in the betrothal system. Indeed, women who were older, widowed, and lower class were especially vulnerable (Midelfort 2002), and this may have encouraged them to lean on nonhuman relationships for comfort, protection, and familial connection.

Yet, the idea that a cat or dog might replace a husband or children would have drawn suspicion and derision then, as it does today. Although this association with other animals was in some ways forced upon them, the connection women had with other animals nonetheless remained a potential threat. The great importance of women in maintaining and reproducing society invited all manner of accusatory practices to stifle their power and facilitate their exploitation. Some women believed to be witches were also accused of cannibalism, particularly the eating of human children. This trope that has been thought to reflect the trepidation around the considerable power that women wielded in being primary caretakers (Hughes 1965). Indeed, accusations often involved the inversing of women's traditional roles (Jackson 2002). Rather than feeding their families, they were said to poison them. Rather than healing the community, they hexed and harmed. Rather than raising children, they killed and ate them. Rather than tending to "livestock," they trifled with them. Midwives, with their deep understanding of natural healing and birthing, were especially vulnerable to being blamed for any deaths, illnesses, or deformities associated with those in their care (Russel 1985). Women's potential to resist patriarchal institutions or wield important responsibilities *within* patriarchal institutions needed to be moderated in order to maintain their subservient status, which led to establishing and reproducing gender difference and female inferiority.[3]

Explaining Familiars

Familiars were most often described as autonomous beings that served as the witch's "magical agent," and the witch provided food and shelter in return. Usually, they were thought to suckle blood from the witch (in trials, they would be examined for signs of this). Valiente (1962) even considers that this practice may have *actually* transpired, supposing that witches may have offered blood to their familiars to build a psychic bond. As mentioned, pet-keeping might be confused with witchcraft, as older, isolated women were more prone to cohabitating with other animals. Hughes notes that the "dirty and devoted pets of lonely, if sympathetic, old women" became subjects of suspicion (1965: 155). "Pet-keeping" was not unfamiliar to England, but in early modern years, very close relationships with "pets" were probably thought strange. Some research suggests that the practice was exclusive to women (and clerics) in medieval times (Walker-Meikle 2013). Weinstein agrees, noting that "witches have always kept many animals as house pets, even in times when other people saw animals simply as objects to be killed and eaten" (2020: 80). As "pet" keeping grew more common in the early modern years, this likely complicated the social role of Nonhuman Animals, given that animals categorized as "pets" would be granted relatively more privileges and capacity for agency than other nonhuman species.

This would be one explanation as to why those animals who were more likely to be kept as pets were also those more likely to be accused of consorting with Satan and his witches. The anthropomorphizing of Nonhuman Animals, incidentally, also served to dehumanize the suspected witches they were thought to collaborate with (Parish 2019). In lowering themselves to the stratum of Nonhuman Animals, witches became less than human themselves; feeding or caring for Nonhuman Animals for purposes of compassion or friendship was suspect, as it indicated an immoral, unholy alliance. Historian Helen Parish supposes that the concept of breastfeeding (or offering blood) to other animals played with "godly Christian motherhood and care for infants" and "the connection between blood and the life of the soul in the Judeo-Christian tradition" (2019: 7). "Whether the witch shed blood to feed an animal or a demon, such actions were morally and theologically dangerous" (Parish 2019: 7). The maternal theme between women witches and their familiar remains prevalent in the public imagination, emphasizing the unnaturalness of transspecies suckling, especially that performed by a postmenopausal crone. This had the dual effect of dissolving multispecies comraderies and stigmatizing women's aging.

Species Boundaries

The extreme persecution of women believed to ally with other animals (or even forgo their humanity by transfiguring into other animals) demonstrates a considerable societal disquiet on the species boundary. Sociologist Adrian Franklin (1999) has suggested that violent treatment of Nonhuman Animals was far more common in the medieval and early modern eras due to the uncertain status of Nonhuman Animals in the establishing species hierarchy. Indeed, many reports of familiars emphasized their human-like capacity to communicate, dance, dine, harm, and be harmed themselves (Scott 1974). Familiars were, in fact, believed to exhibit considerable agency, a characteristic that may reflect growing anxieties about the status of Nonhuman Animals, who, in early modern times, were still under categorical construction as "animal" and other-than-human. As vegan feminists have noted, the idea of the "human" was still very much under construction in this era (Ko 2019). Given that witchcraft persecutions in the West aligned with major social and political upheavals (Russel 1985), the joint persecution of women and other animals may have been useful for defining, elevating, and protecting anthroparchal power. Structural violence against women and other animals as exemplified in the persecution of witches ensured their lowered status; it also objectified them. Indeed, there are historical records of cats being burned with their suspected human accomplice. In some cases, cats were collected and burned en masse (Engels 2000). Their extermination was an effort to extinguish women's allegiance with other animals, protect the border erected between humans and other animals, and defend religious order.

Familiars and Power Animals in Witchcraft Today

Witchcraft today continues the traditional association between women and other animals by reclaiming familiars as an essential part of the practice and celebrating women's overlooked powers and social contributions. This is not to say the stigmatization has dissipated. Several scholars have noted that the "crazy" or lonely "cat lady" stereotype continues to vilify women's independent living and interspecies solidarity (Mershon 2024, Probyn-Rapsey 2019). The former belief that witches colluded with other animals to conjure evil, furthermore, seems to have been replaced with the modern fear that witches torture and kill Nonhuman Animals in ritual sacrifices and cauldron brews. Heavy negative press in the mid-20th century, Margot Adler (2006) considers, may have pressed the witchcraft community to heavily emphasize its positive relationship with other animals. Tarot decks, jewelry, Instagram accounts and other witchcraft accoutrement are, in any case, laden with black cats, wolves, owls, and other charismatic megafauna that have been romanticized in this new age spiritualism. Not all witches today work with familiars, but it surfaces heavily in introductory texts, and specialist books on familiar work abound. In British witchcraft, this trend usually incorporates familiar narratives in the medieval sense, reclaiming the concept from the nefarious roots of the familiar, working to reposition it as a source of empowerment. Other variants of familiar work pull on shamanic traditions, and these tend to be more popular in Celtic and American practice.

Due to these eclectic origins, there are a wide variety of interpretations as to what a modern- day familiar actually is. Madame Pamita (2025) defines the familiar as a spiritual and magical collaborator, "almost always one who was in physical form" (10). Sometimes this familiar work refers to inspecting dreams and visions for images or messages from other animals from within or from external sources. Working with the familiar self is thought to manipulate the practitioner's consciousness in such a way as to invite self-efficacy and connection with nature. Patterson agrees, noting that working with familiars allows the witch to "bring in the power and magic of nature into being" (2017: 8). The form of the familiar, either real or imagined, is thought to depend upon the personal characteristics and needs of the witch. Conway (2013) suggests a possibility of four types: astral creations, elemental spirits, spirits of the departed, or companion animals with whom the practitioner can communicate without the need for vocalization. Hall (2023) explains that an element of anthropomorphism is involved, with familiars providing a sort of "shorthand" that allows practitioners to make sense of nature and wield its power (94). Roderick (1994) adds, "to the Witch, the familiar is more than just the physical animal; it represents a power born of the unconscious. It is one of the many aspects of a living deity's expression" (151). Weinstein defines familiars as "usually a small animal of extraordinary psychic ability" (2020: 80), distinct from familiars who exist only as spirits. Some witches understand familiars to be purely imaginative, manifesting as psychological tools for manifesting goals

(Bell 2001). Whitehurst (2015), for instance, notes that witches can "conjure a creature [...] out of thin air" to aid in intention setting (126). Morningstar (2005), likewise, sees familiars as physical Nonhuman Animals who are in close, physical proximity to humans as well as more physical nonhuman energies that can be called upon as "spiritual allies": "familiars, like archetypes, are an aspect of our own potential" (Morningstar 2005: 216). Weinstein, too, emphasizes this partnership. More than simple "pets," familiars demonstrate a "talent and desire to actually join in the work of magic" (2020: 81). Indeed, this connection is deeply political in that it is not based on control, but rather consent. As Grimassi describes it, it is a subversion of domestication with partnership. Connecting with familiars entails "merging the human consciousness" for psychic enhancement, healing, protection, communication, and other magical workings (2021: 3). For modern witchcraft, then, familiars are a regular feature of the practice, usually as a symbolic idea but sometimes thought of as embodied in physical animals, usually those categorized as "pets." McKay (2024) defines them as historically rooted, an "entity from the spirit realm that guides, advises, and informs the witch" and that has "morphed over the centuries into a cute term to describe our pets" (12). This perceived psychic connection with other animals is, for many witches, fundamental to the craft. "Human and non-human were meant to work together" muses Conway (2013: 16).

Familiars in Service or Collaboration?

Consent may be idealized in familiar work, but it is unevenly sought. Grimassi (2021), Conway (2013), and Morningstar (2005) advise collaboration with physical companion animals, given their heightened senses and willingness to share physical space during ritual work, but concede that the metaphysical alternatives are suitable in cases where cohabiting with Nonhuman Animals is impractical. In any case, this reclaiming is done with the intention of personal benefit for the human practitioner, rarely with any intention of collaboration for *multispecies* benefit. Nonhuman Animals are regularly referred to as "it," suggesting they lack personhood or intrinsic value in the witch epistemology. Although some modern texts encourage an open collaboration with other animals, that collaboration is invariably one-sided, with Nonhuman Animals most frequently exploited as a form of sympathetic magic. They are, more often than not, absent referents. Patterson (2017), for instance, identifies familiars as useful for delivering messages, reflecting the practitioner's shadow self, aiding in a ritual, or providing psychological assistance—for any length of time as is needed by the witch, up to and including their entire lifetime. By way of another example, Starhawk sees Nonhuman Animals as a vehicle for raising power, and, when kept in the home as "pets," they may be tapped as "a source of elemental energy" (1999: 161). Ted Andrews, who identifies as a mystic and clairvoyant specializing in the metaphysics of human relationships with other animals and the natural world, mirrors this attitude toward familiars: "They serve many functions upon the planet. They help us to recognize our own innate abilities. They help empower us and protect us. Their energies can be used to help heal, inspire, and grow" (1993: 7).

Familiars may also manifest as a fetch in the Celtic tradition, or what Danu Forest (2020) refers to as a co-walker. The fetch, they explain, is an "ally who has always been with you throughout your life, though you may not know it" (28). As with the traditional familiar, it is not clear as to whether fetches are physical or metaphysical, but, in any case, their role remains an anthropocentric one, with fetches thought to exist primarily to serve human needs. Sometimes witches are more forthright in their species supremacy. Leek (1973) suggests that witches have a unique power *over* Nonhuman Animals. Leek also used several companion animals, namely a jackdaw and a boa constrictor, as physical familiars and promotional mascots in her public witchcraft. Leek, like many witches, warns against imposing power over others, but does not seem to extend this logic to nonhumans. The exploitative use of Nonhuman Animals for anthropocentric gain is implied.

Many texts do recognize nonhuman agency, but often this is an imagined agency that is used to insinuate that Nonhuman Animals *choose* to become servants. For instance, Franklin (1997) does acknowledge some agency in a familiar's capacity to "wander off" if not paid ample attention by the witch who conjures them (13). Weinstein clarifies that the familiar, by definition, "volunteers for the work" (1991: 43). "A familiar is not a pet," she continues, "it is an equal from the animal realm, and it is a co-worker for the witch" (1991: 43). This relationship is an exclusive and significant one: "A witch may have many pets, but rarely more than one familiar" (1991: 43). Because this collaboration takes place at the psychic level, communication is possible without necessitating speech; there is a "total understanding of each other's needs" (1991: 43). "The most powerful force between familiar and witch," she observes, "is always love" (1991: 45). Grimassi (2021) encourages petting companion familiars as a means of energy exchange, while both Grimassi (2021) and Hall (2023) advise ritual offerings to attract the good will of familiars. Murphy-Hiscock (2018) suggests providing nonvegan offerings such as cookies, cows' milk, and bees' honey. Because the former two foods are not likely to be easily digested by many species, this suggests their symbolic importance to the human practitioner over practical utility to nonhuman familiars.

Weinstein adds that including familiars in magical practice has a dramatic effect on ritual efficacy, but with this benefit comes considerable responsibility. They should be included in blessings during ritual, attended to outside of ritual, and even left with a trusted carer when taking holiday. Weinstein is an exception in the equality she grants other animals (if only symbolically, although Weinstein does suggest that the familiars to whom she refers are physically real): "Never 'train' your familiar by ordering it around, nor by giving it commands as some people do with their pet animals. Always talk to it as an equal" (1991: 43–44). If the familiar does not wish to participate, those wishes are to be respected. The familiar should not be forced, she advises. Free will in colla-boration is thought especially important given the perils thought to be attached to metaphysical work. Grimassi, for instance, hesitates to use other animals, as the dangers are considerable: "It is not uncommon for loyal Familiars to 'take a magical hit' in place of their human partner" (2021: 101). Witches, he suggests, must consider this risk when entering into partnership with a physical familiar. Starhawk (1999) also advises caution, noting a number of dangers to (pre-sumably real) Nonhuman Animals, particularly when engaging in trance work.

Most texts do advise a careful study of Nonhuman Animals in order to understand them and become spiritually receptive to their powers. For instance, Patterson (2017) notes that learning more about other animals through personal research, donating to "wildlife" charities, and engaging in "shapeshifting" to take on the perspective of other animals is an important aspect of the practice. For instance, Andrews (1993) advises seekers to visit "zoos" to consider which of the inmates they are most drawn to. Blake (2015) and Roderick (1994) also suggest visiting "zoos" and "farms" for these purposes. This advice fails, how-ever, to consider the highly artificial nature of "farms" and "zoos" and the incredible psychological and psychical suffering they tend to cause for Nonhu-man Animals incarcerated within.

Franklin (1997) recommends zoological study, but also meditation, trance work, and a little imagination to bring forth the power of other animals, an approach that continues to rely on stereotypical and reductive thinking but at least expands beyond the confines of carceral institutions. In identifying a famil-iar, many authors suggest a communion in spaces where they might frequent (Conway 2013, Grimassi 2021, Hall 2023). Reverence is usually advised when doing this, although intrusion is nonetheless condoned, even if it could cause distress to those being observed. Witches are not unaware of this violation. For instance, Forest (2020) advises sitting quietly to reduce "much of the alarm an animal will feel at your coming into an area" (36). Forest explicitly discourages the use of animal mimicry for the purposes of harming Nonhuman Animals but does disclose a number of "hunting" techniques to trick Nonhuman Animals into permitting humans into their proximity for use in familiar work, such as using camouflage, staying downwind, remaining quiet, and making use of distractions such as food or rain (2020: 47–48). Historically, this type of observation was indeed used to aid in "hunting," allowing humans to understand the mind and movements of other animals for nefarious ends (Gardner 1970).

Witches also observe Nonhuman Animals for augury purposes (Morningstar 2005, Patterson 2017, Valiente 1975). By way of an example, a black cat crossing could mean bad luck on the horizon, or the sound of a crow could foreshadow a death. Patterson (2017) even suggests using the entrails of nonhuman corpses for divination. Here again, Nonhuman Animals are not thought to exist for the pur-pose of living their own lives, but rather to exist as messengers for humans. Sometimes authors will insist the relationship is more reciprocal. Andrews (1993) and Murphy-Hiscock (2018), for instance, encourage practitioners to give back by donating to charities for free-living animals. But a reliance on charity does nothing to ensure liberation, only continued vulnerability and dependence. Neither suggest supporting vegan or anti-speciesist charities that work to liberate Nonhuman Animals.

Although there is an element of human entitlement to these exercises, the aim is ultimately to learn more about other animals, which could be said to reduce the otherizing influences of speciesism and segregation. In general, however, there are few exceptions to anthropocentric intentions. Tess Whitehurst is one of these important exceptions. She has criticized the possibility of witches actively procuring Nonhuman Animals specifically for their own benefit— including purchasing them from "breeders" (2017). She also warns against adopting "familiars" in cases where time, attention, companionship, veterinary care, space, and healthy food cannot be adequately shared. As is the case in vegan feminist thought, caring is a duty, but when that care is limited by a desire to render other animals subservient and hierarchies of power are not challenged, this care is oppressive and cannot be said to be reciprocal or respectful (Sutton and Taylor 2022). Indeed, the home can be a space for considerable oppression, not just for women, but also for Nonhuman Animals and other feminized groups. But the home can also be a micro-utopian space where egalitarian ideals might be enacted. Whitehurst approaches this ethic of care in her recommendation that homes be truly equal spaces for all parties: "Seriously consider letting the dog on the bed and sofa. If the state of your décor is more important than the comfort and happiness of your best friend, your priorities may need revisiting" (2017: 145).

Cats and dogs are prioritized as physical familiars, given that they share the witch's home, but other species have also been considered. Andrews (1993), for instance, leaves some space for insects and reptiles as potential power animals. However, the inclusion of free-living animals not considered cute or majestic is rare and tends to be a point of contention for some witches. Some make more space for mythical creatures like unicorns than for *real*, albeit less glamorous, everyday animals (Conway 2013, Whitehurst 2015). That said, the positive inclusion of Nonhuman Animals in spellwork that does not objectify them could be a ritual means of acknowledging their personhood, seeing them as subjects worthy of recognition and improved wellbeing. Conway (2013), for instance, insists on intentionally working with animals categorized as dangerous, scary, or repulsive to erode speciesist stereotypes and reduce the practitioner's anxiety. Whitehurst (2017), however, cautions against keeping certain species in the home who have not evolved to thrive in such habitats. Tanks and aquariums for insects, fishes, amphibians, and reptiles, for instance, cannot sufficiently support wellbeing. For that matter, many species kept as pets, she notes, cannot in any way consent, and confining them in tanks "would cause them to be imprisoned almost certainly against their will" (154). In such cases, a proxy for Nonhuman Animal familiars should be employed, such as a photograph or statue. Conway (2013), likewise, allows that "pets" can be familiars (as could any animal that is drawn to the practitioner), but while this cohabitation with familiars can be an enjoyable responsibility, Conway clarifies that these animals are not owned. Instead, they are cared for and truly *minded*: "familiars tend to stay around those humans who make them feel welcome for themselves, not just for their magickal powers" (24). For these witches, Nonhuman Animals are indeed sentient persons. Morningstar (2005) supports this perspective, acknowledging that Nonhuman Animals, like humans, "have family ties, social structures and organized hierarchies" (205). Like Whitehurst, she is an exception in recognizing how this also applies to domesticated farmed animals and even insects. Caring for other animals, for Morningstar, is central to Wiccan practice: "Let us not forget that if we wish to live the life of a Wiccan healer, we should behave kindly to all animals" (2005: 206).

Although they do not address veganism, it does appear that a more equitable attitude toward other animals can be found in these margins of modern familiar work. This perspective that prioritizes coexistence and collaboration is believed to be the most powerful. With a particular emphasis on earning consent, Conway advises providing regular offerings of food, shelter, safety, companionship, care, and respect to attract familiars. Blake (2015) supports this perspective: "Animals are not to own, but a gift we are allowed to enjoy" (122). Whitehurst (2017) mirrors this sentiment, observing that nonhuman allies "bestow their unique magical energies and gifts upon us" (141). Blake and Whitehurst use the term "gift" in such a way as to highlight that their presence with humans adds something valuable and is provided in trust. It is not something to expect, assume, or coerce. Indeed, there is a sacred responsibility to working with familiars. Whitehurst asserts that they are "our furry brothers and sisters, not our slaves" (2017: 122). Blake extends this sentiment further to suggest that even adoption entails some sort of ownership, and a true familiar can only come to collaborate with the witch of their own free will. These interpretations illustrate the possibilities of familiar work in a vegan witchcraft, resisting the legacy of witchcraft persecution that so fervently sought to disrupt multispecies solidarity. Nonhuman Animals play a very important role in vegan witchcraft as collaborators with agency and dignity, not servants to be exploited for human benefit. This is a feminist perspective that rejects hierarchy and celebrates, rather than vilifies, difference. It is a radical centering of compassion. "I believe in my heart that this is the rule of the God and Goddess most want us to follow," Blake summarizes, "BE KIND" (2015: 170).

Cute, Charismatic, and Stereotypical

Although Black, Conway, Morningstar, and Whitehurst offer important counternarratives to speciesist familiar work in modern witchcraft, this collaboration is rather selective. With few exceptions, witchcraft texts prioritize Nonhuman Animal species stereotyped as particularly wise, helpful, or magical for familiar work. Laura Hobgood (2024) has observed that major religions tend to prioritize companion animals and other species living in close proximity to humans, integrating them to some extent into divine representations, ritual practice, and religious beliefs. This speciesist preference persists in Wicca and witchcraft as well. Even Conway's less speciesist approach to familiar work fixates on charismatic megafauna, particularly big cats, wolves, and other popular American and African species. Domesticated animals used for ritual sacrifice warrant little mention and no critical analysis. The myth of cow veneration in India is also perpetuated, illustrating a detachment from the lived oppression of Nonhuman Animals.[4] To some extent, the attribution of supernatural abilities to other animals is an extension of pre-existing mythologies. The Celts believed ravens to have the power to see the future outcomes of battles, for instance, and bears have been central to a wide variety of prehistoric traditions. Morningstar (2005) also highlights the relationship that many deities have had with particular animals and how this informs the stories we create about these species today. This reductiveness is not seen as problematic. Andrews, for example, is clear that the identification of power animals relies on tropes:

> We can use animal imagery and other nature totem images as a way to learn about ourselves and the invisible world. We do not have to believe that these images and totems are beings of great intelligence, but there are archetypal powers that reside behind and oversee all manifestations in Nature. These archetypes have their own qualities and characteristics which are reflected through the behaviors and activities of animals and other expressions of Nature.
>
> *(1993: 2)*

And, although Andrews encourages those seeking a nonhuman totem to learn about and respect that totem, they nonetheless rest on human-serving reductive and essentialist tropes: "The characteristics and activities of these totems will reveal much about our own innate powers and abilities. By studying the totem and then learning to merge with it, we are able to call upon its archetypal energy whenever needed" (1993: 2). For many totem specialists, Andrews included, these archetypes tend to reflect American or British species (depending upon their nationality) and an assortment of popular animals from across the world. They are not in any way representative of the staggering diversity of nonhuman life and reflect the Western tendency to reduce considerable difference across groups to fit restrictive categories, as has been the case with peoples of Africa, America, and Asia in the colonial imaginary.

As Andrews' work illustrates, a number of sources on familiars also appropriate non-Western and North American Indigenous cultures to establish credibility in path-working advice. Indigenous vegan scholars have noted that, in the Americas, certain tribes did hold special relationships with other animals, often granting them elements of personhood and viewing them as "guides or teachers," but Native Americans, too, engaged in systematic violence against other animals nonetheless categorized as foodstuffs (Robinson 2024). With the coming of colonialism and its introduction of the "fur trade" and Nonhuman Animal agriculture, respectful ties, sustainability knowledge, and even access to the land for Indigenous communities were systematically destroyed. It is something more than irony that whites today draw so heavily on the very culture they purposely eradicated over the span of several centuries. Subsequently, many white practitioners now refrain from "spirit animal" terminology, opting instead to discuss familiars in terms of "power animals" (Blake 2015). Adjusting language in this way is hoped to resist cultural appropriation and celebrate humanity's connection to other animals in ways that do not replicate or aggravate colonial relationships.

These sensitivities are not extended to Nonhuman Animals, who are heavily stereotyped in both "spirit animal" and "power animal" traditions, however. Clearly, the imagined special properties of other animals that might be gained from a spiritual connection are culturally determined. As with familiars, it is primarily charismatic megafauna who are chosen to serve this role of "power animal." Very few texts revere the qualities of less charismatic species. Blake (2015) encourages readers to "keep an open mind" (125) about which species will be most appropriate familiars. Blake maintains a humble sheep as her familiar. Patterson's (2017) *Animal Magic* is another exception, and she herself claims the common pigeon as her power animal. Andrews, likewise, discourages seekers from disregarding a totem "simply because it may not seem glamorous or as powerful as your ego wanted" (1993: 6), but his book prioritizes just those species, with he himself identifying with wolves, owls, and big cats. Scaerie Faerie's "Birds, Bugs, and Spiritual Growth" is another exception. Reminding the witch community that there is "a whole world of animals out there, and they're not all mammals and birds" (Scaerie Faerie 2004: 79). "There is no reason why the woodlouse couldn't be a totem," they muse (79).

Interpretive guides regularly draw on Nonhuman Animal symbolism to explain human subconscious experiences, and these interpretations rely on stereotypes. Positive stereotypes are stereotypes nonetheless, condensing a huge diversity of multispecies life into anthropocentric archetypes. Whether negative *or* positive, stereotypes function to reduce a diverse group of individuals into a narrow understanding that is created by humans as the dominant class (Dunayer 2001). Moura's (2020) *Green Witchcraft*, for instance, includes a variety of mammals, birds, and insects in its dream divination advice. Some of the symbolism relates to behavioral practices, others to speciesist practices. For example, given that male wrens build many nests in hopes of enticing a partner, they are often stereotyped as industrious and busy, while the exploitation of cows for their breastmilk often sees them stereotyped as "nurturing." Even for the most culturally sensitive engagements with "spirit" and "power" animals, the propensity for appropriation is high. In many reports of meeting with or transfiguring into these animals, the practitioner may purport to hold respect for nonhuman persons, but ultimately, they are being exploited for the benefit of the practitioner. For instance, in the same chapter that Sarah Lyons (2019) encourages non-Indigenous witches to serve as allies to Native Americans in protest of white supremacy (and to do so without aggravating injustices through dominating and exploitative practices), she also advises witches to regularly engage in soul flight to sustain their activism. This soul flight practice entails occupying the bodies and minds of Nonhuman Animals in meditative practice, implicitly encouraging witches to metaphysically dominate and exploit Nonhuman Animals. This symbolic colonization of other animals has serious implications for real-world Nonhuman Animals, not the least of which being their exclusion from the witch's moral concern and vulnerability to human violence in a deeply speciesist society.

The symbolism applied in these familiar practices relate less to what individual Nonhuman Animals themselves experience and more to human *ideas* about other animals as relevant to *human* experiences. There is very little consideration for nonhuman ordeals at all. Based as they are on human cultural projections, the witchcraft discourse on power animals and familiars is indicative of what vegan feminist Joan Dunayer (2004) terms *new speciesism*, granting recognition and favor to Nonhuman Animals believed to be closer to humans (either biologically or by spatial proximity). Much of it also exhibits what sociologists Matthew Cole and Kate Stewart refer to as "cute style" (2014: 89). Emphasizing the cuteness or adorability of Nonhuman Animals, they argue, reduces them to stereotypical characters and effectively infantilizes them. This portrayal of other than human animals also culturally reproduces speciesism by leading the viewer to find enjoyment in *looking at* other animals, who are rendered as objects to be gazed upon, objects that exist for human pleasure. Rendered dependent and consumable, the affectivity that cutification encourages fails in "articulating those feeling with actions that can challenge and transform violent human-nonhuman animal relations" (Cole and Stewart 2014: 109). These representations, they add, can be understood as "instrumental in the continuance of exploitation, rather than offering any challenge to it, despite superficial appearances to the contrary" (110). Kott and DeVine's (2020) *Unfamiliar Familiars: Extraordinary Animal Companions for the Modern Witch* is a compelling example of this tendency. The publisher's description of the book indicates to the reader that the handbook is "humorous," "charming," "quirky," and employs a "playful, magical spin" sure to "delight animal lovers who have a sense of humor" (Chronicle Books n.d.). It further exemplifies the stereotyping characteristic of cute representations in its description of specific familiars. The pot-bellied pig is described as "some charmer" (Kott and DeVine 2020: 68) whose weakness is "malnourishment" (69) (presumably because pigs are voracious and greedy eaters). A very cute drawing of a smiling pig is illustrated as representative of all pot-bellied pigs. The cuteness of this representation masks the lived reality of pigs, who endure intensive confinement, bodily mutilations, and genetic manipulations, cognitive deprivation in rationalized, unstimulating environments, attacks (and sometimes even cannibalism) from their equally stressed and bored inmates, long periods of transportation on packed trucks (often in extreme cold or heat) without access to water, food, or fresh air, before meeting a frightening end in a slaughterhouse. Mocking the hunger of pigs, furthermore, makes light of the rationalized violence their bodies have endured, including an intensified hunger that has been genetically manipulated to encourage faster growth for greater human profit.

Stereotypes also pose certain conundrums for human practitioners. For instance, big cats, wolves, bears, eagles, and owls are very commonly chosen as familiars despite their considerable physiological difference from primates. Can vegetarian or vegan witches take a carnivorous animal as a totem? Longtime vegetarian Scaerie Faerie argues in favor of this possibility: "All five of my totems are obligate carnivores, some of them being pretty savage killers. Nature likes nothing better than to remind us of the need for balance!" (Scaerie Faerie 2004: 79). Andrews (1993) finds the predators especially enticing for this reason. Not only are they the stereotypical charismatic megafauna that tend to attract humans seeking totems, but patriarchal narratives about the nature of life can be validated through their use. Nature is only "red in tooth and claw" in some cases and from some perspectives. The symbiotic and reciprocal living that predominates in nature—which would serve a more representative depiction and could offer more inclusive norms of caring and compassion for witches—is easily subsumed under this platformed bloodlust. The awkwardness of this patriarchal interpretation is evident in the convoluted advice these authors provide. Patterson (2017) advises vegans against shapeshifting into predators, but Andrews suggests the practitioner work to align their diet to that of their familiar. Those whose power animal is a rabbit, for instance, should practice vegetarianism to tap into their rabbit energy. Elks, too, can offer their particular energy through vegetarianism according to Andrews, who argues it increases energy and stamina while reducing stress. Those associated with reptilian power animals, however, "may find that certain dietary restrictions may not work." For Andrews, vegetarianism and flesh-consumption are means of embodying power and submission. These observations are more symbolic than they are biological or nutritive, fitting uneasily with large and powerful species (such as elk) that thrive on plant-based diets. By way of another example, he suggests that those who align with gooses should go vegetarian, as real gooses are vegetarian. Yet, he does not advise those who have a totem eagle to embody this connection by actively killing other animals as an eagle might, nor does he suggest they increase their flesh consumption. Practicalities and ethics of modern life in the West, in other words, heavily shape the interpretation of animal totems.

Indeed, the conflation between great apes (who are predominantly vegan and vegetarian) with obligate carnivores like eagles makes for tricky shamanic advice. Predators, for Andrews, teach humans universal lessons of balance, but the predator experience is anything but universal, as most life on Earth lives symbiotically. The notion that balance can only be achieved through violence and death, for that matter, is more a reflection of Andrews' Western androcentrism than that of an eagle or reptile. Likewise, many other lessons he suggests, such as adaptability and responsibility, might be learned from predator totems without glorifying the most violent aspects of nature. Even lichen (found in the most extreme ecosystems) can be adaptable and seahorses (a species that reproduces through male gestation) responsible. Feminist perspectives on nature and feminine totems, however, lack the same cultural value and tend to be overlooked in mainstream, anthroparchal totem mythmaking. Conway (2013), for instance, does not emphasize the predator/prey dynamic as does Andrews, opting instead to lump all Nonhuman Animals together in their catalogue of power animals. Although Conway's approach can have an objectifying effect by circumventing vast species distinctions, it at least eases the anthroparchal hierarchies imposed on them.

Zoological Witchcraft

As previously mentioned, in some familiar work, the witch does not only call on the power or spirit of other animals but actually aims to *embody* the other animal, shapeshifting or occupying their body or psyche (Horne 2019). Gardner (1970) was skeptical that transfiguration would have been "real" beyond linguistic or totemic use, but many witches entertain the possibility, which raises a number of serious ethical concerns, as anthropocentrism is core to these practices. Starhawk (1997) emphasizes that many boundaries between humans and other animals are culturally created, such that engaging in transfiguration may soften them, but she consistently privileges humans and other animals who are biologically and proximally closer to humans in her spiritual philosophy. Indeed, transfiguration may only be a human supremacist fantasy of occupying the nonhuman other. Roderick (1994) argues that the familiar is actually experienced as the practitioner's own self, "certain animal spirits actually live inside each of us and are formative influences on our individual personalities, lending to each of us special abilities and attributes" (7). Although this type of familiar work is predicated on Indigenous ideologies, it unknowingly finds itself resting on colonizer mentality, with modern witches often suggesting that not only worshipping but also *killing* and *eating* totems could imbue the practitioner with a particular animal's stereotypical attributes. Thus, while familiar magic purports to reach beyond species borders to facilitate the physical and spiritual roots of humanity's shared ancestry with other animals, it tends to be more reductive than respectful. Furthermore, it overlooks the reality that humans, too, are animals, thus reifying the false human/animal binary. Presumably hominids are not thought to be available for shamanic use by human practitioners and *certainly* not by nonhumans.

It seems a difficult task for pagans to engage with other animals without reducing them to tropes and spirits to be absorbed or attempting to physically control them body and mind. Some moral negotiation is usually necessary to align claims of respect for others with ideologies of human supremacy.

Taxidermy, for instance, is one popular means of using Nonhuman Animals for totemic (or even simply decorative) purposes. Many texts encourage witches to gather and preserve bodies and body parts of deceased animals they find in natural spaces or even grocery stores. Although it seems to be the case that most of these bodies or body parts (such as mounted or decorated skulls and antlers) are remains from Nonhuman Animals who died naturally or by automobile collisions, the ideological and material objectification of Nonhuman Animals is more or less the same. Ko (2019) has noted this tendency in the colonial politics of racial construction, whereby the racialized other is culturally and materially plundered and then "stuffed" with ideologies of white supremacy to facilitate an unequal society. Ko theorizes a "zoological witchcraft," whereby the dominant class infiltrates body and mind to exploit and control the oppressed. As a vegan feminist scholar, Ko conceptualizes this by examining the suffering of Nonhuman Animals who are both materially taxidermized (in terms of being killed, stuffed, and put on display for the enjoyment of humans) and ideologically taxidermized (through processes of domestication which render them more controllable and thus more vulnerable to human violence). In the witchcraft community, the fascination with "the familiar" replicates these problematic power imbalances. For instance, elements of colonial logic can be found in Andrews' position that the essences of other animals are readily available for human use, to the point at which humans may even ritualistically shapeshift into them. Likewise, Harner's (1990) *The Way of the Shaman* provides an array of rituals to discover or recover power animals. White supremacy and human supremacy, in other words, both support an entitlement to the bodies, beliefs, and communities of otherized beings for exploitative purposes. Nonhuman Animals, like colonized peoples of color, become exotic foreign conquests.

Here, the colonialist element of appropriating Indigenous religious culture is worth reiterating, whereby the "other" takes on a mystical quality in its perceived primitiveness. Harner's analysis exemplifies this, claiming that "underneath our ordinary human cultural consciousness is a near-universal emotional connection with wild animal alter egos" (1990: 67). There is perhaps a lesson to be found in Andrea Smith's (1993) essay, "For All Those Who Were Indian in a Former Life," which argues that "respect" for Indigenous culture by outsiders usually manifests in some variation of fetishization, profiteering, spiritual appropriation, or avoidance of white society's responsibility for past and present Indigenous oppression. White women, she suggests, will do better to find strength in their own heritage. With Smith's own self-identification with Native American culture ironically under scrutiny at the time of this writing (Viren 2021), the importance of reflexivity could not be clearer.

Recall that, in traditional lore, witches have been believed capable of transfiguring into other animals to do their mischief. Valiente (1962), for instance, reports an English belief that women could become hares by the moonlight to harass and harm farmed animals. The same belief proliferated in early modern

Ireland, leading to taboos against eating hares that persisted into the 19th century. Transfiguration remains a prevalent theme in both pagan witchcraft and feminist witchcraft variants. For feminist practitioners, the practice of "body-knowing" encourages women to "activate and integrate all aspects of the self: physical, emotional, mental, and spiritual" (Ma 2000: 205) through deep attuning to the various bodily senses. This body work encourages practitioners to tap into the natural, biological, and even animalistic elements of their being, transgressing the cultural boundaries of the human being. Thus, the witchcraft community may have begun to consider the ethical problems with appropriating Indigenous and non-white culture for magical purposes, but the same cannot be said of Nonhuman Animals.

Anna Franklin (1997) introduces her book on British familiars by encouraging a shamanic connection with Nonhuman Animal powers: "Through this connection the shaman or witch can draw on the power of the whole species for their strength and abilities" (5). Nonhumans are also rendered servants in the belief that they can be controlled by humans, with some witches attempting to manipulate birds to deliver messages, for instance. Franklin also suggests that particularly powerful witches can master the ability to psychologically, or even *physically*, take on the body and mind of another animal, a process that, whether possible or not, suggests an entitlement to other animals who are rendered puppets for human wants. Projecting one's consciousness into the bodies of other animals, Franklin admits, "is not entirely ethical" and can "confuse and damage the animal involved" (22), a process not unlike the project of domestication in these ways. Otherwise, the human supremacist subjugation of Nonhuman Animals as servants, vessels, and food goes unremarked.

A Special *Dis*connection with Other Animals

To be clear, not all witches work with familiars or power animals, but many do claim a special connection with inhabitants of the natural world. Observes Blake (2015),

> Maybe it has something to do with our being a nature-based religion, because animals are a very relatable part of nature [...]. Mostly, I think it is because we are so open to connection in general: connection with deity, the natural world, spirit ... and animals are part of all that.
>
> *(121)*

As already discussed, sometimes this includes an ability to communicate with Nonhuman Animals on a psychic level, but sometimes this simply refers to a wider metaphysical awareness. Indeed, a unique capacity for heightened empathy is a characteristic (or "gift") often claimed by modern witches. These empaths believe themselves to be especially attuned to the experiences and inner life worlds of others. This can be a psychological connection, or, for some, this empathy is even physically perceived. Whether or not this supernatural level of empathy is real or simply imagined, these empathetic powers are greatly shaped by who anthroparchal culture can and cannot "see" in the social world. With the exception of those authored by Whitehurst (2015, 2017) and Morningstar (2005), none of the witch-authored books included in research for this book were able to sense the suffering of *trillions* of Nonhuman Animals who live and die by human hands each year on Planet Earth,[5] most often hidden in feedlots, industrial barns and tanks, deep sea nets, laboratories, "fur" farms, mines, factories, municipal "shelters," "zoos," "aquariums," faraway fields, and forests decimated by climate change and rife with "sports hunters." Most humans in the West, witches included, only interact with dogs, cats, rabbits, and sometimes songbirds, horses, or other proximal animals. These are not coincidentally the same species with whom witches claim a magical empathic connection.

No research currently exists to estimate the prevalence of anti-speciesist or vegan beliefs in the modern witch community, but it is safe to assume that most witches, despite their disproportionate claim to empathic powers and concern for the natural world, are not practicing vegans. Subsequently, many animals remain objects for pleasurable consumption and are not believed to exhibit psychologies, spirits, bodily experiences, or any other markers of personhood that a witch might connect to. The ability to communicate with ghosts, another characteristic that many witches assert, demonstrates a similar spiritual speciesism. Sensing ghosts says more about the witch's culture than the objective presence of the paranormal. As one example, research has identified that male spirits are disproportionately reported (Finucane 2001) (presumably their male privilege extends into the afterlife). Although the nonhuman deceased far outnumber that of humans, and given that most die extremely violent deaths for the most trivial of human wants and would presumably have a greater incentive to haunt, they comprise just a fraction of contemporary ghost stories (Wrenn 2020). In all this empathy and spirit-seeking, few witches are able to sense the recently departed who linger in their stomachs, toilets, and refrigerators. A true empathic connection with the dead would surely alert them to the immense suffering of Nonhuman Animals killed for the breastmilk in their morning coffee, the "ham" in their sandwich, the "leather" on their feet, and so on.

Veganism, as a political ethic, allows humans of all denominations to experience a special empathy with other animals in breaking down the institutions, ideologies, and structural barriers that segregate other animals and invisibilize their suffering. Here I suggest vegan witchcraft as a means to reestablish this special multispecies connection. The human species is moderately unique in its capacity for pro-sociality, evolved as it has to live in groups. Like other social species, humans are equipped with empathetic capabilities and symbiotic multispecies potential for collaborative living. What might be described as magic might actually be a consequence of measurable brain chemistry, and yet it is a power that remains largely untapped in modern Westerners socialized to center the human. Vegan feminism has argued that emotional ways of knowing and compassion-based connections have been wrongly suppressed under patriarchy in favor of reason, rationality, and objective disconnectedness (Donovan 1990, Gruen 2013, Kheel 2007). Veganism, like witchcraft, aims to reestablish this lost connection to nature and other species. Embracing empathy and unlocking its powerful potential is key to this transformation. Witchcraft has been limited by its reluctance to relinquish human supremacy and forgo the objectification of Nonhuman Animals. I suggest that veganism may be a political ethic *and* an emotional and spiritual mechanism for overcoming this barrier. Communicating with other animals and finding empowerment in that communication is not so difficult when the patriarchal restrictions of speciesism and sexism are relaxed.

Interestingly, research does support that the vegan and Nonhuman Animal rights community exhibits comparatively high degrees of empathy when compared with the general public (Erlanger and Tsytsarev 2012, Signal and Taylor 2015, Stone 2022). Whether or not individuals are drawn to pro-animal causes because they are particularly empathetic or whether affiliation with pro-animal causes increases empathy is difficult to discern, of course, and, for that matter, most of the species humans exploit, torture, and kill can communicate their distress perfectly well without the aid of any magic or special intuitiveness. Social psychological research, however, has demonstrated that children's innate compassion for other animals gradually wanes as the child matures and is socialized. By early adulthood, most empathetic concern for Nonhuman Animals has dissolved. Disregard for the wellbeing of animals (other than those categorized as companions or cute) is something that is taught; it is cultural (McGuire et al. 2022, Miralles et al. 2019).

Of Domestication and Disenchantment

This stifling effect of socialization is well known in the social sciences. Weber, for instance, may not have extended political consideration to Nonhuman Animals, but recall that he did observe that the move to modernity had a disenchanting effect on society. A key element of this modernization was the intensification of domestication, whereby the "wildness" of life, including that associated with nonhumans, has been subsumed under predictable, rationalized social relations. Zooarchaeologist Nerissa Russell (2024) points to the "ownership of animals and the creation of separate wild and domestic spheres," which would have had "profound consequences for human relations with other animals, the natural world, and each other, and thus also for their religions" (224). "Wild" animals took on a more prominent spiritual power once this category of "wildness" had been created with the widespread introduction of domestication. For witches who aim to tap into predomesticated society and reenchant daily life, the mundanity and tameness of cows, chickens, pigs, fishes, and other animals objectified in the economic system do not offer the same pagan romanticism. Likewise, domestication symbolizes submission to male order, an association that also runs counter to feminist interpretations of witchcraft. Indeed, Nonhuman Animals who have been domesticated by humans tend to be obscured in the familiar discourse (Andrews 1993, Farmer 2006, Grimassi 2021, Murphy-Hiscock 2018, Patterson 2017, Roderick 1994, Whitehurst 2015, 2017). As Andrews explains, domesticated species are "just links to the true power animal" (Andrews 1993: 8), those being boars, aurochs, wolves, jungle fowls, argali, and so on. More likely, their domestication, a marker of oppression, demystifies them. Domestication represents disempowerment, thus undermining the allure of the power animal with its imagined agency.

When these domesticated species *are* included, they are invariably noted for their association with fertility and prosperity, a theme that is repeated by other Wiccan catalogues of familiar species (Conway 2013). Recall that, despite the great complexity within each nonhuman species, it tends to be the qualities of interest and potential benefit to humans that will be emphasized. Likewise, psychologists and sociologists have noted that Nonhuman Animal worth tends to be ranked according to their utility to humans (Cole and Stewart 2014, Serpell 2004). In familiar work, domesticated animals are linked to fertility in ways that free-living animals are not. This is understandable given the purpose of domesticating food animals is to control their bodies and reproduction for human wealth, but describing Nonhuman Animals in terms of their reproductive or wealth-producing capacities is euphemistic, obscuring intentional and violent human manipulation over their bodies and lives. Thus, pigs, cows, chickens, goats, and other "livestock" become totems of privilege, wealth, and human supremacy and are rarely, if ever, examined as contributing characteristics or wisdom to benefit humans as is afforded to free-living species, particularly birds and charismatic megafauna. Morningstar (2005) is one exception, seeing cows and bulls, for instance, as sacred symbols of power, and pigs as symbolizing protection, play, and sociability. The diversity of life, if acknowledged, has much to offer, they conclude: "The rich and varied aspects of our animal world provide a veritable cauldron of information that Wiccans can delve into when weaving magic" (228).

As Western societies gradually disconnected from nature, Nonhuman Animals have become ritualistically important as a symbolic link to this lost way of life. Nonhuman totemism was certainly a major element of ancient human cultures. Pennethorne Hughes explains that this totemism was much more than a fear-based reverence, as has been surmised by some scholars. Instead, it emerged from a "psychological and economic bond" (1965: 26). In 20th-century British witchcraft, male practitioners were advised to craft garments and headwear to evoke the image of the "horned god" of the sacred hunt. Buckland (2002) even suggests using the preserved skins and hair of other animals for maximum affect. Historically, many species identified by witches as having totemic relevance were sacrificial. Franklin (1997), for instance, notes that bears, gooses, pigs, sheeps, and other such species were ritualistically killed so that their spilled blood and dismembered bodies might be used figuratively (and sometimes literally) as fertilizer to rejuvenate the land and bring another successful growing season. Some species (chickens and goats in particular) were also used as symbolic vessels for the elimination of illness, evil, and suffering in human animals.

As might be expected, the everyday violence of speciesism is not incorporated into the advice given in the discourse to witches, who claim to connect with other animals. Witches who identify with chickens, for instance, may be advised to pay attention to their maternal side, but will not be advised to take on another's illness, donate their eggs, or volunteer themselves as food for others. To be clear, even this symbolic use of Nonhuman Animals reduces them to vessels. Because familiar lore does not encourage the practitioner to understand chickens or other animals as individuals with unique personalities and life experiences, they serve only as hollow shells within which witches can impart their own desires, much in line with Ko's critical race theory of taxidermy. In support of a vegan witchcraft, then, the figurative objectification and symbolic exploitation of Nonhuman Animals should be confronted. Vegan feminism, importantly, has indicated that the *symbolic* and the *material* objectification of Nonhuman Animals (in addition to women and other feminized groups) are not unrelated. There are real-world consequences for oppressed groups that result from anthroparchal ideologies, in text, thought, and speech.

Respect for Nonhuman Animals in this regard is extremely spotty in modern witchcraft. Domesticated animals surface regularly in unproblematized accounts of sacrifice, and these vestiges of disempowerment would further explain the limited representation of domesticates in modern familiar work. More often than not, chickens, cows, pigs, and other animals exploited for food are so fully objectified that they do not even warrant mention in familiar guidebooks. In the few cases that they are mentioned, stereotypes about their objectified status are manipulated in the rendering of advice for ritual work. There are patriarchal undertones to the assumption that these animals can be objectified, owned, and exploited. For instance, Farmer (2006) associates cows with nourishment and nurturing with no acknowledgment of how the consensual nurturing of human mothers and the biological nourishment of human breastmilk for human babies is replaced with the exploitation of bovines and the theft of their breastmilk from calves. Andrews (1993) and Patterson (2017), by way of further examples, mention chickens as totems for fertility and sacrifice. Andrews also sexualizes gooses, suggesting their feathers have been used to increase sexuality and fertility. Farmer (2006) notes the same of turkeys, associating their mass slaughter with the sentiments of Thanksgiving in the United States. These sentiments include ceremony, sharing, and family, but not suffering. Andrews implicitly sexualizes this relationship by referencing the symbolic similarity found from killing chickens to bring life through death by earning the favor of the gods and by providing food with the figurative death experienced in orgasm or the literal death of the sperm at the point of conception. His sexual imagination for chicken sacrifice is varied. Chickens' feathers, he advises, are appropriate for stuffing the mattresses of marital beds. By contrast, the rooster takes on characteristics of masculinity, with Andrews associating them with qualities of protection, mystery, and even resurrection. These more powerful associations are not granted to the modest female chicken.

Reincarnation

Working with totems allows the practitioner to appreciate characteristics attributed to other animals and draw lessons, wisdom, and power from this connection. But, in relying heavily on stereotypes and presuming nonhuman totems exist primarily as servants to human wants and needs, animism and totemism can replicate speciesism and human supremacy. In witchcraft, humans and other animals remain fundamentally separate and far from equal. This ideology can also be found in discussions of reincarnation, whereby Nonhuman Animals continue to serve humanity in the afterlife. Although these reincarnation beliefs could be said to appropriate elements from Eastern religions, reincarnation in Western paganism refers more specifically to the role of humans within the wider ecology. That is, when the body dies, that body is reabsorbed into the ecosystem and sustains further life. It is also thought by some that the energy of the person who has died re-enters the universe, eventually returning in physical form as another living being. Witches are divided on whether or not Nonhuman Animals can return as humans or if humans can return as Nonhuman Animals. Some argue that reincarnation is species-specific, while others believe that any living being is capable of being born with the spirit or soul of any other living being. Valiente (1978), for one, is clear that Nonhuman Animals are included in this cycle, and every incarnation is chosen. Weinstein (1991) also argues that Nonhuman Animals can reincarnate. Although nonhumans are thought to control their path through this karmic process, subsequently exhibiting some agency, Weinstein also surmises that nonhumans will be swayed in their choice of reincarnation given connections to particular witches and desire to reunite with them. This might be interpreted as a special bond between the witch and other animals, but it also suggests that other-than-human animals are expected to serve humans even in the afterlife. Likewise, Franklin (1997) has observed that a wide variety of Nonhuman Animal species are thought to have a connection to the underworld, with the ability to convey messages or escort human visitors. In this tradition, Nonhuman Animals are not thought equal to humans in their experience of the spiritual life cycle.

If witches truly believe that they, as present-day humans, have lived previous lives as other species, this begs the question as to why they would not be more sympathetic to their plight. Some interpret the reincarnation process as an affront to the arbitrary species barrier. "In Witchcraft," Buckland explains, "the belief is that *all* things have souls" (2002: 18). However, he clarifies that some practitioners only believe that reincarnation can take place *within*, not between, species. In this belief, a human would only be born again as another human, never a cow or a chicken. Leek (1973) disagrees. The notion that humans should seek to overcome their inner animality, she notes, is an affront to the Nonhuman Animals they have embodied in past lives. Being animal is part of the journey, not something to be balanced or removed. That said, she is clear that "lower" and "higher" states of being can be experienced along this journey whereby animality is aligned with moral and evolutionary impoverishment. Evil people, she suggests, are "in a lower state of spiritual evolution and may even have just made it into this physical form, bringing memories of [their] animal nature into the present carnation" (1973: 127). The emphasis on individual responsibility for one's life outcome has implications for complicity with speciesism, as reincarnation beliefs tend to be associated with the greater reverence for the "do no harm" karmic rule. Some witches are adamant that Nonhuman Animals be included, even suggesting that humans who intentionally harm them will be held to account in their next lifetime. Valiente sees this as a means for resisting speciesism and restoring universal balance. If scientists came back as laboratory animals or if "hunters" returned as "game," she notes, "there would be real justice" (1978: 39).

Although witches believe that each individual is responsible for their own behaviors within their lifetime, karma also serves as a way of "rewarding" or "punishing" individuals for their behavior. Understood in this way, karma promises a higher level of being or more opportunities for learning by being born nonhuman or otherwise disadvantaged. Focusing on individual culpability tends to obscure larger social systems and institutions which create, maintain, and reproduce stratifications. It also falsely aligns with the centuries-old socially constructed and culturally enforced belief that the ideal state of being is white, wealthy, able-bodied European maleness. In Weinstein's system, it would follow that if an individual lived appropriately and, upon death, chose wisely, they should come back as a privileged white male. This presumption fails to acknowledge that white males have historically been the key drivers of a system that marginalizes, oppresses, and stigmatizes other groups. Weinstein does acknowledge that mass atrocities may create a unique challenge for this karmic system, but "people in these groups have been defined as necessary victims *by their enemies*," suggesting some responsibility for those who are causing these deaths. This could speak to the experiences of Nonhuman Animals, who have certainly been defined as necessary victims by anthroparchal myths that mark their flesh and fluids as both necessary and natural foods for great apes. By this logic, the unimaginable and unquantifiable suffering experienced by trillions of Nonhuman Animals each year is a karmic suffering imposed by humans, who wield their privilege of oppressing others for pleasure and profit primarily for the purposes of teaching a karmic lesson, which seems less likely than a simple invisibility of nonhuman personhood under witch thealogy. In any case, Weinstein *is* clear that witches should not abandon social responsibility by deferring all suffering to the karmic process, but the disagreement over whether or not Nonhuman Animals may participate in reincarnation denotes their lowered status and precarious position in witchcraft thealogy. "We are the spiders weaving our own webs" (1975: 154), Leek notes of reincarnation and personal responsibility, though whether or not humans are as morally relevant to spiders and other animals is unclear.

Leek (1975), at least, warns that "any teachings which claim that the highest duty of man [sic] is to 'overcome the animal' in him [sic]" (116) should be avoided, as other animals are part of the reincarnation journey. She offers a semblance of respect for other animals and clarifies that the belief in karma should not be used to coerce this respect: "While I do not advocate killing flies, that is out of respect to the life forces within the fly, not out of the fear that I may perhaps return, in another reincarnation as that fly" (1975: 150). Humans and other animals alike must do this work as Leek understands it, to strive for so-called higher orders of life, the aim being that Nonhuman Animals can "tread a different, more progressive karmic path next time around," she explains (1975: 116). Leek's position is confused. On one hand, she insists that denying the "animal" aspects of humanity (for instance, the cultural tendencies to restrict sex and conceal pregnancy) is incompatible with the true human experience. On the other, she discounts Nonhuman Animals as relevant to humanity's karmic journey, presumably due to their own "animal-like" behaviors. "It should be emphasized that we do not accept the Eastern belief that man [sic] can come back as a lesser animal," Leek explains of modern witches. Indeed, embracing one's inner animality is a common theme in contemporary witchcraft, but rarely does this entail acknowledging, challenging, or disrupting human supremacy. Adherence to human rationality—the realm of the mind—continues to dominate even in witchcraft's effort to embrace and celebrate all that of the body. As such, the harmony and humility with nature that Leek and other witches advocate stops short of equality. Humans are ultimately believed supreme to other animals cognitively, physically, and spiritually: "man [sic] has to know that he is more than flesh and blood, more than an animal living to sleep and eat and perpetuate his species" (Leek 1973: 149). Witches will do well, she suggests, to "act with inner wisdom, intelligence, and an awareness of love" to "gradually become free" with "less dramatic repercussions" (1973: 143). Nonhuman Animals, presumably, lack capacity for these moral characteristics. Witchcraft philosophies of reincarnation, then, despite their potential to level sentient beings as equal in grander schemes of natural cycles, continue to marginalize other-than-humans.

Going Skyclad

A final characteristic of modern witchcraft practice that links human practitioners to Nonhuman Animals and to their own animality is the custom of working sky-clad. Although perhaps less discussed and less practiced in the 21st century, nude ritual work was characteristic of the 20th century witchcraft revival.[6] Although nakedness certainly does draw on the base nature of human animals and redeems sexuality as something neither in need of concealment or stigma, Valiente (1978) recommends working naked is anything but sexual. Instead, it helps to create an altered state of mind conducive to ritual work. Practically speaking, performing witchcraft in the nude improves freedom of movement and reduces the danger of candles catching clothing alight. It is also a means of creating equality and shared humility among practitioners, a direct eschewing of institutional religions that reinforce power relations through ceremonial garb. As Adler notes, nude practice has a "leveling quality" (2006: 109). Salomonsen affirms this: "Ritual nudity symbolizes that the participants, at a deep level, are one body, one being, one member, as it symbolizes the innocence of beginnings, of conversions, of being born again" (2002: 225). "When we take off our clothes," Starhawk adds, "we drop our social masks, our carefully groomed self-images. We become open. The mystical meaning of the naked human body is 'truth'" (1999: 71).

Starhawk clarifies that nudity is never *required*, as the vulnerability it entails should not be forced on practitioners, but when freely adopted, it is a custom that adds potency to spellwork. Grimassi supports this, claiming that it "helps to magnetize your aura, and being nude while you gather herb makes you a creature of nature again, free from the signs of domestication" (2000: 37). Indeed, several Wiccan writers liken nude spellcraft as a means for humans to return to their animal being by materially disrupting the clear divide between humans and other animals, civilization and nature. Valiente claims that it can encourage the witch to tap into their "animal magnetism" (1978: 101), as the human body supposedly emanates an auric energy that clothing can mask or disable. For Salomonsen, it encourages "vulnerability, sensuality, honesty, and equality, as well as with the remembrance of how human life is brought into this world: as a naked body, through a naked body" (2002: 225). Morning Glory Zell-Ravenheart (2004) indicates its ritual purpose in symbolizing purity and sacredness, allowing the witch to "work just as nature made them" (23). I suspect there is an effort to attune to prehistoric ancestors to re-create ancient religiosity. It may also be an effort to permeate the species barrier, given that wearing clothes is one of the primary cultural means by which humans maintain distinction. There are many explanations for the practice, but it seems that most, one way or another, tap into a desire for the modern witch to eschew the trappings of civilization, capitalist consumerism, and domestication that have historically weighed upon women, Nonhuman Animals, nature, and other feminized groups. Skyclad practice might offer a means of rewilding and, for vegan witchcraft, a means of reclaiming animality without colonizing, exploiting, or killing other species. Witches, after all, are great apes, born as naked as any other animal. Disrobing serves as a means of relinquishing hierarchies; perhaps this could include human supremacy as well.

Conclusion

Nonhuman Animals have been foundational to the practice of witchcraft—either real or imagined—in medieval, premodern, and modern eras. Much of this relationship is founded on animism—the recognition of nonhuman personhood and sacred aliveness of nature. Animism has been foundational to many of the world's traditional spiritual practices, paganism included. This pagan connection would later inform Christian persecution of witchcraft, whereby the familiar was conjured as evidence of the witch's evil ways. Materially speaking, however, there were certainly connections between real, living women and real, living Nonhuman Animals. Anthroparchy has rendered both women and other animals property to be husbanded, their bodily autonomy and reproductive capacities owned and exploited for men's benefit. In this shared social space, women have been in regular contact with other animals as primary caretakers, and those marginalized from this heteronormative system through disability, age, widowhood, or a desire to live alone may have found company and companionship from other animals. Women may have also been made more assailable by the industrialization of Nonhuman Animal agriculture, namely the rise of the "wool" trade in the Middle Ages, which cleared land by all means of dubious, forceful, and violent measures. In such conditions, women's status was precarious. The fracturing of communities under a variety of structural shifts pushed "deviant" and "burdensome" women even further to the margins and made them more vulnerable to persecution. Vegan feminism argues that as Western society shifted into a domesticated, anthroparchal society the potential threat of resistance that any alliances between women and other animals may have posed could have invited societal suppression. If this is the case, it is perhaps predictable that the suspicion placed on women's connection to other animals was so fundamental to anti-witch persecution. Indeed, there is ample evidence in early Western witch persecution that women's very humanity was on trial. Nonhuman Animals were strategically utilized in making meaning of women's perceived deviance. There would be ramifications for Nonhuman Animals, of course, namely the active killing of demonized species as well as the broader ideological entrenchment of the notion that other animals were potentially evil and must be controlled.

Yet vegan feminism also sees the connection between feminized humans and other animals as a potential point of solidarity, strength, and resilience. Although collaboration with familiars was a major point of persecution in earlier times, today's witches have reclaimed their connection with other animals in magical practice. Modern familiar work is a blend of reclaimed tropes about the witch's relations with other animals from the days of persecution, animism of prehistoric pagan traditions, and shamanic elements from other Indigenous communities. On its face, this aspect of witchcraft seems to put into practice the basic tenets of vegan feminist thought: the very link between animalized and feminized groups (particularly women and other animals) that has been used as a rationale for marginalization might be reclaimed to resist oppression. Explains Forest,

> Animism, the belief that all things have a spirit and life within them no matter how different from our own, allows our awareness to stretch

beyond the merely physical and material and our consciousness to strive beyond a human centric version of the universe into something far larger.

(2020: 3)

Ancient animist epistemologies have been resurrected by today's witches in a radical way, directly challenging the encroachment of rationalization that has gradually demystified the natural world and commodified it for the commercial and political benefit of largely male-dominated institutions. For the most part, however, this work with other animals is symbolic and self-serving, such that witches today step into the very anthroparchal role that has historically influenced their own oppression. In some cases, it is explicitly human supremacist and colonialist, with witches hoping to control Nonhuman Animals for their bidding or even believing they can physically embody Nonhuman Animals to achieve their own aims. Although witchcraft is a nature religion, exceedingly few texts engage familiar work in order to better understand Nonhuman Animals on their own terms or for their own benefit. Some witches also claim extraordinary levels of empathy, but this power rarely encompasses a connection with other animals, especially those who are domesticated and slated for commercial use. In failing to sense the existence or experience of Nonhuman Animals exploited for human use, witches differ little from the general non-vegan, nonmagical population. Nonhumans could serve as comrades rather than commodities in resistance to an anthroparchal society, but the witch community would first need to challenge the normalcy of species inequality.

Vegan witchcraft, by contrast, emphasizes that, as human beings, *all* witches possess the power for empathy. Empathy allows those humans who are open and willing to understand to sense the experiences of other animals, feel a connection to them, and develop compassion across species barriers. Working with familiars might mean allowing Nonhuman Animals to speak on their own behalf in their own way, perhaps even serving as ambassadors rather than objectified generalized representations of their entire species. Instead of treating Nonhuman Animals as symbolic objects for anthropocentric aims and replicating the patriarchal tendency to exploit nature, witches could recognize Nonhuman Animals as persons in their own right. Rejecting the objectification of Nonhuman Animals—even that which transpires for spiritual purposes—supports a more inclusive, respectful, and compassionate society.

Notes

1 The first "witch" to be charged as keeping a familiar was a woman living in 14th-century Ireland (Sax 2009).
2 This chapter also relies on several books on shamanism that have been heavily cited and recommended by leading texts in witchcraft, namely *Animal Speak* (Andrews 1993).
3 Women, too, made accusations of witchcraft. Hester suggests that this role may have fallen on women as "moral gatekeepers" (2002: 282), whereby women bargained with

patriarchy to secure their social status by association with male power. Women, after all, had extremely limited power in the medieval and early modern eras, such that making accusations (or even *admitting* to witchcraft themselves) may have offered a sense of control in their lives (Gaskill 2002, Karlsen 1998, Larner 2002).

4 The slaughter of cows for dairy and flesh consumption is actually widespread in India, particularly with recent industrial development in the region (Narayanan 2023). India is the world's largest dairy producer, an industry that requires the systematic killing of calves and their mothers. India is also one of the top five "beef" producers globally.

5 There are several books that take a vegan approach to interspecies telepathy, but none specifically in the Wiccan or witchcraft tradition surfaced in my research.

6 Working skyclad is arguably less commonplace in 21st-century witchcraft, although some witches work skyclad underneath ceremonial robes to balance modesty and comfort with the magical attributes of nude practice.

References

Adler, M. 2006. *Drawing Down the Moon*. London: Penguin.

Andrews, T. 1993. *Animal Speak*. Woodbury: Llewellyn.

Bell, J. 2001. *The Grimoire of Lady Sheba*. St. Paul: Llewellyn.

Blake, D. 2015. *Everyday Witchcraft*. Woodbury: Llewellyn.

Buckland, R. 2002. *Complete Book of Witchcraft*. Woodbury: Llewellyn.

Chronicle Books. n.d. "Unfamiliar Familiars Full Description." Retrieved August 30, 2023, from: https://www.chroniclebooks.com/products/unfamiliar-familiars-hc.

Cole, M. and K. Stewart. 2014. *Our Children and Other Animals*. Surrey: Ashgate.

Conway, D. 2013. *Animal Magick*. Woodbury: Llewellyn.

Donovan, J. 1990. "Animal Rights and Feminist Theory." *Signs* 15 (2): 350–375.

Dunayer, J. 2001. *Animal Equality*. Derwood: Ryce Pub.

Dunayer, J. 2004. *Speciesism*. New York: Lantern Books.

Engels, D. 2000. *Classical Cats*. London: Routledge.

Erlanger, A. and S. Tsytsarev. 2012. "The Relationship between Empathy and Personality in Undergraduate Students' Attitudes toward Nonhuman Animals." *Society & Animals* 20 (1): 21–38.

Farmer, S. 2006. *Animal Spirit Guides*. London: Hay House.

Finucane, R. 2001. "Historical Introduction: The Example of Early Modern and Nineteenth-Century." pp. 9–17, in *Hauntings and Poltergeists*, J. Houran and R. Lange (Eds.). Jefferson: McFarland & Company.

Forest, D. 2020. *Wild Magic*. Woodbury: Llewellyn.

Franklin, A. 1997. *Familiars*. Berks: Capall Bann Publishing.

Franklin, A. 1999. *Animals and Modern Cultures*. London: SAGE.

Gardner, G. 1970. *Witchcraft Today*. London: Citadel Press.

Gaskill, M. 2002. "Witchcraft and Power in Early Modern England." pp. 343–352, in *The Witchcraft Reader*, D. Oldridge (Ed.). London: Routledge.

Grimassi, R. 2000. *Wiccan Magick*. St. Paul: Llewellyn.

Grimassi, R. 2021. *The Witch's Familiar*. Woodbury: Llewellyn.

Gruen, L. 2013. "Entangled Empathy: An Alternative Approach to Animal Ethics." pp. 223–231, in *The Politics of Species*, R. Corbey and A. Lanjouw (Eds.). Cambridge: Cambridge University Press.

Hall, N. 2023. *Path of the Moonlight Hedge*. Woodbury: Llewellyn.

Harner, M. 1990. *The Way of the Shaman*. San Francisco: HarperCollins.

Hester, M. 2002. "Patriarchal Reconstruction and Witch-hunting." pp. 276–288, in *The Witchcraft Reader*, D. Oldridge (Ed.). London: Routledge.

Hobgood, L. 2024. "Companion Animals." pp. 212–223, in *Animals and Religion*, D. Aftandilian, B. Ambros, and A. Gross (Eds.). London: Routledge.

Horne, R. 2019. *Folk Witchcraft*. Moon Over the Mountain Press.

Hughes, P. 1965. *Witchcraft*. London: Penguin.

Jackson, L. 2002. "Witches, Wives and Mothers." pp. 353–366, in *The Witchcraft Reader*, D. Oldridge (Ed.). London: Routledge.

Karlsen, C. 1998. *The Devil in the Shape of a Woman*. London: W. W. Norton & Company.

Kheel, M. 2007. *Nature Ethics*. Landham: Rowman & Littlefield.

Ko, A. 2019. *Racism as Zoological Witchcraft*. New York: Lantern Books.

Kott, M. and J. DeVine. 2020. *Extraordinary Animal Companions for the Modern Witch*. San Francisco: Chronicle Books.

Larner, C. 2002. "Was Witch-Hunting Woman-Hunting?" pp. 273–275, in *The Witchcraft Reader*, D. Oldridge (Ed.). London: Routledge.

Leek, S. 1973. *The Complete Art of Witchcraft*. New York: New American Library.

Leek, S. 1975. *The Complete Art of Witchcraft*. London: Leslie Frewin.

Lyons, S. 2019. *Revolutionary Witchcraft*. New York: Running Press.

Ma, V. 2000. "Woman Mysteries." pp. 201–216, *Daughters of the Goddess*, W. Griffin (Ed.). Oxford: AltaMira Press.

McKay, D. 2024. *A Witch's Ally*. Woodbury: Llewellyn.

McGuire, L., S. B. Palmer, and N. S. Faber. 2022. "The Development of Speciesism: Age-Related Differences in the Moral View of Animals." *Social Psychological and Personality Science*. Online first.

Mershon, K. 2024. "Gender and Sexuality." pp. 58–69, in *Animals and Religion*, D. Aftandilian, B. Ambros, and A. Gross (Eds.). London: Routledge.

Midelfort, H. 2002. "The Experience of Bewitchment." pp. 113–119, in *The Witchcraft Reader*, D. Oldridge (Ed.). London: Routledge.

Miralles, A., M. Raymond, and G. Lecointre. 2019. "Empathy and Compassion toward Other Species Decrease with Evolutionary Divergence Time." *Scientific Reports* 9: 19555.

Morningstar, S. 2005. *The Art of Wiccan Healing*. London: Hay House.

Moura, A. 2020. *Green Witchcraft*. Woodbury: Llewellyn.

Murphy-Hiscock, A. 2018. *The Witches' Book of Self-Care*. London: Adams Media.

Narayanan, Y. 2023. *Mother Cow, Mother India*. Redwood City: Stanford University Press.

Pamita, M. 2025. *The Witch's Guide to Animal Familiars*. Carlsbad, CA: Hay House.

Parish, H. 2019. "'Paltrie Vermin, Cats, Mise, Toads, and Weasils': Witches, Familiars, and Human-Animal Interactions in the English Witch Trials." *Religions* 10 (134): 10020134.

Patterson, R. 2017. *Animal Magic*. Hants: John Hunt.

Probyn-Rapsey, F. 2019. "The 'Crazy Cat Lady'." pp. 175–185, in *Animaladies*, L. Gruen and F. Probyn-Rapsey (Eds.). New York: Bloomsbury.

Robinson, M. 2024. "L'nuwey Views of Animal: Personhood and Their Implications." pp. 25–35, in *Animals and Religion*, D. Aftandilian, B. Ambros, and A. Gross (Eds.). London: Routledge.

Roderick, T. 1994. *The Once Unknown Familiar*. St. Paul: Llewellyn.

Russel, J. 1985. *A History of Witchcraft*. London: Thames and Hudson.

Russell, N. 2024. "Domestication and Religion." pp. 224–233, in *Animals and Religion*, D. Aftandilian, B. Ambros, and A. Gross (Eds.). London: Routledge.

Salomonsen, J. 2002. *Enchanted Feminism*. London: Routledge.

Sax, B. 2009. "The Magic of Animals: English Witch Trials in the Perspective of Folklore." *Anthrozoös* 22 (4): 317–332.

Scaerie Faerie. 2004. "Birds, Bugs and Spiritual Growth: Totem Animals and the Witch." pp. 78–82, in *Pop! Goes the Witch*, F. Horne (Ed.). New York: The Disinformation Company.

Scott, A. 1974. *Witch, Spirit, Devil*. London: White Lion.

Serpell, J. 2002. "Guardian Spirits or Demonic Pets: The Concept of the Witch's Familiar in Early Modern England, 1530–1712." pp. 157–190, in *The Animal/Human Boundary*, A. Creager and W. Jordon (Eds.). Rochester: University of Rochester Press.

Serpell, J. 2004. "Factors Influencing Human Attitudes to Animals and Their Welfare." *Animal Welfare* 13 (1): 145–151.

Signal, T. and N. Taylor. 2015. "Attitude to Animals and Empathy: Comparing Animal Protection and General Community Samples." *Anthrozoös* 20 (2): 125–130.

Smith, A. 1993. "For All Those Who Were Indian in a Former Life." pp. 168–172, in *Ecofeminism and the Sacred*, C. Adams (Ed.). New York: Continuum.

Starhawk. 1997. *Dreaming the Dark*. Boston: Beacon Press.

Starhawk. 1999. *The Spiral Dance*. Third edition. New York: HarperOne.

Stone, A. 2022. "The Relationship between Attitudes to Human Rights and to Animal Rights is Partially Mediated by Empathy." *The Journal of Social Psychology* 163 (3): 367–380.

Sutton, Z. and N. Taylor. 2022. "Between Force and Freedom: Place, Space, and Animals-as-Pet-Commodities." pp. 177–198, in *Vegan Geographies*, P. Hodge, A. McGregor, S. Springer, O. Véron, and R. White. New York: Lantern Books.

Thomas, K. 1983. *Man and the Natural World*. Harmondsworth: Penguin.

Valiente, D. 1962. *Where Witchcraft Lives*. London: The Aquarian Press.

Valiente, D. 1975. *Natural Magic*. Custer: Phoenix.

Valiente, D. 1978. *Witchcraft for Tomorrow*. London: Robert Hale.

Viren, S. 2021. "The Native Scholar Who Wasn't." Retrieved May 6, 2024, from: http://www.nytimes.com/2021/05/25/magazine/cherokee-native-american-andrea-smith.html.

Walker-Meikle, K. 2013. *Late Medieval Pet-keeping*. London: University College London.

Weinstein, M. 1991. *Earth Magic*. Custer: Phoenix.

Weinstein, M. 2020. *Positive Magic*. Newburyport: Weiser Books.

Whitehurst, T. 2015. *Holistic Energy Magic*. Woodbury: Llewellyn.

Whitehurst, T. 2017. *Magical Housekeeping*. Woodbury: Llewellyn.

Wrenn, C. L. 2020. "Discriminating Spirits: Cultural Source Theory and the Human-Nonhuman Boundary." *Mortality* 25 (3): 348–363.

Zell-Ravenheart, M. G. 2004. "Fire-Light and Moon-Shadows: A Summary of Wiccan Lore." pp. 20–26, in *Pop! Goes the Witch*, F. Horne (Ed.). New York: The Disinformation Company.

3
GREEN WITCHCRAFT

Introduction

Green witchcraft is an ecofeminist pagan practice that emphasizes the practitioner's connection to nature and the power to be found there. "Mother Earth is powerful!" Whitehurst exclaims, "When we notice and honor our interconnection with her, we are deeply nourished by her power, and we can ride its tide as we allow it to fuel our intentions and magical workings" (2015: 154). Green witchcraft is distinct in that it makes natural connection paramount by incorporating herbs, plants, seasons, and ecosystems in magical practice. Vanderbeck defines it as a "relationship with all things natural and supernatural for harnessing that energy in a way that can affect your everyday life" (2020: ix), a "call from the earth" that involves slow living, plant medicine, and honoring "the spirits of the trees, the animals, and even the rocks" (2020: ix). Subsequently, green witches often incorporate natural elements in their incantations, which are inclusive of the elements, the directions, plants, and herbs, and engage Nonhuman Animals. They may also incorporate herbs in their spellwork and herbalism in making magical sachets and charms, teas, poultices, and infused oils. Green witches sometimes practice outdoors, or they bring the outdoors inside by decorating their ritual spaces with flowers, leaves, branches, and other treasures from nature. The idea is to align with nature to empower one's own magical practice.

This collaboration with nature, with its rejection of domination and ownership, distinguishes green witchcraft from patriarchal religions. Many of the leading witch thealogists make this relationship of reciprocity and respect integral to the practice. The green witch is "not a steward of the earth," Ann Moura explains, "the Witch *is* the earth" (2020: 7). "In the Green level," she continues, "life is an immortal energy" (8). Lady Sabrina adds: "Witchcraft is a process of learning to understand nature and tread her paths with confidence

DOI: 10.4324/9781032649801-3

and pride" (2001: 10). Sybil Leek aligns witchcraft with "the four Great Sabbats of the four seasons," which "establish simple psychic guarantees of health and fruitfulness in man [sic], beast [sic], and plant life" (1973: 18). This psychic alignment, she insists, is an important antidote to the urbanization of modern life, detached as it is from natural processes. It is cyclic, resisting the rationalistic approach that now predominates with its end goals, end points, and pursuit of growth and progress. Green witchcraft also resists the capitalistic approach to surveying nature for its profit-making potential, as nature is not understood according to its exchange value. Instead, its value is found in its flowing and rejuvenating energy. Indeed, like many paths of witchcraft, it is distinctly feminist, flipping the predominant androcentric and anthropocentric perspectives by positioning the feminine, the natural, and the wild as sacred and empowering rather than sinful and dangerous.

This chapter employs a vegan feminist critique to examine the basic principles of green witchcraft, beginning with an exploration of how vegan feminism and green witchcraft have comingled for some decades, particularly within ecofeminist philosophy and activism. Despite these historic entanglements, green witchcraft abandons its spiritual commitment to other animals when confronted with vegetarianism and veganism. The ideological subjugation that persists in witchcraft poses problems, disrupting the ethic of reciprocity with the maintenance of the human-nonhuman binary. Green witchcraft aims to work *with* nature, not *over* it and, further, it typically asks for the consent of nature and its inhabitants before using them in practice. Using animal products in green witchcraft troubles this notion of consent, however, as Nonhuman Animals do not (and cannot) consent to being forcibly impregnated, confined, separated from their children, maimed, and killed for products to satisfy culturally defined human pleasures. Nature-based witches defend the right to kill and eat other animals more often than they challenge it. In fact, much of this defense is couched in patriarchal mythologies and colonial imaginaries of the sacred "hunt" that romanticize the killing of other animals for the spiritual and material development of humans. The witchcraft community's near universal rejection of Nonhuman Animal sacrifice for ritualistic purposes, furthermore, is sidelined in order to integrate these narratives of "hunting" and flesh consumption. Although these narratives are thought useful for constructing a link to wilderness lost, vegan feminism identifies them as patriarchal in origin. In subsuming more peaceful and symbiotic (albeit less exhilarating) histories of ancestral women, these narratives are also patriarchal in practice. Ultimately, it is argued that green witchcraft maintains patriarchal hierarchies of control and domination and thus remains antithetical to vegan feminism. To this end, it serves as a rather flawed forerunner to vegan witchcraft.

Roots of Green Witchcraft

As summarized in Chapter 1, veganism and modern witchcraft share a common point of resurgence in Western counterculture. The back to the land movement, the natural foods movement, the environmental movement, growing interest in alternative spiritualities, and other counterculture initiatives pushed back on capitalistic, anthroparchal authority and critiqued prevailing social inequalities with inclusive, nature-based perspectives (Amey 2014). As witchcraft was coming into its modern fruition in the mid-20th century, it did so along furtive feminist, anti-speciesist, and environmental organizing. These approaches responded to the entrenched legacy of the Enlightenment, with its emphasis on rational organization, rational thought, and the control over mind, body, and nature. Yet, for all the freedoms the Enlightenment has introduced with its scientific exploration and emphasis on individual rights, it has also entailed a systemic encroachment into all aspects of life, demystifying, categorizing, standardizing, and, with the aid of capitalism transpiring in tandem, also commodifying. Witchcraft, feminism, environmentalism, and Nonhuman Animal rights activism have all been constrained and diminished by the rational emphasis of the Enlightenment project, but so too have they benefited from greater intellectual exploration, which has inspired efforts to rethink inequalities and decolonize women, other animals, and nature. As conversations mingled across picket lines, protests, workshops, community centers, and hallways of universities, attention to the various overlaps in these radical alternatives to hegemonies of human dominance, patriarchy, exploitation, and war perhaps inevitably began to coalesce into intersectional approaches. Ecofeminism was one key area of development, resisting the androcentrism of both environmental thought and organization by incorporating elements of feminism more holistically to theorize the rampant destruction of nature and rising concerns with climate change. In challenging the modernist effort to tame and conquer all that is wild, be it nature, women, or other animals, ecofeminism interrogated relations of power, categories of difference, and dualistic relationships that had become entrenched in the West.

Ecofeminism and the Goddess Tradition

Over the following decades, ecofeminism has deeply informed the development of both paganism and veganism. It is characterized by an avoidance of dualism, particularly as manifested in binaries constructed between nature and civilization, masculine and feminine, and human and nonhuman. It also resists the rationalist worldview that finds nature and its inhabitants rendered categorizable, commodifiable, improvable, and exploitable. As such, it has recognized that oppressions tend to interlock, necessitating an intersectional response (Alloun 2015). Ecofeminism, furthermore, has argued that humanity's connection to the natural world is, if not sacred, then at least deeply profound, pushing back on the rationalist demystification and objectification of humanity's place in the world.

Green witchcraft in the United States is heavily influenced by ecofeminism as practiced by second wave feminists in the San Francisco Bay area. Although spirituality is not a necessary component of either witchcraft or ecofeminism, a reverence for "the goddess" is prevalent. Starhawk (2020) explains this spiritual approach as a natural result of the enormous change in worldview that both entails. More than a change in worldview, it also entails a consciousness to nature and regular connection with it. This reconnection with nature could indeed be very profound. As discussed in her seminal *Holy Book of Women's Mysteries*, Z. Budapest (1986) recollects that she and her feminist colleagues began to organically convene outdoors on the sabbats (sometimes drawing the attention of wary neighbors and unsympathetic police officers). These feminist witches recognized that patriarchy was not simply an oppression of women but of nature more broadly. Women were quite literally disconnected from the land upon which they drew their power. Indeed, Daly (1984) has identified the intentional separation of women from elemental nature as a primary means of their suppression. Ecofeminism is premised on the overlapping oppression of women and the environment, both of which are thought to be regarded with "fear, resentment, and denigration" (Spretnak 1993: 261). As is the case with witchcraft, ecofeminists have challenged the divide maintained between the material and the spiritual (Adams 1993), a direct confrontation with the Western patriarchal tradition that has sought "rather desperately" to "transcend nature and the body—especially the female body" (Spretnak 1993: 261). Ecofeminism recognizes instead a sacredness to the *connection* between women and nature, whereby both nature and body are considered "sources of spiritual revelation" (Spretnak 1993: 261).

Some worship a true goddess or set of goddesses, while others see the goddess as symbolic, "a metaphor for divine immanence and the transcendent sacred whole" (Spretnak 1993: 273). Greenwood emphasizes that "the goddess" is "a *political* symbol" (2000: 141). For many ecofeminists and witches alike, the "goddess" is thought to exist within each living being, thus situating sacredness and power within each individual. The Wiccan utilization is rather expansive, referring to the cosmic, Gaia, and the erotic, and not all practitioners agree on interpretations (Clifton 2006). Maternal energy, however, is usually fostered, whereby practitioners are encouraged to take on a nurturing leadership role in their personal or cosmic spheres. Although ecofeminism does often conceptualize this nurturance as a maternal power, it remains critical of patriarchy's tendency to abuse that labor with enforced selflessness and usually aims to disturb traditional gender roles (Berger 2000). Some ecofeminists, furthermore, reject gender essentialism outright, aiming to include kinds of gender and nurturing styles (Irni 2024). With consideration of the possibility of exacerbating gender essentialism by associating women, femininity, and spirituality with deep connection to the Earth (and beyond), ecofeminism is thus charged with tackling hierarchical social arrangements that separate reason from the body while affirming femininity as a valid means of navigating the self and broader society (Warren 1993).

Ecofeminist Ethics

Although its primary focus is the interrogation of false dualisms placed on and between humans and nature, whether to include Nonhuman Animals in the ecofeminist ethic of care has been debated (Cudworth 2016). Explain Sjöö and Mor (1991): "Moralisms, dualistic dogmas, repressive prohibitions block our imagination at its source, which is the fusion of sexual and spiritual energies" (421). This could suggest that veganism, frequently derided as moralistic and prohibitive, will illicit little confidence from the goddess tradition, despite the separatism that nonveganism maintains between humans and other animals. Finding liberatory power in feminine socialization patterns (particularly those relating to care and emotional expression), vegan ecofeminists have instead argued for a mindful consideration of other animals, intentionally resisting the cold, rationalistic, and objectifying approach that typifies a patriarchal society's multispecies relations. Many ecofeminists have exalted the importance of free-living animals, to be clear, but not all have been willing to take a vegetarian (much less vegan) position (Warren 1993), and domesticated animals have been generally obscured from the discourse. Nonetheless, ecofeminism rejects that humans are inherently dominant over nature. Rather, other-than-human animals are thought to exist as an extension of the universe in unity and harmony. The elements of the universe, after all, are physically embodied in each person, be they human or nonhuman. The mysteriousness of this universal design—whether intentionally created by a "god" or simply accidental—instills awe, while the lush greenness of life on Earth invites wonder in its aliveness and abundance (Fideler 1997). Miernowska adds, "We are not part of nature. We are nature" (2020: 13), and the endless growth in natural cycles becomes a source of personal wellbeing that the consumerism of modern capitalist life has promised but largely failed to deliver.

British witchcraft as had been reimagined for the 20th century certainly drew inspiration from nature, but American witchcraft explicitly centered it. Gardner, Wicca's founder, was himself a naturist, but his vision of witchcraft saw it rooted in Stone Age fertility rituals. The greater alignment with nature in the United States may stem from the legacy of movements in romanticism and environmentalism. Wicca's claim to be a nature religion in the 1970s, in fact, strategically pulled on environmentalism as a newly resonant frame, particularly following the success of the inaugural Earth Day (Clifton 2006). Although this has not always meant that witches have been environmentalists, they were certainly more green-oriented than the average American. In the United States at least, this alignment with Earth Day would mark a break from witchcraft's attempt to align with old, prehistoric religions, reframing it as nature-based worship.

By the 1980s, witchcraft was deeply entangled with the environmental movement. Vivianne Crowley notes a rich history of magical gatherings and group rituals which helped to "encourage environmental activism and an identification with the natural world" and create "social cohesion in the Wiccan community" and "heal the breach between self and other" (2000: 162). Because modern paganism, whether goddess worshipping or not, sees nature as sacred and representative of the feminine divine (Jones and Matthews 1990), it is fundamentally concerned with planetary health. Starhawk (1999) is perhaps the most prominent in this regard, but Reverend Selena Fox, a Midwestern American priestess and spokesperson for Wiccan religious rights, has made this environmental protectionism central to her work as well. In the 1970s, Fox founded the nature preserve and gathering space Circle Sanctuary in Wisconsin, rooting pagan practice in physical proximity to wilderness. Indeed, she often capitalizes Nature in her writing as a measure of respect and to indicate its immanence (Puca 2023). For witchcraft, this alignment with nature is an active reclaiming of a relationship that was historically persecuted among nature-working pagans. The Enlightenment with its reformations and rationalizations may have opened up space for critical inquiry and discovery (to the general benefit of persecuted practitioners, who were less likely to be deemed demonic or supernatural), but these same ideals would lead to rapid industrial expansion and the exploitation of natural resources, giving rise to a green witch revival.

For Starhawk, humanity's estrangement from nature and spirit is a consequence of domination in both the figurative and literal sense. "The removal of content, of value, serves as the basis for the exploitation of nature" (1997: 5), she explains. And when spirit is eradicated from politics, this could facilitate the manipulation of objectified groups: "We lose our own sense of self-worth [...] and acquiesce in our own exploitation" (1997: 6–7). Drawing on the sociological work of Herbert Marcuse, Starhawk sees a society socialized in disempowerment. Turning to the goddess is believed to disrupt this estrangement and foster an attitude of resistance, one that involves "choosing to take this living world, the people and creatures on it, as the ultimate meaning and purpose of life, to see the world, the earth and our lives as sacred" (1997: 11). For Starhawk and other ecofeminists, culture is identified as the leading contributor to the normalization of inequality and the maintenance of boundaries between humanity and nature. As such, this culture is thought malleable, and the ecofeminist—whether they identify as a witch or not—has a duty to maleate it. There is an element of creativity here, imagining the unknown, interacting with other animals and nature, and forging a culture that is symbiotic and egalitarian. Many witchcraft paths also see a return to animism as a means to achieve planetary healing. Hall (2023), for instance, advises a hedge witch pathway, whereby practitioners might rebuild their connection and familiarity with nature, encouraging a partnership. By spending time in nature, Hall and others find a potential for rewilding. Hedge witchery, in particular, prioritizes the margins as liminal spaces of considerable power. Likewise, for Nonhuman Animals, these are spaces that provide much needed refuge for free-living animals and wild plants in an increasingly controlled landscape.

Healing and Cyclical Living

The protectiveness that green witches find in nature is not thought to be one-sided. By merging the late-20th century's renewed interest in homeopathic medicine with reclaimed knowledges of traditional folk remedies, modern witchcraft's relationship with nature offers healing that is spiritual but also psychological and physical. For many priestesses and influential authors, in fact, healing is the central aim of the craft (Leek 1973). This emphasis on healing is also used to counter prejudice against witchcraft, given its stereotypical association with harming and hexing. This stereotype masks a very opposite reality in the history of witchcraft persecution. Ehrenreich and English argue in their influential feminist text on women in medicine *Witches, Midwives and Nurses* (1973) that folk healers constituted the majority of women trialed and killed for witchcraft. In Britain, this assault is believed to be part of the Church's attempt to squash women's empirical and evidence-based approaches to healing, approaches that competed with the more supernatural and mysterious power that the Church wielded. In America, an opposite tactic was employed whereby women's supposed lack of empirical capability was used as reason to institutionally and legally bar them from medical practice. Professionalization of the medical discipline solidified male control, not only over the ability to practice, but over access to the scientific knowledge itself. The stereotypes manufactured against women as witches or quacks were fluid, adapting as needed to suppress women's power. The witchcraft trials are a harrowing reminder of how dangerous this patriarchal strategy could be, but Ehrenreich and English note that the implications continue through today, as women continue to be underrepresented in the medical profession and underserved as recipients of care and benefits of scientific research.

Green witchcraft, then, embraces an effort to reclaim traditional folk healing practices that were once familiar to women, offering them a sense of agency in a society that has for many centuries pathologized, disempowered, and controlled the female body. Although feminist Goddess traditions happily embrace witchcraft as a means of self-healing, self-care, and self-empowerment, mid-20th-century British witchcraft was clear that it should be used for community work, not personal gain. Self-care is included in many British texts, but the focus is primarily on healing others. Witchcraft as a healing art was a primary frame used by Alex Sanders, for instance, who heavily emphasized witchcraft's healing purposes in media interviews to counter stereotypes of evil sorcery (Johns 1969). Both pagan and feminist variants of witchcraft see this healing role as extending to natural spaces. As the environment informs seasonal changes, rituals, and even the chemical makeup of the human practitioner, it is believed that a healthy, accessible environment is key to effective witchcraft and the holistic development of the witch (Crowley 2000).

Rooting witchcraft in nature makes for a profoundly unique spiritual perspective quite unlike that of patriarchal religions. Ruether explains that "modeling God after alienated male consciousness, outside of and ruling over nature" runs counter to "the immanent source of life that sustains the whole planetary community" found in the goddess (1993: 21). Starhawk (1997), too, identifies institutionalized god religions as religions of death. "The quest for longevity" in modern patriarchal science Andrée Collard (1988) argues in *Rape of the Wild* is a reaction to this death orientation: "No longer able to believe that in dying he would flow back to the stream of life ever-present in the Goddess he had murdered, he faced death alone in fear, guilt, and envy of Mother Earth's endless/ageless renewals" (93). By contrast, Warren (1993) counters that "ecofeminist spiritualties are or can be life-affirming, personally empowering, and collectively constructive" (127). Ecofeminism is life-enhancing, not life-constrictive. Interdependence is prioritized over hierarchy.

For that matter, it questions assumptions of linear progress whereby a global society dominated by Western white patriarchy is presented as the epitome of human development. Sjöö and Mor (1991) remind us that human societies across time have not always followed a straight path from primitive to developed. Instead, they have often assimilated with other societies, dissolved, disappeared, or even devolved. It is problematic to assume, in other words, that the current state of life on Earth is any better (or worse) than that which came before or that which will come in the future. This assumption of progress, however, has been used as justification for all manner of colonial conquest, cultural destruction, and the molding of subjugated peoples, nonhumans included. Goddess worship must thus confront the limitations of a patriarchal worldview, a journey that Spretnak describes as a "perceptual shift from the death-based sense of existence that underlies patriarchal culture to a regeneration-based awareness, an embrace of life as a cycle of creative rebirths, a dynamic participation in the processes of infinity" (1993: 273). Creativity and change are celebrated over stagnancy and definitive mortality.

As was explored in the previous chapter, a key element of witchcraft is the rejection of death as an ultimate end point. This is an intentional alignment with fluid natural cycles over linear, patriarchal timelines. Time is thought to be cyclical, organized around the rotation of the Earth, sun, moon, and other stars and planets of the universe (Jones 1990). The notion of a start and end point is thought incompatible with the nonlinear nature of existence. Comfort with the inevitability of death and the connection that humans have with the life cycles of Earth and the wider universe creates a worldview that is rather different from Judeo-Christian traditions that understand human (and nonhuman) life as finite on Earth. Leek explains: "Once we become obsessed with thoughts of death as an ultimate end, we defeat our ability to become involved in life" (1973: 140). For Nonhuman Animals, the patriarchal quest to defeat aging, illness, disability, and death itself has inspired all manner of heroic efforts in scientific exploration, efforts that have been used to rationalize all manner of grotesque, systematized brutality in vivisection laboratories (Collard 1988). It is an all too familiar pattern to vegan feminists: "In an earlier time, we burned witches in the name of religion," muses Kheel, "Today we torture animals in the name of science" (1983a: no page).

But the alternative worldview that emphasizes an infinity of existence has also proved problematic, as nonhuman death can be conceptualized as part of this cycle: inevitable and expected. While embracing the normality of death is an important counter to mainstream religions, it can undermine death's gravitas for Nonhuman Animals. Leek adds: "As far as the spirit is concerned, the body is expendable; when we reach the point which we call death, the body is sloughed off like a coat we no longer need" (1973: 140). Unfortunately for Nonhuman Animals, whether or not this death is premature or violent (as is the case when they are killed for food) does not always make a difference and can be dismissed as "nature's way."

The killing of other animals is thus liable to diminishment even in goddess religions. Indeed, Weinstein (2020) notes that death should not be seen as "horrible or frightening," as it is a natural and necessary aspect of life (105). Writes Leek: "Both power and suffering can be hurtful," she notes, and "both, as parts of life, should be respected" (1973: 181). Suffering, in other words, must be accepted to an extent. While it is true that suffering in life cannot be avoided, few witches differentiate between incidental suffering. Starhawk, by way of example, emphasizes that suffering may exist, but "it is not our task to reconcile ourselves to it, but to work for change" (1999: 37). Indeed, Starhawk (1997) is perhaps the strongest advocate for using magic in the service of change. For her, witchcraft is a form of direct action and civil disobedience that can resist despair. For Nonhuman Animals, however, their suffering is more easily reconciled if they are categorized as human foodstuffs.

As was explored in the previous chapter, justice is also thought achievable through cycles of reincarnation. Green (2002) considers that illness and disability may be a form of punishment for anyone who has been "tyrants or torturers, cruel slave drivers or even brutal to animals" (73). Likewise, Buckland (2002) suggests that reincarnation explains disability but also poverty and even homosexuality. Each lifetime, he explains, is a learning experience. Vegan feminism would intervene on this philosophy, as the idea that disability serves as a form of retribution for wickedness wrongly insinuates that disability is something horribly negative, punishing, and inherently otherizing. Similar arguments can be made for poverty, femininity, and homosexuality, which some 20th-century witches have deemed as penalizations. Recall that Weinstein (2020) explains social stratification as karmically created. Every individual is believed to reincarnate into the new body they have chosen, subsequently inviting the social hardships that they will experience in life. For Weinstein, this is a cosmic system of cause and effect, which motivates individuals to own their choices and take responsibility. Even death, she suggests, is chosen. This includes those who die violently or accidentally as each individual is thought to subconsciously choose to put themselves in situations that would lead to these deaths. From a feminist perspective, however, ethical behavior cannot be effectively incentivized by threat of punishment, as it is only reactionary to patriarchal coercion rather than moral obligation. From a *vegan* perspective, furthermore, the Wiccan understanding of nonhuman sentience and cognitive capacity becomes especially important. Nonhuman Animals have close to no agency whatsoever in an anthroparchal society, as powerlessness is ensured with corporal controls, heavy confinement, and psychological domestication. Weinstein's (2020) position that one's social position is a result of one's behavior in past lives fits awkwardly with Nonhuman Animals in a human supremacist society, as they have little ability to change their circumstances in their current lives, much less their future ones.

Although Californian feminist witchcraft would presumably take issue with this victim-blaming approach to reincarnation, they make no concessions for Nonhuman Animals either. Nonhuman death is positioned as fundamentally lesser in importance to that of humans despite the rhetoric of togetherness that abounds in green witchcraft. Veganism, furthermore, remains philosophically and thealogically marginal in the discourse. Starhawk goes so far as to *promote* speciesist consumption, given that "death is a part of life, for all of us" (2005: 116). "I would rather be eaten by a cougar [...] than embalmed and stuffed in a box" (2005: 116). This analogy, however, creates a false equivalence between the experiences of free-living prey species, who enjoy autonomy and capacity for escape and self-defense, and farmed animals, who are restricted by forced confinement, genetic manipulation, psychological and biological domestication, familial disruption, and wholly unnecessary, frightening, and painful deaths for the benefit of humans, who, unlike obligate carnivores, do not need to eat them to survive. Yet, Starhawk (1999) praises domestication as a reward earned by conscientious humans, who are "deeply attuned" to nature and animals (28). It is possible she considers that women caring for free-living animals in distress may have launched the system of domestication (Starhawk 1987). Sjöö and Mor (1991) also claim domestication as a wondrous invention of women, to be celebrated in the goddess tradition. The maternalism of women, they argue, naturally drew them to own and control other animals for human benefit. Sjöö and Mor do recognize the environmental consequences this has created and even acknowledge the cruelties of dairy production, but they attribute this systemic violence to profit- and domination-driven patriarchy, not to domestication itself. As explored in the previous chapter, vegan feminists have countered this patriarchal take on human-nonhuman relations. Domestication is, regardless of the gender of those designing and maintaining it, fundamentally a system of domination. It entails full control over the minds, social lives, bodies, and reproductive capacities of Nonhuman Animals. With its attention to paternity, property, and sexual ownership, it is also a system that has been entangled with the control of women (Kheel 2007, Nibert 2013). In their effort to claim historical developments for women, Sjöö and Mor perhaps too eagerly reassign domestication, one of patriarchy's most cruel and disastrous institutions, to the goddess tradition. Relatedly, the god figure often celebrated in witchcraft as the feminine complement is celebrated precisely for his untamed nature. It is the very untameability of the masculine essence that is exalted, while the actual taming of Nonhuman Animals for the purposes of manipulating, exploiting, and killing them goes without mention. "He is that within us that will never be domesticated," Starhawk muses (1999: 126). It seems counterintuitive then, to leave patriarchal entitlement over domesticated bodies uncritiqued, but this may reflect the underlying assumption that patriarchy—through its manipulation of nature—has been the key driver of culture. If green witchcraft aims to reclaim women's history as movers of culture, it will need to abandon this, what Collard describes as "patriarchal propaganda" (1988: 41). Starhawk has charged that the misuse of sexuality is "heinous" in mutating a force of love into violence (1997: 37), but this very same sexual exploitation in Nonhuman Animal agriculture—forced sex, exploitation of childbirth, forced sterilization, and devaluation of non-productive female bodies—goes unremarked. "It is important to remember," Collard suggests, that women are "capable of offering interpretations of the past that reflect our values, our beliefs" (1988: 41).

Eating Animals

The fascination with domestication not only obscures its consequences for women and nature; it also eclipses feminized food production and plant-based consumption. Although women in many cultures were disproportionately responsible for collecting plants, fruits, nuts, and other non-animal foods, which comprised the majority of early human diets well into modernity (Collard 1988, Sjöö and Mor 1991), this legacy is sidelined by Starhawk, who normalizes power over other animals in flesh-consumption: "Meat [...] often has a symbolic as well as nutritional value and was certainly seen as an important source of life" (1999: 249). This seems an area in which green witchcraft might offer an important counternarrative with its appeal to feminist creativity. This same creative freedom, however, has served as an impediment to establishing firm feminist ethics. Although Wicca entails some guidelines of practice, for instance, Murphy-Hiscock clarifies for readers that there are "no ethical or moral rules associated in the green witch path" (2018: 17). "Green witchcraft isn't about forcing an individual to change; it's about an individual choosing to harmonize her own life with the energy of Nature" (17). McKay agrees, suggesting that witches could harness the energy of familiars by becoming an anti-speciesist activist and going vegan or "embrace eating meat," as "the only limit to how we choose to work with animals is our own imaginations" (2024: 31). Harmony with nature, with its inherent love and respect, seems to render a set of ethics redundant.

Starhawk's Earth Path

The failure to accommodate species-inclusive best practices has essentially normalized systemic violence against other animals. Often, these oppressive relationships align with patriarchal norms to justify the cognitive dissonance that using and consuming other animals entails. For instance, in *Truth or Dare* (1987), Starhawk introduces a typology of effective activism, clarifying a difference between "power-over," "power-from-within," and "power-with" politics

(9). Killing and eating other animals is clearly power-over behavior, as it requires force, obedience, and violence, but Starhawk's typology could see it conflated with power-*within* politics, as it offers a "sense of mastery" and "arises from our sense of connection, our bonding with other human beings, and with the environment" (1987: 10). Starhawk's rejection of vegetarianism, however, from a vegan feminist perspective, suggests that a connection to the environment could be embodied through the consumption of other animals. The "sense of mastery," in other words, could arise from species domination. Indeed, Starhawk clarifies that recognizing the value in others (which she identifies as a requirement for mobilizing power-from-within) does not preclude violence. To explain this, she provides the analogy of crushing snails in her garden, as they "are out of pattern here" (15). This position easily overlooks the possibility of power-*with* other animals in nurturing the strength found in group solidarity.

Ultimately, Starhawk's failure to center veganism (or at least vegetarianism) undermines her argument that "every being is sacred." Her position that "each has inherent value that cannot be ranked in a hierarchy" (1987: 21) remains deeply anthropocentric in that numerous nonhuman species have been ranked lower than humans in being categorized as food, clothing, or entertainment. And yet there seems much room for redemption in anthropocentric green witchcraft. "Relationships based on exploitation destroy immanent value," Starhawk concludes, and "if I can feel comfortable living well when someone else suffers, I value that person's life less than mine" (1987: 118). Acknowledging shared sentience and right to existence across the species barrier, it would seem, might improve the practitioner's personal comfort, spiritual alignment, and strength as experienced in solidarity across diverse groups.

In the rare cases that farmed animals are mentioned, however, they are often objectified as resources and invisibilized by euphemistic language. In *The Earth Path* (2005), Starhawk makes a brief mention of human speciesism, framing it as available "energy in living systems" (114). She does suggest giving animals space as they await slaughter, with regard to the concentrated design of industrialized farming, but otherwise, the systematic control over Nonhuman Animals itself goes unchallenged. Nonhuman Animals are linguistically objectified in *The Earth Path* as well, referred to as "meat" rather than individuals, or as "beef," "lamb," "chicken," and as assets that must be "managed well" (115) and made "productive" for human purposes (116). This rationalization of speciesism is also found in claims of dietary necessity, as she argues that vegetarianism creates "chronic fatigue" in women. The rich history of vegetarianism in the Global South[1] is overlooked in this claimsmaking. Instead, Western norms of animal-based agriculture are universalized, and vegetarianism is rejected as impractical given that "not all land is suitable for growing crops." Land, even from her ecofeminist position, thus remains an exploitable resource that must be efficiently utilized for maximum profit. The same is imposed on other animals. If commodified beings were not brought into the world for the purposes of exploitation, Starhawk charges that they would not have the chance to live at all: "Were we to stop eating them, they would not be living happy, productive, fulfilled animal lives; they would cease to exist" (2005: 116).

Starhawk's distorted understanding of speciesism aligns with industry myths that Nonhuman Animals are "living happy, productive, fulfilled animal lives" (1997: 116), or, with improved farming methods, at least capable of experiencing these qualities. In addition to its capitalistic overtones, Starhawk relies on the rather patriarchal assumption that Nonhuman Animals could never live happily, productively, or fulfilled without being dominated and exploited by others. Her feminist, anti-capitalist thealogy of living for pleasure and creativity, in other words, does an about-face for other-than-human species. Eating other animals is *not* a requirement. A thriving global vegan community proves just that, as has the flourishing of many great civilizations that have persisted for several millennia on exceedingly little animal protein. The assumption that (masculinized) animal protein is somehow exceptional to (feminized) plant protein is magical thinking of the worst kind and condemns Nonhuman Animals to unnecessary deaths in obedience to patriarchal mythology. Vegan feminism reminds us that eating other animals is a resource intensive, violent system of human privilege that has been fanned by anthroparchal capitalist ideologies and Western colonialism (Cudworth 2011, Kheel 2007, Nibert 2013). Starhawk's ecofeminism, therefore, may argue that humans are part of nature and that domination must be resisted, but vegan witchcraft argues that these values do not take breaks at mealtime.

The considerable environmental toll that Nonhuman Animal agriculture has exacted, for that matter, goes largely unremarked. Indeed, Starhawk conceptualizes both "meat" and wildfires as manifested "energy in living systems" (1997: 114), wildfires being a particular threat in her home state of California. She discusses these fires as an unfortunate consequence of climate change, seemingly unaware that they are the direct consequence of Nonhuman Animal agriculture that proliferates in the American West, especially in California (McCormack 2021). In the same chapter of *The Earth Path* that promotes the consumption of Nonhuman Animals as taking advantage of "energy in living systems," she bemoans the degradation of Californian forests—another direct consequence of Nonhuman Animal agriculture. Rather than acknowledge the detrimental realities of an animal-based diet, she instead advises ritually singing to the trees to both praise and sustain them. The loss of these trees is indeed tragic, but it is telling rituals of this kind so often center non-sentient life forms. There are no witches singing in slaughterhouses.

To be clear, this speciesist system is deeply gendered. Indeed, sociological and psychological research has identified that masculinity undergirds speciesist attitudes toward other animals and the consumption of their bodies (Greenebaum 2018, Rosenfeld 2023). It has also been demonstrated that those ascribing to hegemonic masculine attitudes are less positive about vegetarians (De Backer et al. 2020). Although many ecofeminists have recognized this and have accounted for veganism or vegetarianism in theory and practice, witchcraft, as Starhawk's ideology exemplifies, remains resistant. To drive home how important eating other animals is to the witchcraft community, she recounts how participants in her annual festival would stock up on bird corpses for the event to keep their energy high: "Witches do seem to crave it" (1997: 115). Again, her dismissiveness of veganism and vegetarianism is startlingly inconsistent with her advocacy for sustainable living. For all the immense effort she expends in singing to trees, living off the grid, digging wells and diverting creeks for drinking water, listening to songbirds, and even praying to compost piles to increase their potency, perhaps the most straightforward way to tread lighter on Earth and respect Nonhuman Animals is to live vegan. Especially for middle-class white women living in the San Francisco Bay area (who dominate The Reclaiming tradition), plant-based foodways are readily accessible. Vegetarianism is nonetheless framed as unnatural, difficult, and antithetical to proper exploitation of the natural world for human privilege.

Starhawk is highlighted given her leadership in green witchcraft and American ecofeminism, but her anthropocentric position is typical. Forest (2020), for example, acknowledges that green witchcraft's honoring of sacred land is complicated by the consumption of those sentient beings who occupy it. She advises eating vegetarian "whenever possible" (156) as a means of connecting with plant spirits (even if this advice is a bit confused in prioritizing plant spirits rather than sentient nonhuman persons, who would be spared by this dietary shift). Vanderbeck's bestselling *Green Witchcraft*, likewise, does note that some green witches are vegetarian or vegan but suggests these are morally equivalent to speciesist witches who "say prayers of gratitude to the spirits of animals they consume" (2020: 9). She abstains from introducing any ethics or values into her version of green witchcraft: "Once you learn how the earth communicates with you, it'll tell you what it needs" (2020: 9). Presumably, what the Earth needs varies from individual to individual according to their personal preferences. Even Morningstar and Whitehurst, highlighted in the previous chapter for their species-inclusive practice, continue to eat animal products. Morningstar (n.d.) describes herself as "mostly vegan" and "a lover of animals & the wild world" (no page). In *Magical Housekeeping*, Whitehurst refers to animal products as "physical toxins" and advises "cutting back on meat and other animal products" (2017: 12). Yet, in the first episode of her podcast *Magical Mondays*, she clarifies to listeners that she does sometimes eat dairy despite her ability to "tune in" to animals (Levinger and Whitehurst 2019). The clarity of this attuning seems questionable given her failure to reject the suffering that dairy production entails.

Sybil Leek (1973) does not advocate veganism but does critique human reproduction, given rampant habitat loss as humans veraciously compete for resources. For Leek, this trend lacks consistency: "This, then, is the situation in which man finds himself today—on one hand declaring that he is above animals; on the other, fouling his environment. Where is the remarkable reasoning faculty which puts man above animals?" (1973: 117). It is far more common for witches to speak about anti-speciesism in the abstract, usually in reference to free-living communities in the face of climate change. Patterson (2017a) encourages attuning to nature to detect otherwise unsensed energies in her *Witchcraft into the Wilds*, but this primarily refers to plants and trees and does not seem to include an active attuning to the suffering of the animals living there. For instance, she advises drawing on the energies of nature as an important means of protection. Natural energies are thought to shield against negative forces, but such energy-working tends to be anthropocentric. Nature is often envisioned as devoid of animal life, if not disproportionately focused on free-living nonhumans. Thus, the negative energies being shielded may actually be the suffering of other animals that goes unnoticed by so many green witches.

Vegan Ecofeminism

This theoretical inconsistency has not gone without critique. Like green witches, vegan feminists have been resisting patriarchy's violence against women and other marginalized human groups, Nonhuman Animals, and the environment for many years (Adams and Gruen 2014, Wrenn 2023). As ecofeminist witches found strength through a spiritual affiliation with nature, ecofeminist vegans extended this to recognize a sacred solidarity with other animals that empowered their activism and personal resistance. There is some evidence that ecofeminists straddled both witchcraft and anti-speciesism in their practice. Although not a vegetarian, famed LGBT+ rights and environmental activist Sally Gearhart incorporated Nonhuman Animal advocacy in her writings and intersectional advocacy, welcoming other animals into her lesbian separatist projects. Daly (1978), by way of another example, emphasized the centrality of male violence against Nonhuman Animals and nature in her feminist writing, often strategically using the language and symbolism of witchcraft to theorize women's liberation. Aside from being one of the most influential feminists of the 20th century, she also served on the board of Feminists for Animal Rights (FAR), the preeminent vegan feminist grassroots organization founded by Marti Kheel in Berkeley, California. She was a vegetarian and lifelong collaborator with former understudy Adams, who remembers her as a "sister theorist" (Adams 2012: 97). Although Daly was likely not vegan and was somewhat reserved in her integration of anti-speciesism in her theorizing (in addition to harboring deeply problematic attitudes about the transgender community), she was nonetheless deeply impacted by vegan feminist thought.

Given the many parallels, it seems curious that more connections between witchcraft, feminism, and anti-speciesism have not been identified. Kheel and Starhawk, both constructing ecofeminist thought and action in the San Francisco Bay, would certainly have been familiar with one another's work.[2] It is probable that they had some sort of correspondence.[3] The two ecofeminists contributed chapters to Diamond and Orenstein's (1990) *Reweaving the World*, for instance, and both were featured in the March 1988 U.C. Berkeley "Friendship Earth" speaker series (Friendship Earth 1988). Both presented at

Culture, Nature and Theory: Ecofeminist Perspectives, a conference held at the University of Southern California in March of 1987 (Feminists for Animal Rights 1987), with Kheel offering several talks on Nonhuman Animal rights and vegetarianism and Starhawk presenting on her own activism and concluding the gathering with a grounding ritual. Kheel's (1983b) essay, "Animal Rights is a Feminist Issue," furthermore, was reprinted in *WomanSpirit*, a leading publication in American feminist spirituality that regularly featured the work of witches such as Selena Fox and Z. Budapest. Within vegan feminist spaces, equally few collaborations are evident. Adams' (1993) edited collection *Ecofeminism and the Sacred*, by way of an example, includes essays on all variety of spiritual ideas related to women's connection to the environment but includes no contributions from the Starhawk goddess tradition.

A sprinkling of Wiccan and witch-leaning writers did appear in FAR newsletters.[4] FAR itself was supportive of alternative spirituality and largely skeptical of mainstream religions. Kheel's position echoes the skepticism of Daly: "Animals, I suspect have as much hope of being redeemed by the institutional (i.e., patriarchal) religions as do women" (1984: 1). The work of the feminist poet and author Barbara Mor (1992) explores the connected oppressions between women and other animals and was featured in FAR newsletters. The art of Sudi Rakusin, too, which featured many Wiccan and Goddess themes, was a persistent feature (Scarborough 1996). One FAR director in the late 1990s even incorporated the teachings of Z. Budapest. In her newsletter editorials, she advised that members use the summer solstice to "cast our activist spell on the collective patriarchy; and to rededicate ourselves to activism on behalf of other animals, other people, and Earth" as "positive ways to advance the cause" rather than dwelling in the negative as so often permeates anti-speciesist mobilization (Bailey 1996: 2). For Bailey, vegan feminist writing and exchange was a means of manifestation: "We need to see the words as the seeds of an alternative reality—our perspiration and nurturing cause them to germinate and thrive" (1996: 2). Herbalism, too, features in vegan feminism. For instance, Kheel's contributions to FAR demonstrate considerable suspicion of mainstream medical and pharmaceutical industries, which were believed to use misogyny and accusations of witchcraft to work against women's healing abilities. She often promoted homeopathic and herbal healing instead; natural preventatives and remedies were often presented as a means of reconnecting to the environment and the essence of human life (Kheel 1986).

By way of another example, Ecofeminist Voices Emerging (EVE), a grassroots collective based in New York City that incorporated anti-speciesist analyses, openly embraced alternative spiritualities as part of its ethos: "This incredibly diverse, metaphysical mélange includes everything from non-monotheistic spiritual practices such as paganism, Eastern religions, Wicca, Yoruba traditions, shamanism, and mysticism to more physical/emotional modalities" (McGuire n.d.). At EVE meetings, witches and vegans likely came face to face in conversation, if not embodying both practices concurrently. Co-founder Cathleen McGuire (n.d.) assures that these overlaps would not have been unusual or unwanted: "The beauty and allure of ecofeminism is that it has the capacity to incorporate an analysis and a practice of both the political and the spiritual" (no page). Likewise, the Yale University archives of Bloodroot Collective, a Connecticut-based vegetarian lesbian feminist group and adjacent restaurant, includes undated correspondence with Starhawk. It is clear that some crosspollination between vegan and pagan ecofeminism had taken place in 20th-century campaigning and community work.

Starhawk would not have been ignorant of vegan feminist claimsmaking. Indeed, her avoidance of vegan ethics can only be intentional given her extensive commitment to interconnecting injustices. With each successive edition of her seminal *Spiral Dance*, she is careful to outline growth and flexibility in her political position, which has included less importance placed on gender polarity, more solidarity with the LGBT+ community, and greater engagement with food justice and capacity-building in nature, notably through permaculture. All of these concerns easily align with a vegan framework, given that animal-based food production is one of the leading threats to environmental wellbeing and community health (Tschakert 2022) and that gender role expectations inform men's domination of women *and* other animals (Hunnicutt 2019). Indeed, social and environmental justice is at the core of Nonhuman Animal liberation efforts, as speciesism is deeply entangled with a litany of other systemic oppressions (Nibert 2002). Yet, Starhawk has been largely silent on the plight of Nonhuman Animals. Her failure to adopt a position of anti-speciesism—particularly as it relates to using and eating other animals—seems to be a reflection of her libertarianism. Her witchcraft aims to align politics and morality, but free choice is ultimately prioritized in resistance to patriarchal control. "There is no external authority, no set of absolute truths," she notes in *Dreaming the Dark*, "that can tell us precisely how to determine the meaning of our personal commitment to the dance. For some, preserving the dance of life/death may mean neither eating meat nor using the products of domesticated animals" (1997: 39). In those few cases in which Starhawk does consider the morality of speciesism,[5] choice feminism (a conflation of women's liberation with their ability to participate in the marketplace and make individual consumer choice) and moral relativism prevail. For other, anthropocentric issues of morality, however, her position alters, abandoning flexibility for a harder stance. Following her declaration of "no external authority, no set of absolute truths" with regard to respecting the bodily autonomy of other animals, for instance, she declares abortion restriction immoral. This defense of abortion spans several pages, while the plight of Nonhuman Animals warrants no further attention than a sparse sentence that positions killing and eating other animals as a matter of personal choice.

Animal Sacrifice

With its roots in ecofeminism, green witchcraft has encouraged its practitioners to live harmoniously with nature and other animals, but green witchcraft has remained, with few exceptions, cut off from the vegan branches of ecofeminist thought. Eating other animals is believed to be congruent with respecting nature, and domesticated food animals remain largely absent from the green witchcraft discourse, which tends to prioritize free-living species and ecosystems. But then, all manner of feminist paths, pagan or not, have obscured speciesism. Vegan ecofeminists have noted that most feminists, despite championing agency for the marginalized, nonetheless adhere to the patriarchal norm that Nonhuman Animals are without capacity for their own agency (Adams 1991). They are instead objects for others to enact their own agency upon. Anthroparchy ensures that Nonhuman Animals, women, nature, and other oppressed entities are not free agents, but rather free fodder for profit and gain. Nonhuman Animals especially have been systematically used for such sacrificial purposes, killed so that their life energy can benefit humans by appeasing the divine. The prioritization of non-sentient nature, the protection of flesh-consumption, and the invisibility of non-human suffering in green witch thealogy creates a situation in which Nonhuman Animal sacrifice becomes disturbingly normative.

Before introducing an analysis of this accommodation of animal sacrifice in the craft, it is relevant to note that witchcraft and Wicca explicitly reject this practice. Starhawk proclaims that there are "no provisions for either human or animal sacrifice; no altars, no pits for blood, and no caches for bones" (1999: 55). Again, because sacrifice has become a point of stigmatization that is almost unique to the persecution of pagans, it is likely that modern witches feel it necessary to account and apologize for it. Valiente (1978) assures readers that sacrifice is confined to antiquity, and even then was executed respectfully with great pomp, prayer, and genuine belief that Nonhuman Animals willingly consented to their killing. The essential role that Nonhuman Animals play in magic, she frets, has unfortunately—in very rare cases—left them vulnerable to miscreants. "Such practices," she assures readers, are "part of the evil realm of black magic" and inevitably evoke "karmic retribution" (Valiente 1975: 151). Valiente (1962) has elsewhere supposed that the archetypal triple moon goddess symbol is one that has historically linked the sacrifice of animals to "black magic." Gardner, too, dismisses sacrifice outright as "hateful and cruel" (1970: 90). He writes, "It would be wrong or sinful to kill an animal for that purpose" such that witches would "not think of doing it" (1970: 96). Like Valiente, he struggles to find congruencies: "I do not myself see how it would fit in with our system of magic" (1970: 96). Sometimes, in fact, non-Western sacrificial practices are even used to elevate Western witchcraft as more civilized by comparison. Alex Sanders, for instance, denounces Nonhuman Animal sacrifice given that other, life-affirming means of energy-raising are readily available (Johns 1969). In doing so, he refers to examples of Caribbean sacrifice he had personally witnessed, describing them as crude and wholly unnecessary.

Lady Sheba, an influential witch of the 20th century, advises practitioners to ritualistically scourge themselves instead as a means of sacrificial purification. Sheba's self-sacrificial scourging, I should note, is outdated, linked as it is to the early 20th-century Gardnerian practice, but it suggests that witchcraft does to an extent see the suffering, harm, and violence caused to oneself and those socially beneath them as necessary for raising power (Bell 2001). With some reluctance, Gardner supposes power *could* be raised from killing other animals, but he is unclear as to how it could be effectively wielded. In any case, he remarks sarcastically, "I should expect to hear that the municipal slaughter-house men were setting up as magicians" (1970: 65). For most witches of the Goddess tradition, however, sacrifice of *any* kind is seen as problematic, masochistic, and unnecessary self-denying in a natural world of abundance. Sacrificing oneself for the greater good, however, is seen as commendable given the healing emphasis of modern witchcraft (Starhawk 1999). Grimassi (2001) denounces live nonhuman sacrifice but, like Starhawk, also finds value in self-sacrifice, a practice that ensures magic will be worked for the wellbeing of others rather than for personal gain. Here, Grimassi advises practitioners to rise "above the desires and needs of the flesh" (36).

And yet nonhuman sacrifice remains extremely prevalent in neo-pagan mythology, creating an air of tolerance and even *excitement*. Starhawk, for one, seems to find charm in this lore. Despite her opposition to the practice in modern times, she repeats Valiente's fiction that Nonhuman Animals were willing sacrifices in ancient times (1999). As is the case with domestication, attempts to discover power in women's history often finds the goddess tradition merging into patriarchal traditions. Sjöö and Mor (1991) emphasize that the goddess took the form of other animals in ancient depictions, offering sexualized mythologies of union between men and women, nature and humans. Warriors pierced and bloodied the bodies of nonhuman victims to create a "symbolic resolution," as a penis entering a vulva (82). This sacred likeness between goddess and nonhuman, in their estimation, was culturally necessary to support the belief that nonhuman victims willingly sacrificed themselves for their human oppressors and relieve any associated guilt in the suffering it invariably caused. They exalt the magical powers of blood harvested from the gaping wounds of dying sacrificial bulls, drunk by priestesses to increase their mystical power and spread across fields to improve the resourcefulness of the land. What Sjöö and Mor do not contend with, however, is how this willing victimhood would also be attributed to women and all manner of other vulnerable social groups to normalize and naturalize severe inequality and violence (Collard 1988). Neither do they contend with the anthroparchal implications of shifting to a "hunting"-based society, transforming Nonhuman Animals from social equals to commodity objects. Killing Nonhuman Animals, who symbolically represented the goddess, was, by extension, also an attack on the sacred body and spirit of the goddess. Killing to obtain the power found in victims' blood, furthermore, is the ultimate patriarchal contract. For these reasons, it seems ill-suited to feminist reclaiming.

Nonhuman Animal sacrifice as manifested in flesh-consumption and the incorporation of animal body parts in ritual work has been praised as a sort of reciprocal, ecosystemic relationship that witches aim to remember, reimagine, and re-enact in alignment with their imagined past ancestors. With this mythologizing, witches are better able to accommodate the gruesome reality of sacrifice. Melissa Madara (2021), for instance, romanticizes the ritual killing of other animals in her "meat"-centric Wiccan cookbook, imaging that:

> Sacrificial animals would be looked after and kept quite content, such that they arrived at the altar as calm and 'willing' sacrifices. In ancient Greece, the sacrificial blade would be concealed until the instance it is need, and attendees would writhe and scream in sympathetic pain at the very moment of death.[6]

She mirrors Valiente's wishful thinking in supposing that victims in Roman society would be draped in flowers and elevated like deities "as they approached the moment of no return" (no page). Vegetarianism, she assures readers, could not reach this level of "harmonization between the earthly and divine." As such, Madara encourages readers to prepare meals with sacrificial animals, such as quails, who can become "a delicious whole-animal offering" (no page).

Vegan feminist Brian Luke (2007) has written extensively on the patriarchal myth of "sacrifice for the greater good," which inevitably comes at the expense of society's most vulnerable. Warriors killed other animals "for the good" of the community, priests killed other animals on the altar "for the good" of the community, soldiers kill men, women, children, and all manner of other animals "for the good" of the community, and scientists kill other animals in laboratories "for the good" of the community. This line of thinking is reflected in Starhawk's muses that "to plant a garden, you must [...] crush the snails" (1999: 106), insinuating, it would seem, the necessity of animal sacrifice to realize nature's abundance. Gardner (1959) grants that animals would probably only have been killed during ceremonies and festivals for the provision of a uniquely substantial meal to attract participants. Yet, Gardner recalls fondly the regular killing and roasting of corpses for everyday modern pagan events, suggesting that this cooking process itself is magical. Recalling the fate of a sheep killed for one such gathering, he records:

> It was a weird sight with the flames lighting up the trees, and I suddenly saw the framework of the sheep, through the bonfire, its ribs bare, the bones of the four feet hanging down. The flickering of the fire and smoke made it seem to move as if it were alive [...] and mighty good it was too.
> *(1959: 123)*

Adams and Procter-Smith (1993) have noted that the oppressed state of Non-human Animals is especially poignant in the normalized sacrifice of more-than-human animals for religious rituals and feasts. Speciesist violence, they suggest, is able to thrive due to religion's reliance on the written word, word that Nonhuman Animals can neither contribute to nor counter. Institutionalized religions find the word of "God" in these religious texts and "speaking thus becomes identified with holy power" (301). Nonhuman Animals, unable to communicate in these languages, become marginalized. This theory applies shakily to witchcraft; while it does not have a "bible" in the traditional sense, given that it prioritizes self-autonomy and is anti-authoritarian, it does draw very heavily on the written word of leaders, both past and present, to determine norms. Thus, if Gardner and Starhawk purport to have a special connection to the nonhuman world but do not promote anti-speciesism and veganism, Nonhuman Animals are likely to remain marginalized. Speechlessness, according to Adams and Procter-Smith (1993), has also been used to oppress other human groups, women included, creating an echo chamber that reverberates the voices and values of the dominant class. Women and children, who are disproportionately impacted by rape, have historically been unable to speak out against their oppression, accused of speaking untruthfully if their stories are heard at all. In other cases, their voices are distorted by oppressors who push a biased account. Nonhuman Animals, likewise, are subject to all manner of injustices, agonies, and torturous deaths. Unable to "speak" or to be heard by humans—sometimes even physically restrained, caged, muzzled, beaten, whipped, starved, isolated, traumatized, anesthetized, paralyzed, laryngectomized, electrocuted, and stun-gunned to quiet them—anthroparchal narratives are told on their behalf, insisting that nonhumans willingly gave their lives, wanting it even.

Honorable Bodysnatching

The accuracy of sacrificial history in witchcraft thealogy, incidentally, is rather debated in the community. Gardner dismisses its ancestral use but otherwise concedes that there is archaeological evidence of teeth and bones used in folk magic and charms.: "I expect the old village herbalist type of witch may have used skulls and bones and other things to impress people because they were expected to. They were good psychologists" (1970: 14). Nonetheless, it has become common practice to use the teeth, nails, hair, feathers, and even bones of other animals in ritual work, perhaps more so than in other witchcraft paths. Patterson (2017b), for example, advises birds' feathers and entire wings for wafting smoke, using the bones of other animals for magical jewelry, and, in some cases, eating their flesh to "honour the animal by using as much of it [sic] as you possibly can" (58). Presumably the animals she advises eating are sourced from grocery stores and butcher shops, but she also suggests utilizing animals killed on roads for augury magic.

Kate Freuler (2020) agrees, claiming to have "respectfully honored, cleaned, and salvaged the remains of all these creatures" (92) before using them in sympathetic magic. Objectifying Nonhuman Animals as resources is, furthermore, framed as a moral act, as they are "better off being honored by someone using them in magick than just going to waste" (Freuler 2020: 95).[7] Such a position overlooks the postmortem role that deceased animals play in the ecosystem as food for other animals, insects, and the soil, which seems counter to the cyclical nature that witchcraft extols. Freuler (2020) prefaces her *Of Blood and Bones* with a disclaimer that "this book does not support hurting or killing animals or people for any reason" and the advice to "be ethical and humane when it comes to collecting bones and animal parts" (xiii). Freuler nonetheless advises using Nonhuman Animal "parts" including "hearts, bones, and horns" as doing so is "rooted in the history of many traditions around the world" (91). Sacrifice, too, is thought acceptable given its long cross-cultural history: "As with everything regarding ethics, it's a fluid gray area that can be debated endlessly" (92). The same treatment of humans, of course, is never up for debate although many cultures historically sacrificed their own. Human supremacy privileges the witch's species such that they will forever avoid any "fluid gray area" with regard to their right to life or postmortem dignity.

The notion that one must be useful (even in death) in order to be honored likely derives from capitalist ideologies that fetishize productivity and resource exploitation. Using animal bodies also masks the alienating nature of capitalism in linking the practitioner to a natural world long since estranged from humanity, especially in the West. This capitalist practicality is infused within Freuler's justification: "the animal was already dead, using their parts is okay and even honoring the animal in a way by including them in something spiritual" and "using them in ritual is better than them going to waste" (2020: 95). "Refusing to use the parts is pointless," she continues, "and not helping the problem anyway" (2020: 95). Although Freuler claims that she "does not support hurting or killing animals or people for any reason," her copious recommendations for the nails, horns, bones, feet, organs, and other body parts for the purposes of sympathetic magic suggest otherwise. For that matter, she does not simply advocate the use of animals killed accidentally but those killed purposefully for hamburgers, hot dogs, and egg salad. "It is your choice whether to use factory-farmed animals in your witchcraft," Freuler assures readers in line with Starhawk's libertarian speciesism, "just as it is your choice whether to eat them or not" (95).

Fundamental to green witchcraft, I reiterate, is the expectation that Nonhuman Animals be used in some way to work nature magic. Nonhumans seem to serve as a link between the disenchanted, civilized world of modern humans and the mysterious, untamed, natural world of yesteryear. By way of another example, Raven Digitalis (2022) advises the construction of bone charms for Lughnasadh (a late summer festival) to

> mark the occasion with plentiful gratitude not only for the flora and fauna that feed us physically on a daily basis, but also gratitude for the fact that the harvest allows us to survive and thrive, thereby increasing our positive spiritual influence in the world.
>
> *(107)*

Killing and consuming other animals, even if the killing is undertaken by others, is a sacrifice thought necessary to create positivity. Some witches might negotiate these conflicting aspects of their thealogy and practice by relying on "ethically" sourced animal materials, and a few alternatives to killing other animals have been offered. Gardner (1970) sees the witch's power as primarily manifested in the psyche, for instance, as "mind over matter" (96). He also suggests the possibility of using one's own blood for raising power. Budapest (1986) advises that menstruating people use their menses to unlock power for ritual purposes (23). Patterson (2017a) also sees value in the use of one's own menstrual blood, which is noted as useful for love magic as well as tool consecration. Whitehurst describes "moon blood" as "one of the most magically potent substances known to humans" (2015: 93), and Eller (1995) notes that menstruation, central to many of humanity's first rituals, is symbolically powerful in representing the cycle of life and death, aging, and phases of the moon. Of course, people who can menstruate also demonstrate considerable power in childbirth. Grimassi (2001) has even compared this process to the more masculinized "hunt" with regards to the courageousness and risk it entails. Perhaps these are the types of deathless blood sacrifice that could replace the killing of other animals. Nonhuman Animals, nonetheless, seem to be a staple resource for raising energy. Digitalis assures readers, "Yes, humanely and sustainably sourced chicken or cow bones are okay!" (2022: 107). A vegan green witchcraft, however, would question how the assault of other animals could ever be considered "humane," or, given the strong connection between Nonhuman Animal agriculture and climate change, how it could ever be considered "sustainable."

The hidden labor of Nonhuman Animals is also viewed as a readily available sacrifice. Budapest (1986), for instance, draws on the exploited power of mother cows in advising using their breastmilk as a "libation" for the Earth (31). Here, Nonhuman Animals remain as familiars wrested into the witch's service. The cows trapped in dairy compounds will have had no ability to consent to this collaboration. The same could be said of the laboring bees exploited to produce the honey used in Budapest's anti-harassment spell (42), and the mother chickens whose eggs are taken to absorb the illnesses of the sick in her Hungarian health spell (59). Blood may not be spilled on the altar, but these are sacrifices with real-world consequences for other animals, nonetheless.

I would suggest the *symbolic* sacrifice of Nonhuman Animals is also relevant in this regard. Budapest's symbolic use of Nonhuman Animals, in particular, is regularly invoked in quite negative ways. By way of an example, she advises carving images of snakes into candles to "send back evil vibrations" (1986: 25). The heavy stigma that this symbolism entails feeds into lethal persecution of living snakes in the material world. Thus, even when witches relieve living Nonhuman Animals of physical exploitation, there remain cultural implications of stereotyping them and exploiting those stereotypes for human gain. Budapest notes, "The number one tool that we have is imagination" (28), an angle that may seem harmless, except that all manner of human imaginations about the status of Nonhuman Animals have come into horrible fruition, feeding the sanctioned, systematic, highly rationalized, and incredibly violent oppression of other species that thrives today. Consider also Freuler's (2020) prescription for the use of nonhuman "claws" and "fur" in protection magic. By referring to their nails and hair in this way, she unnecessarily differentiates between shared mammalian features, feeding a false human/animal binary. Sociologists have disparaged this linguistic tactic as it effectively otherizes Nonhuman Animals and underscores their lower status (Nguyen 2019, Nibert 2002).

Graveyard Magic

Again, this material and symbolic entitlement to other animals does not extend to humans, as witchcraft discourages the use of human body parts taken without consent. Graveyard dust is one occasional exception. For those who are comfortable using it in spellwork, there is generally a degree of respect and ritual in its collection. Witches typically advise asking consent of the dead and leaving behind a gift in exchange. Some are so averse to potentially disrespecting the dead in this way they substitute with crumbled mullein plant, a reverence that is rarely granted to other animals. "You don't want to disturb anyone living or dead," Patterson explains. "You don't want to be disrespectful and you definitely don't want to get caught" (2017a). She also advises relying only on the graves of close friends and relatives to avoid upsetting the dead of others. The graves of "toxic" persons, such as murderers, furthermore, should also be avoided (2017a: 99).

The toxicity of speciesist violence that almost all Nonhuman Animals used in witchcraft will have experienced, whether they were hit by an automobile or a bolt gun, does not pose the same barrier in green witchcraft. It is the liminality of cemeteries that lends graveyard dirt its purported magical properties, suggesting the possible potency of using Nonhuman Animal bodies in magical practice in the same sense. Nonhuman Animals, after all, not only speak to the blurred boundaries between life and death through their extreme exposure to human violence, but also to the blurred boundaries between humans and other animals and between nature more broadly. Their lowered status in life, however, renders them all but invisible as magical subjects in death. Witches prefer incorporating Nonhuman Animals as magical *objects* for anthropocentric purposes instead.

Often, graveyard magic is intended to be sympathetic, in that it uses symbolic representations to effect change. Killing animals represented a sacrifice of wealth, as Nonhuman Animals have historically served as currency. But this killing was also representational, symbolizing all manner of spiritual sacrifices for devotional purposes. Kitchen witch Sarah Robinson describes Nonhuman Animal sacrifice as useful for appeasing the Goddess, bartering for prosperity, and repelling any "restless spirits" (2022: 32). This legacy, of course, suggests that Nonhuman Animals are not actually revered as persons, but remain objects. They themselves cannot consent to be killed, nor do they participate in sacrificial rites for their own benefit. Their capacity to become "restless spirits" is denied, despite the animist roots to contemporary witchcraft.

But might sympathetic magic be employed more explicitly to remove Non-human Animals completely for a more representational magic? Madara (2021), for instance, suggests the use of pharmakos cakes shaped as "scapegoats" to represent (and substitute) Nonhuman Animals killed for religious practice. "Consider these as an addition to your sacrificial and cleansing rites," she advises, "when a bloodless sacrifice is appropriate" (no page). The adjoining recipe relies very heavily on excretions from a variety of Nonhuman Animals, such that her cakes cannot at all be said to be "bloodless," but a plant-based variation might serve these purposes for modern practitioners—as an offering in return for spiritual favor without harming others to achieve this personal gain.

"The Hunt"

Without an authoritative bible or code of ethics in the craft, narratives of tradition and natural law become the de facto moral authority. In developing a spiritual relationship with the natural world, witchcraft has leaned toward the objectification of other animals as symbols or tools at the individual practitioner's discretion. Conceptualizing this as "sacrifice" works as a moral shield that psychologically removes the killer from the ethical connotations of their violent behavior (Adams and Procter-Smith 1993). Although most witches denounce ritual Nonhuman Animal sacrifice, some advocate or accommodate "hunting," using the same distancing language that has been used to protect other types of sacrifice. Andrews (1993), for instance, rejects Nonhuman Animal sacrifice as morally repugnant and indefensible: "It displays ignorance and a great disrespect toward Nature" (219). Religious killing, he also warns, will solicit karmic retribution. Killing for shamanic work or other spiritual purposes, for Andrews, is exploitative and seems aimed at depleting nature until there is: "nothing left but pictures" (1993: 220). Yet, he excuses "hunting" as it is supposedly different from religious sacrifice in being executed with great respect in "primitive times" (1993: 219). Respect, as Andrews understands it, can be consistent with killing sentient persons in cases of genuine scarcity so long as the entire corpse is utilized. Thus, Gardner and other founders may have insisted that "witches do not use the blood of sacrificed animals, birds, or other living things in their rites" (Gardner 1959: 229) to assuage negative media sensationalism, but this does not make witchcraft a bloodless path. As another example, Blythe (1990) admires the killing of other animals in premodern times, often accomplished with inaccurate, crude, and sometimes long-winded methods of execution including bludgeons, arrows, flint knives, traps, pits, or the driving of entire families off of cliffs. These "swift killings for food and shelter," he surmises, are far better than the "wantonness" of killing that transpires under modern environmental degradation (1990: 139). Whether or not killing others for food and shelter, especially to the point of species extinction, was ever *truly* necessary for most humans is not considered.

Blythe (1990) interprets the pagan "hunt" as symbolic as well, with its true purpose lying in the confrontation the "hunter" might have with their own self.

Similarly, witchcraft that purports to draw on pre-Christian pagan life frequently centers "the hunt" as a source of ancient, animistic power rooted firmly in archetypes of the sacred masculine and feminine (Buckland 2002). Lady Sabrina (2001) and Grimassi (2001) both glorify the ancient "hunt," rationalizing that the sacrifice feeds the rebirth of nature and renewal of life. Patricia Crowther insists that "a natural inclination to worship the Old Gods" is a prerequisite for becoming a witch (1981: 34). Valiente (1978) also celebrates this history, noting that the worship of the horned god is central to modern witchcraft. Her mentor Gardner agrees. The horned god, Gardner explains, would have been a provider of food, representing not only the masculine hunter, but the horned hunted Nonhuman Animal. He thus becomes the "dealer of death" (1959: 45).[8] Kheel (2007), recall, sees the fetishization of "the hunt" as a ritualized affirmation of male supremacy. Grimassi (2001), for one, does not dispute this, championing the "hunt" as a means of reinforcing traditional gender norms, whereby women, as he understands it, would have gathered and men would have killed other animals. Although witchcraft, at least in feminist traditions, has sometimes challenged this domination of nature and its gender essentialism, British neopaganism accommodates it.

As is the case with repurposing scavenged nonhuman bodies for ritual work, many modern witches reframe "hunting" as a measure of resourcefulness and "respect" (Andrews 1993). A similar logic is employed by Freuler's *Of Blood and Bones*: "people who hunt typically eat the whole animal, and often the skins and fur are used as well" (2020: 95). Taking the lives of others in times of precarity and putting as much of their corpse to use as possible, in other words, becomes a moral excuse, even if largely irrelevant in modern Western society. Although ecofeminists often argue that the historic relationship between humans and other animals was symbiotic, witches will more often draw on the patriarchal history of human-nonhuman relationships that begins only after the advent of "hunting." This ancestral legacy then becomes justification for continued violence, despite the predominance of plant-based eating for most early humans and ample modern advancements that make plant-based, peaceful consumption much more convenient and accessible today. Lady Sheba is a notable advocate, even offering her readers spells to ensure successful kills when "hunting" and "fishing" (Bell 2001). Bell (2001) highlights in their *Grimoire of Lady Sheba* a need for mindfulness about killing, imploring the practitioner to respect ecosystem limits:

> I would remind you of the witch law of the wild kingdom: 'you will take only what you need for food, no more. Thou must never waste the life of any living creature. Never kill all of the covey of the tribe. Some must be left to continue the race.' Never knowingly take the life of a mother animal.
>
> *(2001: xvi)*[9]

The heroism of these "hunts" seems to be amplified by capitalistic and patriarchal elements of rationalism and efficiency, with "nothing" wasted and no "needless killing," amplified by the stewardship role assumed by humans in managing natural cycles and nonhuman populations. Although this entitled management suggests that killing is done to appease anthropocentric interests, Chamberlain (2020) adds that "hunting" offers "an opportunity to directly honour and give thanks to the spirit of the animal whose life you took" (33).

Ecofeminists have criticized this patriarchal mythmaking as deceptive to the effect of codifying an oppressive, male-centered world. "When violence is presented under the guise of a 'noble purpose,' all kinds of abuses go unrecognized and often are even praised," warns Collard (1988: 33). Nibert (2026) supports this, his research finding that while "hunting" is often cited as a driver of human evolution its material and ideological entanglement with rape and other violent crimes, slavery, colonialism, war, and environmental destruction suggests anything but. Kheel (2007), furthermore, has argued that "hunting" is preserved in modern times despite more readily accessible forms of food because it is recognized as important for masculine development and ritualistic male heroism. Couched in ancient patriarchal imaginaries, "hunting" thrives in modern masculinity narratives, including environmental thought. In an effort to "protect" or "conserve" the kin group, these narratives insist that "hunting" must be engaged, to bring life through the systemic killing of others. There are other more symbiotic human relationships with the natural world that have not relied on harming other animals that can bring life without killing, but these lack the rousing, manhood-proving bloodlust of "hunting" mythology.

Daly (1978) would remind that patriarchal myth derives its potency in stealing the mythic power of women. The goddess tradition in green witchcraft is clearly aimed at reclaiming this mythic power, but in glorifying "the hunt," keeping space for warrior culture, and presenting "the goddess" or "divine feminine" as only complementary to violent masculinity, it seems trapped in the necrophilia and oppressive mythology of androcentrism. The desire to use other animals and their body parts is associated with patriarchal religious and political practices, practices that have normalized unequal power relations and the entitlement over others. Starhawk, however, notes in her 2nd edition of *The Spiral Dance* that she has opted to replace the symbolism of the "hunt" and sacrificial cycle of life and death with that of blooded beings who rely on plant-produced oxygen, and how those beings feed plants with carbon dioxide. Both animals and plants, furthermore, support a wide community of fermenters and fungi, who feed on decay. This interpretation seems to better reflect the symbiosis that predominates in life (and death) on Earth without glorifying anthroparchal violence.

Colonizer Visions

As previously alluded to, non-Western cultures are sometimes drawn upon to deepen the mythological value of "hunting." By way of an example, *Speaking with Nature* (a shamanic book dedicated to "all beings in the web of life," who are "loved, honored, and respected") describes a planet "filled with love, peace, harmony, equality, abundance, honor, and respect for all life" (Ingerman and Roberts 2015: i), except, as has been evidenced, that which is good for eating. Coauthor Llyn Roberts (2015) recollects a black bear shot by her Native American neighbor: "I used to cringe at death and find such scenes appalling before I traveled to the Asian steppe [...] and saw how indigenous Siberian people relate to the animals they kill" (128). This use she approves, as she believes eating the bodies of others is "essential" in certain areas of the world and the killing economical since "every part of the animal was used" (129). When killed for sacrifice rather than food, she notes, the animals "died swiftly" (129): "a small cut was made in the chest and the shaman reached in to choke the heart" (129). As the heart of these live and conscious victims are crushed by a human hand, we are assured the animal is communicated with and honored. Killing is "part of the life cycle" (129) such that humans (who are not obligate predators) are somehow absconded. Lesson learned, Roberts obliged her neighbor by sharing the corpse of the bear over his table:

> I consciously and gratefully ate the delicious stew [...] having known the Bear that became this stew, and the hunter who related with the animal from beginning to end, the connection of food to its source was strong. This made the eating of it an entirely different experience.
>
> *(129)*

Indeed, the fetishization of relation, sacrifice, and orientalism seems to add a distinct flavor to death. Adams (1993) has critiqued this typical ecofeminist appropriation, suggesting that it can perpetuate problematic dualisms by elevating certain spiritual practices. Likewise, Laura Donaldson (2001) has referred to the white appropriation of Indigenous spirituality as pop feminist "New Age Native Americanism" (237). The danger, Donaldson explains, lies in the commodification of native cultures, the redirection of spiritual (and material) benefits to whites, and the generalizing of Indigenous peoples in maintenance of old colonial logics:

> Like its ancestor, the Noble Savage, the New Age Indian is an innately spiritual being whose lives in perfect egalitarian harmony with all of life and, in doing, redresses the wrongs of patriarchal capitalism. Neither the old nor the new image, however, bears any resemblance to members of real tribal communities.
>
> *(2001: 242)*

Indeed, the nostalgia attached to Indigeneity adds greater value, further legitimizing the claims (and book sales) of white pagan authors. "Indigeneity," one bruja of color notes, is consumed in the postcolonial world "through voyeuristic academic studies and spiritual tourism" (Monteagut 2021: 85). Once systematically and violently suppressed, Ingenious cultures are now excavated, monetized, and consumed by whites.

Indigenous life is frequently constructed as simple, primitive, other, and subsequently magical, and it is this fetishization that sells. Behind the mysteriousness of non-white spiritual practices, in other words, is a legacy of historical white suppression. Donaldson's critique extends to white collections of native clothing, blankets, and other sacred items; these hijacked cultural artifacts must be interpreted in the context of white settler colonialism. Perhaps the same is true of white-identified witches who collect the stories and customs of Indigenous persons to resist critique but to the effect of preserving the many negative consequences that patriarchy and capitalism impart on women and nature. For these white women, Donaldson explains, an Indigenous object such as a blanket (or, in Roberts' case, a bowl of stew) is "abducted from its original context and social identity so that it may become available as a sign for her own purposes" (2001: 248). The ideas, too, that fill the pages of so many white shamanic books represent "an act of cognitive imperialism" (2001: 249), rendering Native Americans into "a universal sign," collected for the purposes of "illustrating a larger feminine point" (2001: 250).

From a vegan perspective, the fetishization of Nonhuman Animals—who are rendered into the most simplistic, primitive, and otherized group of all—must also be examined in the context of white settler colonialism. Donaldson warns:

> Women persisting in a quest fulfilled at the expense of American Indians risk becoming nothing less than kidnappers who falsely claim feminist ideology and who join the rest of those benefiting from the plunders of imperialism in a New—that is, postmodern neocolonial—Age.
>
> *(2001: 151)*

In many cases, *actual bodies and lives* of Nonhuman Animals are kidnapped and plundered for these purposes. Roberts, for example, not only practices cognitive imperialism over Native Americans in the fetishization of the aforementioned bear's killing, but over Nonhuman Animals as well. Doubly so, as the bear was *physically* collected and *physically* consumed, not just symbolically exploited for the white shamanic visions of *Speaking with Nature*. Ko (2019), recall, has observed the entangled colonization of Nonhuman Animals and people of color—mind, body, and culture—for the benefit of white supremacy. This colonization, she adds, is itself a type of witchcraft, casting a spell on marginalized groups for unjust gain. Black ecofeminism, likewise, argues that "the assault upon the natural environment today is but an extension of the assault upon black women's bodies in the nineteenth century" (Williams 1993: 25), such that the clumsy assault on non-white cultures should be cautiously avoided for danger of replicating the very systems of entitlement, exploitation, and oppression that environmentalists and ecofeminists hope to resist. For context, rampant environmental racism and the animalization of non-white groups have been historically unchallenged by the white-dominated Western environmental movement, creating considerable distrust among communities of color (Riley 1993), such that witchcraft's cultural co-optation sits poorly within this legacy. Consider also that, in the white-dominant goddess tradition of the West, efforts to reclaim "blackness" and "darkness" from their "negative" connotations, though well-meaning, essentially reinforce old colonial logics. Furthermore, goddesses of color have been historically overlooked in this tradition, although Indigenous, Eastern, and African religions have been co-opted by white-identified practitioners as sources of spiritual authenticity (Eller 1995).

The Gathering

Despite the legacy of anti-vegetarianism, exploitation of Nonhuman Animals for body parts in ritual working, lingering apologies for live sacrifice, and the exaltation of "the hunt," it remains the case that green witchcraft is positioned to do *good* for other animals as well. It behooves Western witchcraft to begin reclaiming the symbolic multispecies elements of its practice by retiring "the hunt" and returning the gathering. This gathering will entail a celebration of plant-based bounties that have sustained humans and other animals for hundreds of thousands of years, rejuvenating ancestral vegan foodways and teaching lost knowledges of herbalism and foraging. This gathering will also entail an interrogation of modern witchcraft, to root out and recollect the myths, practices, and values that align with a multispecies society and undermine anthroparchal violence. Green witchcraft, after all, is a craft of creation. There is space now to create a new craft and a new tradition. Vegan witchcraft, borne of this gathering, is decidedly a healing and life-affirming magic. It reclaims humanity's more peaceable relationship with other animals that occurred before the advent of violent patriarchal institutions, namely "hunting," "domestication," and sexism.

Making magic and raising power through killing—be it through "sacrifice," "hunting," or eating flesh—is wholly unnecessary and out of tune with 21st-century crises of the environment, public health, and nonhuman welfare. For most witches—especially those living in the industrialized and relatively wealthy West—other means for creating energy abound. Anxieties about the sexual power of women were likely fundamental to witchcraft persecution (Oldridge 2002); might that sexual power be harnessed to destabilize anthroparchal domination? Power need not be taken coercively or by force. It can also be freely given, received, co-created, and shared. Sex magic, for instance, is another power-raising tactic in the witchcraft tradition that marries mind and matter, corporeal and spiritual, and is founded on mutual pleasure and consent. As the following chapter will explore, power might also be gleaned from plant-based consumption through the alchemy of nutrition.

Vegan witchcraft ultimately argues that power is found in multispecies solidarity. Blythe highlights this in their summary of Western paganism: "The animals are a direct link between ourselves and the earth we live on" (1990: 137). Although many aspects of witchcraft have aimed to muddy this link, it is a connection that should be cultivated. Starhawk points to the "enormous amount of cooperation and interdependence" that exists in natural ecosystems (Starhawk 2005: 31). These are naturally occurring sources of strength and resilience, informing healthy and sustainable *social* ecosystems with resource sharing, celebration of diversity, and multispecies flourishing. Explains Starhawk: "Survival goes not to the most ruthless or competitive, but to those who most effectively cooperate, communicate, and share resources [...] Adaptation is not about one species triumphing over another, but about a whole system coevolving" (2005: 48).

Conclusion

Green witchcraft is a nature-based, healing-oriented magical practice that favors the utilization of plants, herbs, and other elements of the environment in pagan practice. It emphasizes the connection of all beings, practitioners included, to nature and the universe beyond. In the mid-20th century, green witchcraft experienced a resurgence with the help of growing interest in environmentalism and ecofeminism. Herbalism and home remedies associated with shamans and cunning women, once stigmatized as primitive and uncivilized folk magic in the late Middle Ages and early modern era of Western Europe and North America, have now taken pride of place in the cultural landscape as evidenced in the rise of alternative medicine and holistic approaches to wellness. For ecofeminists, the revival of these practices constituted a source of reclaimed knowledge and feminine power. Anti-speciesism was developing in this era as well, creating some interesting points of intersection between green witchcraft, ecofeminism, and veganism, all of which responded to the disastrous implications of an unchecked anthroparchal reign of terror over nature and feminized groups.

Despite these overlaps, green witchcraft has not absorbed a vegan environmental or feminist ethic. Instead, many witches have fallen back on anthroparchal and capitalistic arguments that objectify Nonhuman Animals as well as romanticized visions of ancestral pasts to justify the continued oppression of other animals for magical purposes. In the case of many white-identified witches, this has also included the deployment of colonialist fantasies of Indigenous culture to deflect ecofeminist reflexivity. For all its claim to earthly and universal connection, its commitment to "hunting," using, and consuming other animals denotes a failure to recognize that the systems of machoistic and colonial domination that endanger animals are the very same that have historically fueled the persecution of women and nature, a connection well-established by vegan feminists and contemporary to both 20th and 21st century ecofeminist witch discourse.

Nonhuman Animals, then, have become both symbolic *and* literal sacrifices for the green witch path. The witch's canon overarchingly rejects the live sacrifice of Nonhuman Animals for magical purposes in the modern world, but it continues to align with the anthroparchal status quo with regard to objectifying their bodies, belittling vegetarianism and veganism, and rejecting plant-based consumption as a vital measure of resistance to environmental degradation and speciesist oppression. A veganized green witchcraft, I argue, must be appreciative of nature and *all* of its inhabitants. This must reach beyond humans to also include free-living animals, who are harmed by human-caused dietary-linked climate change, and domesticated animals, who are rendered objects for ritual tools, sacrificial ceremonies, and romanticized "hunts." It recognizes Nonhuman Animals, regardless of species, as persons who have a right to autonomy and respect beyond latent symbols of agrarian life or totemic symbols of natural life. Vegan witchcraft calls for an end to "the Hunt" and a reclaiming of "the gathering" and all the symbiotic, multispecies possibilities it entails. To truly encompass the healing capacities of green witchcraft, the path must lead to veganism as a means of repairing a long legacy of human violence against other animals, the Earth, and, as it informs sexism and dietary illness, other humans as well.

Notes

1 The American Dietetic Association is clear that a vegetarian diet is perfectly healthy for everyone, including pregnant or lactating women (Craig et al. 2009).
2 In a presentation for the National Women's Studies Association, Kheel (2005) does make a quick note of Starhawk's unevidenced anti-vegetarian position in *The Earth Path*.
3 Kheel's papers are digitally archived with Harvard University. Although I was unable to find direct communication between Kheel and Starhawk, there is correspondence between ecofeminist witch and artist Fireweed (1996). In my personal correspondence with Carol Adams in 2023, she was unaware of any linkages between scholar-activists in vegan feminism and witchcraft.
4 For some of its later issues in the 1990s, issue numbers were marked by the Wiccan calendar, rather than the typical Gregorian system.
5 Starhawk is a prolific writer such that I cannot account for every statement she has publicly made on humanity's moral obligation to other animals, but I did analyze her four major publications for this book, *Truth or Dare* (1987), *Dreaming the Dark* (1997), *The Spiral Dance* (1999), and *The Earth Path* (2005).
6 I was only able to source an unpaginated eBook of this text.
7 Freuler's conception of respect is especially dubious in her advice on procuring Nonhuman Animal bodies. To clean their bones, she advises covering them in water, burying them, or using enzymes, all rudimentary and gruesome processes. For those who find this type of foraging a squeamish business and would prefer to "not do the dirty work of bone cleaning (and believe me, *it's dirty*)" (94), she suggests deferring to professional sellers or otherwise "hunting" nonhuman persons to provide fresh corpses.
8 Grimassi (2001) further supposes that the utilization of horns and other imperishable remains was symbolically important for demonstrating life beyond death, reconciling the permanence and impermanence of life.
9 Just how killers are supposed to follow Lady Sheba's "witch law of the wild kingdom" and determine the population health of a species is unclear. It is also unclear how killers would reliably avoid mothers. Indeed, in the modern food system, the killing of mothers is routine, the wasting of life is normalized, and the extinction of free-living animals in the wake of animal-based agriculture is systemic.

References

Adams, C. 1991. "Ecofeminism and the Eating of Animals." *Hypatia* 6: 125–145.
Adams, C. 1993. *Ecofeminism and the Sacred*. New York: Continuum.
Adams, C. 2012. "Finding Necrophilia in Meat Eating: Mary Daly's Evolving Fem-Veg Perspective." *Journal of Feminist Studies in Religion* 28 (2): 93–98.
Adams, C. and L. Gruen. 2014. *Ecofeminism*. London: Bloomsbury.
Adams, C. and M. Procter-Smith. 1993. "'Taking Life' or 'Taking On Life'? Table Talk and Animals." pp. 295–310, in *Ecofeminism and the Sacred*. New York: Continuum.
Alloun, E. 2015. "Ecofeminism and Animal Advocacy in Australia." *Animal Studies Journal* 4 (1): 148–173.
Amey, C. 2014. *The Compassionate Contrarians*. Wellington: Rebel Press.
Andrews, T. 1993. *Animal Speak*. Woodbury: Llewellyn.
Bailey, L. 1996. "Acting Out: Solstice Revolutions." *Feminists for Animal Rights Newsletter* 10 (1–2): 2.
Bell, J. 2001. *The Grimoire of Lady Sheba*. St. Paul: Llewellyn.
Berger, H. 2000. "High Priestess: Mother, Leader, Teacher." pp. 103–118, in *Daughters of the Goddess*, W. Griffin (Ed.). Oxford: AltaMira Press.
Blythe, G. 1990. "Of the Voices of Animals." pp. 137–148, in *Voices from the Circle*, P. Jones and C. Matthews (Eds.). Wellingborough: Aquarian Press.
Budapest, Z. 1986. *The Holy Book of Women's Mysteries*. Oakland: Consolidated Printers.
Buckland, R. 2002. *Complete Book of Witchcraft*. Woodbury: Llewellyn.
Chamberlain, L. 2020. *Wiccan Kitchen*. New York: Sterling Ethos.
Clifton, C. 2006. *Her Hidden Children*. Oxford: AltaMira Press.
Collard, A. 1988. *Rape of the Wild*. London: The Women's Press.
Craig, W., A. Mangels, and American Dietetic Association. 2009. "Position of the American Dietetic Association: Vegetarian Diets." *Journal of the American Dietetic Association* 109 (7): 1266–1282.
Crowley, V. 2000. "Healing in Wicca." pp. 151–165, in *Daughters of the Goddess*, W. Griffin (Ed.). Oxford: AltaMira Press.
Crowther, P. 1981. *Lid off the Cauldron*. London: Frederick Muller.
Cudworth, E. 2011. *Social Lives with Other Animals*. London: Palgrave.
Cudworth, E. 2016. "Ecofeminism and the Animal." pp. 38–56, in *Contemporary Perspectives on Ecofeminism*, M. Phillips and N. Rumens (Eds.). London: Routledge.
Daly, M. 1978. *Gyn/Ecology*. London: The Women's Press.
Daly, M. 1984. *Pure Lust*. Boston: Beacon Books.
De Backer, C., S. Erreygers, C. De Cort, F. Vandermoere, A. Dhoest, J. Vrinten, and S. Van Bauwel. 2020. "Meat and Masculinities." *Appetite* 147 (104559).
Diamond, I. and G. Orenstein (Eds). 1990. *Reweaving the World*. San Francisco: Sierra Club Books.
Digitalis, R. 2022. "Lughnasadh Bone Charms." p. 107, in *Llewellyn's Witches' Datebook 2022*, L. Heineman (Ed.). Woodbury: Llewellyn.
Donaldson, L. 2001. "On Medicine Women and White Shame-ans: New Age Native Americanism and Commodity Fetishism as Pop Culture Feminism." pp. 237–256, in *Women, Gender, Religion*, E. Castelli (Ed.). London: Palgrave.
Ehrenreich, B. and D. English. 1973. *Witches, Midwives and Nurses*. London: Writers and Readers Publishing Cooperative.
Eller, C. 1995. *Living in the Lap of the Goddess*. Boston: Beacon Press.
Fideler, D. 1997. *Alexandria*. Grand Rapids: Phanes Press.

Fireweed. 1996. "Letter, Women & Earth, Gathering in Green." Papers of Marti Kheel. Schlesinger Library, Radcliffe Institute. Archive item sch01622c00476—MC962.7.25.

Forest, D. 2020. *Wild Magic*. Woodbury: Llewellyn.

Freuler, K. 2020. *Of Blood and Bones*. Woodbury: Llewellyn.

Friendship Earth. 1988. *Papers of Marti Kheel*. Schlesinger Library, Radcliffe Institute. Archive item sch01622c00433—MC962_6.8.

Gardner, G. 1959. *The Meaning of Witchcraft*. New York: Magickal Childe.

Gardner, G. 1970. *Witchcraft Today*. London: Citadel Press.

Green, M. 2002. *A Witch Alone*. London: HarperCollins.

Greenebaum, J. 2018. "Vegan Men and Hybrid Masculinity." *Journal of Gender Studies* 27 (6): 637–648.

Greenwood, S. 2000. "Feminist Witchcraft: A Transformatory Politics." pp. 136–150, in *Daughters of the Goddess*, W. Griffin (Ed.). Oxford: AltaMira Press.

Grimassi, R. 2001. *The Wiccan Mysteries*. St. Paul: Llewellyn.

Hall, N. 2023. *Path of the Moonlit Hedge*. Woodbury: Llewellyn.

Hunnicutt, G. 2019. *Gender Violence in Ecofeminist Perspective*. London: Routledge.

Ingerman, S. and L. Roberts. 2015. *Speaking with Nature*. Rochester: Bear & Company.

Irni, K. 2024. "Revisiting Ecofeminist Genealogies: Towards Intersectional and Trans-Inclusive Ecofeminism." pp. 207–247, in *Feminist Animal and Multispecies Studies*, K. Aavik, K. Irni, and M. Joki (Eds.). Leiden: Brill.

Johns, J. 1969. *King of the Witches*. London: Peter Davies.

Jones, P. 1990. "Circles of Earth, Circles of Heaven." pp. 41–54, in *Voices from the Circle*, P. Jones and C. Matthews (Eds.). Wellingborough: Aquarian Press.

Jones, P. and C. Matthews. 1990. "Introduction." pp. 13–40, in *Voices from the Circle*, P. Jones and C. Matthews (Eds.). Wellingborough: Aquarian Press.

Kheel, M. 1983a. "What are They Hiding?" Letters to the Editor. *Oakland Tribune*, January 13.

Kheel, M. 1983b. "Animal Rights is a Feminist Issue." *WomanSpirit* 9 (36): 18–20.

Kheel, M. 1984. "Feminist Reflections: International Conference on Religious Perspectives on the Use of Animals in Science." *Feminists for Animal Rights Newsletter* 1 (3): 1.

Kheel, M. 1986. "From Healing Herbs to Deadly Drugs: Western Medicine's War Against the Natural World." *Feminists for Animal Rights Newsletter* 2 (2): 1–14.

Kheel, M. 2005. *Toppling Patriarchy with a Fork*. Papers of Marti Kheel. Schlesinger Library, Radcliffe Institute. Archive item sch01622c00580—MC962.10.17.

Kheel, M. 2007. *Nature Ethics*. Landham: Rowman & Littlefield.

Ko, A. 2019. *Racism as Zoological Witchcraft*. New York: Lantern Books.

LadySabrina. 2001. *The Beliefs, Rites, and Rituals of the Wicca Religion*. Franklin Lakes: New Page Books.

Leek, S. 1973. *The Complete Art of Witchcraft*. New York: New American Library.

Levinger, N. and T. Whitehurst. 2019. "Episode 1: Intro, Healing Your Inner Child & Communing with Flowers." *Magical Mondays*. Podcast.

Luke, B. 2007. *Brutal*. Champaign: University of Illinois Press.

Madara, M. 2021. *The Witch's Feast*. London: Nourish Books.

McCormack, S. 2021. "Climate Change and Animal Agriculture: Federal Actions Protect the Biggest Contributors from the Disasters they Cause." *Environmental Law* 51 (3): 745–769.

McGuire, C. n.d. "About EVE ONLINE." Retrieved April 18, 2024, from: https://ecofem inism.info/about/index.html.

McKay, D. 2024. *A Witch's Ally*. Woodbury: Llewellyn.

Miernowska, M. 2020. *The Witch's Herbal Apothecary*. Beverly: Quarto.

Monteagut, L. 2021. *Brujas*. Chicago: Chicago Review Press.

Mor, B. 1992. "Poetry by Barbara Mor." *Feminists for Animal Rights Newsletter* 6 (3–4): 16.

Morningstar, S. n.d. "About Me." Retrieved May 8, 2024, from: https://www.sallym orningstar.com/#:~:text=I%20believe%20in%20walking%20my,of%20animals%20%26%20the%20wild%20world.

Moura, A. 2020. *Green Witchcraft*. Woodbury: Llewellyn.

Murphy-Hiscock, A. 2018. *The Witches' Book of Self-Care*. London: Adams Media.

Nibert, D. 2002. *Animal Rights, Human Rights*. New York: Rowman & Littlefield.

Nibert, D. 2013. *Animal Oppression and Human Violence*. New York: Columbia University Press.

Nibert, D. 2026. *Animal Oppression and Malev(i)olence*. Ann Arbor: University of Michigan Press. Forthcoming.

Nguyen, H. 2019. *Tongue-Tied: Breaking the Language Barrier to Animal Liberation*. New York: Lantern.

Oldridge, D. 2002. "Witchcraft and Gender." pp. 267–271, in *The Witchcraft Reader*, D. Oldridge (Ed.). London: Routledge.

Patterson, R. 2017a. *Witchcraft into the Wilds*. Winchester: Moon Books.

Patterson, R. 2017b. *Animal Magic*. Hants: John Hunt.

Puca, A. 2023. "Nature Spirituality & Paganism with Selena Fox." Retrieved May 16, 2024, from: https://www.youtube.com/watch?v=Dw2FlyWVVqM&ab_channel=Angela%27sSy mposium.

Riley, S. 1993. "Ecology is a Sistah's Issue Too: The Politics of Emergent Afrocentric Ecowomanism." pp. 191–204, in *Ecofeminism and the Sacred*, C. Adams (Ed.). New York: Continuum.

Roberts, L. 2015. "Black Bear." pp. 125–142, in *Speaking with Nature*, S. Ingerman and L. Roberts (Eds). Rochester: Bear & Company.

Robinson, S. 2022. *Kitchen Witch*. Shanagarry: Womancraft Publishing.

Rosenfeld, D. 2023. "Masculinity and Men's Resistance to Meat Reduction." *Psychology of Human-Animal Intergroup Relations* 2 (e9645).

Ruether, R. 1993. "Ecofeminism: Symbolic and Social Connections of the Oppression of Women and the Domination of Nature." pp. 13–23, in *Ecofeminism and the Sacred*, C. Adams (Ed.). New York: Continuum.

Scarborough, S. 1996. "An Interview with Sudie Rakusin." *Feminists for Animal Rights Newsletter* 10 (1–2): 1–9.

Sjöö, M. and B. Mor. 1991. *The Great Cosmic Mother*. San Francisco: HarperSanFrancisco.

Spretnak, C. 1993. "Earthbody and the Personal Body as Sacred." pp. 261–280, in *Ecofeminism and the Sacred*, C. Adams (Ed.). New York: Continuum.

Starhawk. 1987. *Truth or Dare*. San Francisco: HarperSanFrancisco.

Starhawk. 1997. *Dreaming the Dark*. Boston: Beacon Press.

Starhawk. 1999. *The Spiral Dance*. Third Edition. New York: HarperOne.

Starhawk. 2005. *The Earth Path*. New York: HarperCollins.

Starhawk. 2020. "#11 Beyond Climate Change." *Gang of Witches – Le Podcast*. Retrieved August 24, 2023, from: https://smartlink.ausha.co/gang-of-witches-le-podca st/11-au-dela-du-changement-climatique-en.

Tschakert, P. 2022. "More-than-Human Solidarity and Multispecies Justice in the Climate Crisis." *Environmental Politics* 31 (2): 277–296.

Valiente, D. 1962. *Where Witchcraft Lives*. London: The Aquarian Press.

Valiente, D. 1975. *Natural Magic*. Custer: Phoenix.

Valiente, D. 1978. *Witchcraft for Tomorrow*. London: Robert Hale.

Vanderbeck, P. 2020. *Green Witchcraft*. Emeryville: Rockridge Press.

Warren, K. 1993. "A Feminist Philosophical Perspective on Ecofeminism Spiritualities." pp. 119–132, in *Ecofeminism and the Sacred*, C. Adams (Ed.). New York: Continuum.

Williams, D. 1993. "Sin, Nature, and Black Women's Bodies." pp. 24–29, in *Ecofeminism and the Sacred*, C. Adams (Ed.). New York: Continuum.

Weinstein, M. 2020. *Positive Magic*. Newburyport: Weiser Books.

Whitehurst, T. 2015. *Holistic Energy Magic*. Woodbury: Llewellyn.

Whitehurst, T. 2017. *Magical Housekeeping*. Woodbury: Llewellyn.

Wrenn, C. 2023. "Building a Vegan Feminist Network in the Professionalised Digital Age of Third-Wave Animal Activism." pp. 235–248, in *Feminist Animal Studies*, E. Cudworth and D. Turgoose (Eds.). London: Routledge.

4

KITCHEN WITCHERY

Introduction

Although I have emphasized that vegan witchcraft is a personal protest and political resistance to systems of speciesist inequality, it is also the case, of course, that witchcraft relates to the food humans eat. Indeed, 21st-century witchcraft has seen a resurgence in interest around culinary magic. After all, what is a witch without their bubbling cauldron? The same can also be said of veganism. Veganism is more than a belief system or a political ideology as it requires sustained and active physical consumption patterns. It changes the practitioner physically, psychologically, and, for some, spiritually. In this way, the practice of veganism becomes a practice of magic. It lifts the veil of speciesist socialization, encouraging new perspectives that are otherwise hidden to non-vegans. It changes bodies, too. Among the many physiological benefits (too many to list here), veganism supports a healthier heart and cardiovascular system, clearer skin, and happier bowels (Petti et al. 2017). As such, it acts as a sort of plant magic in reimagining nascent human foodways and intentional working with natural herbs, greens, berries, and other vegetable matter to do good works for oneself, loved ones, the community, and the wider environment.

The peasants' pottage, a longstanding staple for many cultures, filled the first cauldrons. Brimming with herbs and other wild-growing plants, vegetables, fungi, and hearty grains, the concoction was ripe with health-giving properties and offered unseen nutritive goodness. Each simmering component would release important vitamins and minerals to be readily absorbed in the stomach, while the remains of the plants and grains themselves served as necessary fiber, helping the intestinal tract to remove decaying material and toxic build up. Paired with fruits and nuts, these potions would also offer vital fats, proteins, and amino acids, powering minds and muscles[1] and avoiding the inflammatory responses typically

DOI: 10.4324/9781032649801-4

associated with the consumption of animal ingredients. After consuming, the body is revitalized and energized. It is able to heal wounds, repair and replace cells, and keep muscles moving. This is magic in action.

These basic but transformative properties of food are one reason why it has been so central to witchcraft. Its universality is another. Cunningham (2007) describes kitchen witchcraft as a type of folk magic that makes use of tools available to most people. Food itself becomes "a tool that contains specific energies which we can use to create great change in our lives" (2007: 4). It connects people across generations with recipes, rituals, and rites of passage. There is magical symbolism in kitchenware, too, with the cauldron and other rounded pots symbolizing nourishment and the "great mother," the oven representing fire and transformation, the plate conjuring wealth and abundance, and knives symbolizing that which both threatens and affirms life (Cunningham 2007). In Appalachian magic, the cast iron pan, passed down through the generations along with the remnants of animal fats it collects is thought to hold power (Ballard 2021). Speciesist rituals of food preparation, likewise, such as churning cows' butter and curdling "buttermilk" are believed to raise magic through this generational connection. Fire, too, was a powerful alchemic element. It transformed social life in the creation of hearth, bringing family together in the home and making new cuisines possible. Fire, for Chamberlain, is central to witchcraft as a "living, breathing entity, governed by the deities of the hearth and treated with reverence and respect" (2020: 10).

Making meals out of mundane and otherwise inedible ingredients was a mysterious act, a "magical blessing" (9). Kate West introduces kitchen witchcraft as a means of enhancing life without chemicals in order to "heal the body, soothe the mind and enliven the spirit" (2002: xii). Cookery can do magical things: it can amplify the nutritional qualities of food, it can preserve foodstuffs beyond the natural point of decay, and it can combine elements to create entirely new foods. Foods can affect moods, relax, or empower. Foods can also be dangerous. If left to spoil or prepared incorrectly, they can cause inebriation or illness. Some foods, despite their palatability, can even be toxic. Socially, too, food can be used to build bonds, nurture, and heal, or food can be used to starve, exclude, or justify violent behavior. Entire societies have developed to regulate access to food. Entire societies have also collapsed in failing to do so. It is the very stuff of life and death.

I have discussed the ways in which modern witchcraft romanticizes times gone by as though they were inherently more authentic or laudable. This theme is revisited in kitchen witchery. In the 21st century, food has become highly processed and nutritionally void, often unrecognizable from cuisines of old. Romanticizing traditional consumption patterns is likely a tempting enhancer. Food, after all, is deeply cultural, often embodying a society's values and nostalgias for values thought lost (Carolan 2016). The cottage-core movement, back-to-the-landers, and natural foods movement, for example, have all relied on "real food" as the centerpiece of their values and practice. Kitchen witchery seeks to achieve the same by positioning cooking and tending the hearth as practices that link the practitioner across generations. It is a reconnection to foods believed to have sustained and healed the witch's ancestors. Sarah Robinson (2022) defines kitchen witchcraft as "the magic of hearth, home and food," centering the kitchen as a "sacred space" (4). This sacred kitchen space was the base of operations for much of human life; it is where information and food were exchanged and rituals and healing transpired. Chamberlain (2020) adds, "These cooks simply work with an attitude of reverence for the Earth, inviting the transformative energies of foods and using what they have to create nourishing, magically powerful meals" (4).

Although some elements of this legacy may be historically accurate, much of it is more accurately an *idea* of what witches think their ancestors ate. For instance, Hall, who draws on animism to substantiate his hedge witch path, idealizes his human ancestors as "hunters," who persecuted other animals in "vast grasslands for hundreds of thousands of years" (2023: 159), an ideation that lacks substantiation. For most of human ancestry, humans were primarily plant-based scavengers and foragers (Collard 1988, Spencer 1993). Even with the advent of "hunting," plants comprised about 80% of the human diet, yet historical inaccuracies about consumption, filtered through the anthroparchic norms of the present, persist. Indeed, ideas about food are strongly shaped by the culture of the imaginer. Not only is this imagination deeply problematic for Nonhuman Animals unfortunate enough to be labelled "ingredients," but much of the kitchen witch fantasy relies on white European foodways by making space at the table for "meat," "dairy," and other animal products to the exclusion and derision of foods that have sustained the global majority, inadvertently centering a white colonizer diet as the universal norm for human consumption.

For the most part, however, the mundane incorporation of animal flesh and fluid goes unmentioned in kitchen witch texts. West (2002), for instance, advises readers to eat local foods in tune with the seasons to ensure shorter transportation traumas, reduced spread of disease, and less suffering overall for animals marked as food, but she does not question the need to eat these animals in the first place. Indeed, it is the "premature" killing and added discomfort of illnesses such as foot-and-mouth disease that perturb her, not the killing itself. The unremarked ubiquitousness of their presence renders them taken for granted and almost invisible. Consider, for instance, the claimsmaking of one of the leading and most established kitchen witches, Carin McKay, a nonvegan food activist, collaborator of Starhawk's, and caterer for Reclaiming events. In a special issue on food magic for *Reclaiming Quarterly*, she introduces readers to the power of cooking, the potency of food, and the celebration in consumption (McKay 2003). Importantly, the essay makes little mention of the individuals sacrificed to conjure this "magic." Her website, however, assures customers that most of the "meats" she incorporates are sourced "locally and organically" (Culinary Magic n.d.), underscoring their commodity status.

The overarching absence of discussion about killing Nonhuman Animals for kitchen witchcraft likely results from the normalized nature of speciesism, but it also may be a political maneuver intended to assuage discomfort in the witchcraft community and capitalize on cultural concern with Nonhuman Animal welfare. Most recipes shared in *Reclaiming Quarterly*'s "Kitchen Witch" section are actually vegetarian if not vegan, with vegan substitutions suggested. Greenleaf's *Book of Kitchen Witchery* (2016) offers vegetarian alternatives for animal-based recipes as well. Yet, for every source that advocates, even if implicitly, veganism or vegetarianism, another explicitly rejects it. Buckland's (2002) seminal *Complete Book of Witchcraft*, for instance, dismisses vegetarians as overly critical and out of sync with "the natural order" (8). Sybil Leek's (1973) equally important *The Complete Art of Witchcraft* provides an entire chapter advising readers on how to practice healthy eating based on the "needs of their own body" (118), which is thought capable of reaching self-regulation due to the "orderly mental disciplines of the [Wiccan] religion" (118). Although she advises a diet heavy in unprocessed foods, fruits, and vegetables with no mention of animal products, free will and "balance" are key: "We do not impose restrictions about food for drink" (118). Instead, Leek advises witches to follow their intuition, eschewing supplements in favor of following the dietary traditions of their ancestors. "Wrong diet," she muses, "is just as dangerous in conjuring up body poisons as drugs" (1973: 122). Denatured foods are rejected in favor of fresh fruits and vegetables and plenty of garlic and fiber. For Leek, there is magic in good diet and plenty of exercise. Although she does not make mention of animal products and presumably does not include them in this magical eating, witches will do best, she advises, to avoid restrictive eating, and this advice is presumably inclusive of vegetarianism: "Cutting out the good things of life by stringent, impossible-to-keep diets is not the answer to happy, successful living" (1973: 124). West agrees, introducing her *Real Witches' Kitchen* by reminding readers that there are no leaders or instruction manuals that must be followed: "everyone is entitled to their own, informed, choice of spiritual path, so long as they harm no one" (2002: 3).

Owlvine Green (2024), a YouTube witch with nearly 40,000 subscribers at the time of this writing, describes veganism (which she tried briefly for weight loss) as a very difficult diet for "holier-than-thou" type healthy eaters. Plant-based eating, in other words, seems well suited to aligning with witchcraft's desire for wholesome, natural eating, but its emphasis on personal agency and rejection of dogma renders veganism suspect. Plant-based eating is an act of deviance, as Cunningham (who was a flexitarian himself) summarizes: "Most vegetarians rigidly adhere to their diets in the face of overwhelming odds" (2007: 23).

Being one of the most influential authors in witchcraft, Cunningham's position on vegetarianism is important (and perhaps the most substantive of all authors included in this study), but rather muddled. On one hand, he acknowledges that "living creatures" are "our sisters and brothers," but eating them is not bad healthfully or psychically: "No one diet is for everyone, just as no simple type of haircut, food or religion is suitable for all" (2007: 24). Comparing vegetarianism with a haircut is borderline facetious, but dismissing it as a lifestyle is perhaps more pernicious, as it avoids the ethical arguments against eating "our sisters and brothers." Although Cunningham (and several other witches) vehemently reject promoting vegetarianism or veganism for fear of forcing beliefs and control over others, they have no qualms about doing just that with alcohol. Cunningham (2007) only hesitantly includes alcohol in his encyclopedia of kitchen witchery, warning of its dangers to both body and magical practice: "You'll receive no power or wisdom from getting drunk. Alcohol doesn't open doors to psychic or magical development—in fact, it closes them" (195). Unlike animal products, which warrant little political mention, Cunningham is clear that his coverage of alcohol, "shouldn't be construed as a recommendation to drink [...]. If you don't drink, don't start" (2007: 187).

This chapter explores the ways in which witchcraft works with food and understands it as a key element of magical practice; how it grapples with the dissonant positions on natural diets and species oppression. This chapter also considers room for vegan food magic, examining ways of employing food justice that reposition Nonhuman Animals from mealtime ingredients to honored dinner guests. The kitchen has historically been a site of women's oppression, the oppression of enslaved peoples, and, of course, the oppression of Nonhuman Animals hurt and killed to produce ingredients and foodstuffs. Witchcraft today, however, tends to romanticize the "traditional" kitchen and lacks any critique of the inequalities that have historically festered there. This chapter continues a vegan feminist critique of contemporary discourse in kitchen witchcraft, highlighting the ways in which gender, species, and other identities are reified in the remaking of kitchen routines and rites. Vegan witchcraft is presented as an alternative to this traditional "meat"- and "milk"-based magic—as harnessing the restorative properties of plant foods.

Living Power of Plants

In witchcraft, the emphasis is predominantly on maximizing food's life-giving energy. As Chamberlain (2020) understands it, food in the Wiccan tradition borrows from Eastern knowledges involving the concept of "chi." From this appropriation, the vibrational energy of the universe is thought to also be found in human bodies and other matters, food included. Woodward agrees: "Each bite vibrates with a unique brand of its own energy that you take within to bond with or collide with. There is amazing energy in the food we consume, both metabolic and magickal ..." (2021: 11). When these energies are thought out of balance, food is believed useful for positively manipulating human bodies and emotions to restore equilibrium. Long before witches and folk healers of the West had any contact with the Eastern knowledges, in fact, food was believed to have magical properties of a similar kind, perhaps, as Chamberlain surmises, explaining its ubiquitous presence in ceremonies.

The energy of food is regularly discussed in these esoteric terms. Today, witches "deliberately channel" energy into food preparation and consume mindfully in order to "experience faster and more powerful results" (2020: 19). Emphasizing the adage "you are what you eat," Chamberlain advises eating higher vibrational foods to reap the best benefits. "Our very consciousness" she explains, "is vibration," whereby higher frequency foods can improve not just our physical wellbeing, but also our mental health and our sense of self-efficacy (Chamberlain 2020: 21). Whitehurst (2018) describes this as "enchanted eating" (115), a type of consumption that is conscious of the "effect on our personal vibrations" (115). She recommends "conscious consumption," which she suggests facilitates a "conscious alignment with the Universe and Mother Earth" (Whitehurst 2015: 153). Cunningham also uses this framework to understand kitchen witchcraft: "Food [...] harbors energies. [...] Though we may not be aware of any effect other than a satiated appetite, the food has subtly changed us" (2007: xvii).

Herbs, spices, and other plants are undoubtedly the priority ingredients in kitchen witchcraft. Grimassi (2000) notes that early agrarians saw the "divine creative spark dwelling within the creation" (34), within seeds and herbs, creating a sort of consciousness that could be tapped. "The spirit within the herb had to be treated with respect in order to harvest its magick," he explains (34), such that a number of historic rituals involve herb working. He has even suggested that the spiritual power of plants is so potent that they may even serve as familiars, offering to the practitioner soothing potions, scents, mental calming, and protection (Grimassi 2021). Whitehurst (2017) also celebrates plant magic, highlighting, for instance, the purifying and balancing properties of herbs like rosemary, basil, and sage. Greenleaf (2016) advises keeping a garden for health and healing, as herbs and plants are important not just nutritionally but also emotional and psychically. By way of an example, Green (2002) includes a chapter in her highly influential A Witch Alone that celebrates the wide variety of traditional uses plants have served, including as fabric, dye and decoration, for magic working and as talismans, "pest" control, incense, oils, medicine, and nutrition.

The predominance of plants in kitchen magic would understandably find them prioritized in witchcraft dietary practice. Greenleaf notes that witches seeking to increase their understanding of plant power could "choose vegetarian dishes or salads as ways of celebrating the change of seasons" and share them with friends and family (2016: 139). Whitehurst (2018) also advises whole foods and vegetarianism, particularly advising the elimination of dairy, as it is thought to manifest unwellness and prolong sickness. Although this chapter will find much evidence to the contrary, it is also the case that veganism finds some roots in witchcraft. David Wolfe (2004), for instance, advocates for a raw food diet to align with the natural world and ancestral foodways. Eating raw, he notes, "connects us *directly* with nature and nature spirits, benefits the environment, is compassionate, leads us to limitless beauty, and increases longevity" (134). Indeed, Wolfe's scientific claimsmaking contradicts that of traditional witchcraft food lore that centers animal products in the ancestral diet: "A growing body of archaeological evidence is indicating that we have not evolved but have been de-evolving as a species" (134). Much of the "magic" of food, he continues, is lost through cooking and processing. Veganism is outlined as not only nutritionally sufficient, but nutritionally dense by comparison. Woodward (2021) also incorporates new dietary trends that purport to re-create ancestral eating, such as shopping locally, gardening, and buying organic: "Facts have not changed. You are still what you eat and as a society, we are paying the price with low energy, poor health, and weight problems" (4). Non-organic food, she emphasizes, is not only dangerous for human consumers but for free-living animals, given the toxicological effects it has on natural spaces. She argues that this same logic, however, is applied to "organic" Nonhuman Animal products, under the assumption that their health, wellbeing, and "happiness" (2021: 101) will be considerably higher, creating a more healthful (and magical) product. Starhawk, a permaculturalist, also recommends organic, locally grown and seasonal foods as well as healthful cooking and mindful eating done "with love and gratitude" (2005: 119). She sees eating as a magical practice that allows the practitioner to "ingest place and become it" (2005: 117). What might non-vegan witches become upon ingesting places of slaughter and suffering?

Some leaders in modern witchcraft have identified the importance of plant-based consumption for strengthening not only the physical body, but the psychic body. Cunningham, for instance, explains that his foray into vegetarianism was short lived due to the overwhelming potency of his psychic abilities following several days of abstinence from animal flesh, an experience he refers to as a "harrowing journey" (2007: 27). He advises eating animals' flesh to bolster against psychic attacks. Similarly, Patterson (2017) advises eating fishes to increase psychic power. Despite the prevalence of familiar magic in witchcraft, the magical abilities of living Nonhuman Animals are sidelined in kitchen magic. Instead, animals are thought more useful when deceased, and only humans seem capable of tapping into these powers. Nonhuman Animals who must be killed to provide this psychic ability or psychic protection are not considered capable of wielding such abilities, undermining their subject status and ensuring their objectification as ingredients. Alternatively, veganism is also regularly practiced by Western spiritual leaders, who believe that a pure, plant-based diet amplifies their psychic abilities (Daw et al. 2023). Miernowska (2020) emphasizes that humans are made of the same elements as plants, such that the essence or spirit of plants is alchemically designed to benefit humans. Patricia Telesco's *A Kitchen Witch's Cookbook* (2000) also flags tofu for its psychic attributes. Even the more conservative Raymond Buckland advises eating copious fruits and vegetables. Although he does not explain the insinuated power of plant-based eating behind this advice, he does suggest that it improves personal and spiritual hygiene: "I don't suggest you become a vegetarian, but don't overindulge in meat" (2002: 157). Some medieval rituals also toyed with this relationship between diet and the divine, aiming to transcend consciousness and reach psychological transformation. The occult research of Ramsey Dukes

(2019), for instance, records prolonged rituals of extreme denial, fasting, prayer, seclusion. These older rituals celebrate a return to simplicity, and, of course, pit veganism as a form of denial and sacrifice. But this is not at all in alignment with modern foodways within which vegan cuisine is rich and abundant. Extreme withdrawal from indulgent food and society itself is not required to reap the benefits of plant-based foods.

Eating with the Ancestors

Because plant magic is valued for its anthropocentric capabilities rather than its potential to benefit the environment and advance justice for Nonhuman Animals, eating plant-based is usually taken as a temporary exercise for many in the witchcraft community. Budapest (1986) recalls having gone vegetarian out of concern for her health and weight management, for instance, but she would eventually relax this abstention to include only animals she believed to have "red meat." She admits, "Today, I do with a little chicken and I certainly eat all the seafood I can get my hands on" (1986: 7). Narratives of natural human behaviors and time-honored traditions tend to take precedence in these cases. Consider, for instance, a piece published in The *Reclaiming Quarterly* magazine, which argues for the universality of omnivorism, suggesting those who live with cats share in the bounty of their kills. It is unclear as to whether or not the suggestion is satire:

> Graciously accept the rat, taking it into your hands and admiring it. Then use your fine strong primate molars to crack open the rat's skull. Pry open the split skull and, using your little finger or an oyster-fork, scrape out the rodent's brains and devour them, smacking your lips and licking your fingers appreciatively.
>
> *(Newmeyer 1986)*

The idea is not only to honor the cat's offering but also to return to a long-lost primate heritage. Cunningham, too, muses that today's witches may have lost the old ways of procuring animals' flesh: "we now hunt in refrigerated cases" (2007: xviii).

Indeed, this theme of reaching back to the ancestors through continuations in food culture is a common one. As is the case with green witchcraft and its fascination with Nonhuman Animal sacrifice and "hunting," many books dedicate considerable space to envisioning this culinary history, reconstructing it through amateur research into anthropology, folklore, archaeology, or earlier topical publications in witchcraft, and providing recipes and practices that reflect these imaginations to provide the practitioner a point of connection. This lineage and tradition become a source of empowerment and legitimation. Historicism is the source of magical potency: the longer the practice, the more powerful. Although archaeological evidence finds that "hunting," nonhuman domestication, and flesh-eating are strongly tied to patriarchy, feminist witches work hard to reframe this history to suit the modern food system in which they partake, a food system that has expanded and entrenched white settler colonialism and male violence. Starhawk, for instance, insists that "meat [...] often has a symbolic as well as nutritional value and was certainly seen as an important source of life" (1999: 248) in spite of women's powerful, life-affirming history in procuring plant-based foods, foods that comprised the bulk of the caloric intake for many cultures of the world.

Systems of inequality can easily become entrenched when social constructions of "the past" are keyed to the experiences of the dominant class. Robinson and Pearce (2023) admit that sacrificing Nonhuman Animals for food is an "uncomfortable but true" (109) reality of spiritual life, the assumption being that historical precedence overrides ethical consideration. "All meats," they assure readers, "are connected to abundance and good luck as feasting on meat was [...] often saved for particular occasions or festivals" (2023: 109). Telesco (2000), likewise, reminds readers that "in many instances, small portions of an animal were consumed to internalize the inherent ability of the creature" (177), a practice that persists in non-vegan kitchen witchery. Of relevance, Vincent Woodard (2014) argues that a similar notion that consuming "the other" might grant magical power permeated American and British white supremacy, a magical belief that encouraged many whites to physically consume the bodies of enslaved Africans. Telesco, likewise, finds "beef" potent with "grounding, earth magic, agriculture, and maternal energy," while the bodies of pigs are associated with "success and rejuvenation" (2000: 178). She includes an entire chapter of recipes that explore the various ways to dissect and consume animal bodies. "For a truly sunny meal," she notes on the practice of eating of pig corpses, a can of pineapple can be added. "The flavor is slightly sweet-and-sour" (2000: 183). In another recipe, she instructs the reader to "rub the skin and body cavity with salt" and then "place pats of butter in various places underneath the skin," a process sure to "remind us of cycles and the instincts which humankind has often left by the wayside for logic" (2000: 190) and achieve "intuitive action" and "insightful talent" (2000: 191). Myths about the healthfulness of animal products are rooted in these early imaginaries as well, with nutrition rooted in traditional ideas more than scientific ones. "Chicken has long been considered a kind of healthy cure-all," Telesco (2000: 50) reflects.

These food stories, to reiterate, are bound by politics of power. For instance, Robinson's (2022) promotion of dairy products as of "huge importance to our early ancestors' diet for nourishment, and high-calorie delights" (104) begs the question: *who* is included among "our" ancestors? "Our" ancestors in this case can only refer to those descended from Northern European regions. The global majority—people of color in particular—have difficulty digesting lactose beyond the age of weaning, weaning being a natural part of childhood development now pathologized in the West as "lactose intolerance." This extends to Native Americans, who have been otherwise exploited for the purposes of legitimizing conceptions of "traditional" human foods. Universalizing adult suckling renders weaned adults as abnormal, erasing them from the imagined common human ancestry. Vegan feminists have noted that this tendency to wield food ideologies in the maintenance of racial and ethnic in-group and out-group boundaries through food has a violent history (Deckha 2012, 2020). Colonialism and Westernization have forcibly spread the practice of animal protein consumption as a means of "civilizing" non-white persons and extracting wealth from new markets (Wrenn 2017). This practice also has the effect of marginalizing and pathologizing non-white populations, who, by contrast to white colonizers, are framed as evolutionarily stunted as evidenced by their diets and thereby naturally submissive to Western domination given their failure to master the food chain as carnivores (Adams 2015, Nibert 2003).

The high calorie delights that Robinson exalts, for that matter, are presumed to exist for human exploiters, not the infant Nonhuman Animals who would have depended on their mothers' milk to survive and thrive. The praise of dairy as a food of nurture in kitchen witchery overwhelmingly obscures the inherent exploitation, deprivation, and violence that the production of Bovidae breastmilk for human consumption entails. In discussing forest foraging, Robinson warns that humans should take care when "eating the supper of others without permission" and to be "generous and mindful with food" (2022: 117). But this she ascribes to forest foraging. The mundane stealing of calf food from objectified mother cows remains unremarkable. Likewise, Cunningham (2007), too, lauds this industry, exploring the many associations and magical properties found in dairy products, despite dairy being heavily processed, a quality he generally finds counter to the potent characteristics he associates with dairy, such as fertility, nurturance, and lunar magic. In advising the ritual consumption of dairy milk to obtain its life-giving properties, he promotes animal sacrifice, if indirectly, given the lethal toll it takes on cows, goats, and their children.

Witches tend to avoid the unpleasant realities of speciesist food production, choosing instead to highlight the symbolic meanings of animal products, hearkening back to an abstract time when humans were believed to procure the bodies, babies, and breastmilk of other animals without harming or disrespecting them. Chamberlain's kitchen grimoire, for instance, does not include any animal corpses, but does expound on the magical capabilities of "butter" (for "spirituality, peace, [and] relationships"), "cheese" (for "moon magic, joy, health, [and] completion of goals"), birds' eggs (for "fertility, mysticism, [and] Goddess magic"), honey (for "health, happiness, love, lust, sex, purification, wisdom, [and] stability"), and nonhuman breastmilk (for "love spirituality, sustenance, and motherhood") (2020: 107). Indeed, these animal products are allotted as much space as other "pantry staples" (107) like beans, rice, salt, sugar, and vinegar, suggesting the magical primacy of animal ingredients. Nonhuman Animals produce milk and eggs by consuming plants, but rather than consume these plants directly, witches prioritize secondhand energy obtained through the labor of Nonhuman Animals. Indeed, it is this exploitation that adds the sense of status, wealth, and indulgence. The same can be said of Woodward's (2021) *Kitchen Witchery*. "Milk has energy to pamper," she assures, and "Dairy is a favoured offering to deity" (282). This is a sort of sympathetic magic, whereby handling the physical excrements of other animals is thought to conjure properties historically associated with them, despite the ironic *lack* of peace, relationships, joy, health, love, happiness, or motherhood (to use Chamberlain's words) in the procuring of these items. To materialize the positive symbolisms of breastmilk, *noninterference* will be necessary. Cows' milk and goats' milk is intended for infant cows and infant goats, not humans. Any recipes, spells, or offerings that humans create will be tainted with exploitation, lack of consent, and systemic violence.

To some extent, it does appear that the craft's fascination with historical feasting speaks to the modern practitioner's desire to align with wealth and status. As expensive animal-based foods were exceedingly rare for most humans for much of human history, the cheap glut of "meat," dairy, eggs, and honey today allow the consumer to embody complete indulgence on par only with the most wealthy and powerful leaders of antiquity. Greenleaf (2016) speaks of foods, animals included, as "nature's gifts," an expression of abundance (6). Partaking in animal-based foods, traditionally used in offerings, becomes a sort of devotion-by-proxy, with the witch consuming the offering themselves. Although indulgence in the sensuousness of life is a core element of modern witchcraft, the hierarchy that it has necessitated in the past (through the exploitation of the peasantry and Nonhuman animals) and in the present (through the exploitation of vulnerable immigrant labor and exponentially greater numbers of Nonhuman Animals) does seem to counter the more egalitarian values that typify witchcraft today. The ubiquitousness of animal products in kitchen witchery is not simply an honoring of the past or an authentic alignment with nature. The heavy presence of animal products reflects a modernized, Western-dominated food system within which animal products are produced in astonishing numbers and veritably forced onto consumers through industry-manipulated nutritional guidelines and other educational materials, government subsidies, and colonial control over traditional foodways (Nibert 2003). Consider, for instance, Chamberlain's (2020) selected Imbolc recipes, most of which are laden with cheese, yogurt, and butter obtained from cows' milk, fileted salmons' bodies, and birds' eggs. This imagined Imbolc feast reflects a wealthy, Western, modern diet miles away from the largely plant-based diet of early Irish people celebrating the waning winter months.

The space reserved for Nonhuman Animal products is a form of conspicuous consumption, allowing the witch to rejoice in the bounties of European colonization and speciesist modernized foodways. The same may also be true of women's rise in status in the 21st century: as kitchen labor is generally feminized, it tends to be devalued as a consequence (Robinson 2022). Incorporating high-status foodstuffs could be a means of adding value to this feminized labor. Plant foods, pitted as nutritionally insufficient and less powerful given their association with poverty and famine times, might further amplify the feminine association of vegan kitchen witchery and explain its derogation. Indeed, vegan feminist research has demonstrated that the consumption of animal products is associated with power and privilege, such that men are significantly less attracted to veganism. As Adams (2015) has uncovered, some nonvegan feminist scholars have even suggested that forgoing "meat" and breastmilk will nutritionally disadvantage women. Recall that Starhawk has also taken this position, suggesting that women are biologically more vulnerable to physical weakness such that eating other animals is necessary (1997). Budapest, although not herself vegetarian, is an important exception here, as she recognizes the importance of plant-based diets and the political ramifications of animal-based alternatives. Like many ecofeminists, she surmises that the killing of Nonhuman Animals for food is "the advent of the patriarchal meat-eating customs" (1986: 99).

It is likely that the uncritical inclusion of animal products reflects a desire to increase social status through association with the masculine and the dominant classes. Indeed, Robinson notes that bones and "offal" were ubiquitous in the cauldron as "nothing would be wasted," a "testament to the witches' tenacity" in times that were "cold and damp and in poverty" (2022: 23). Because witches were historically blamed for the sudden death, illness, or disability of "livestock" as well as the spoiling of dairy products, it could be that contemporary witchcraft is attempting to take ownership over this stigmatized relationship with animal flesh to gain status through mastery over animal-based cuisine. Making it delectable, in other words, is seen as a means of using their magical power for good. Notes Madara (2021) of one of her sacrificial recipes: "Braised lamb shanks feel like a regal addition to the feast table" (no page); there is no magical purpose offered as explanation for using children's legs in the meal, only the magic of the juniper berries and other herbs used to garnish are mentioned.

Because of the many similarities in the physical and symbolic treatment of women and other animals in an anthroparchal culture, however, these witches are perpetuating oppressive food traditions that have historically harmed feminized groups. Adams (2015) notes that both women and other animals have been rendered objects of pleasurable consumption for the dominant class, and both have been rendered property in the manufacture of Nonhuman Animal agricultural systems. Sexualized violence against women, then, often comingles in the cultural lexicon of speciesism.

Andrews (1993) *Animal Speak* exemplifies this in exalting the American tradition of eating turkeys for harvest celebrations. Eating turkeys who died a terrifying death following either the torment of a "hunt" or factory farm are feminized in this subjugation and objectified as food. For Andrews, however, ingesting their flesh unlocks psychic abilities and is an act of "honoring the earth mother" (107). Patriarchy's systemic violence against women, which includes sexual conquest, commodification, and social subjugation, is not unlike men's systemic violence against turkeys and other animals rendered food. Not only is this connection unrecognized in modern witchcraft, in aligning with colonial and patriarchal foodways, it threatens the wellbeing of Nonhuman Animals, women, and other feminized groups, whose lower status is made possible by speciesist frameworks that pit some beings as lesser than, animal-like, naturally subservient to the dominant class and consumable. Vegan feminist Karen Davis suggests that it is the anthroparchal power wielded over these beings that renders them fetishized: "Thanksgiving turkeys are maledicted as 'dirty birds' that become magically clean only by being slaughtered, cooked, and consumed by 'superior' humans" (2019: 59).

The merging of sexual pleasure and speciesist conquest appears in several kitchen witch books. West (2002) advises consuming a variety of corpses for sex magic, including pigs' ribs, bodies of sea-dwelling animals, and "steaks," which are believed to "feed passion" (131). Of eels who have been gutted, skinned, and chopped, she muses: "their lightness of texture certainly fulfils one of the main criteria for a romantic food" (131). Greenleaf, likewise, suggests eating oysters or bees' honey for aphrodisiac properties. Cunningham, who associates fish with the magical properties of water, suggests eating fishes and other sea-dwelling animals to "expand your ability to give and receive love" (2007: 183). As the sentience of these species is now understood (Balcombe 2017), it seems more consistent with patriarchal oppression than feminist witchcraft to associate killing and consuming sentient others with giving and receiving love.

Dead Power of Animal Products

Meat, Magic, and Necromancy

Despite these appeals to tradition and power, most kitchen witchery books carefully obscure or negotiate the contradiction in exalting the magical and "high vibrational" properties of plants in what remains a predominantly animal-based practice. Autumn Damiana mentions "energetically 'heavy' foods like meat and fish" as a "snacking no-no" with "complex ethics," whereby the spirit of the animal-cum-snack can "mingle with your own during magic" (2022: 24). To navigate this complexity, they suggest paying attention to methods of incarceration, treatment, and slaughter their victim would have endured. Fruits and vegetables, by contrast, are promoted as "by far the best option" (2022: 24) with regard to nutritional quality, dietary versatility, and mythological richness: "Fruits and vegetables are [...] very 'witchy' foods" (2022: 25). Chamberlain spends several pages discussing the importance of fresh and local produce grown in ecologically sustainable ways for effective kitchen magic, relegating to just a few paragraphs the "counterintuitive" (2020: 31) inclusion of decidedly low (if existent) vibrational energies associated with decomposing animals and their reproductive fluids in spells and recipes.

As with Damiana, Chamberlain finds that this issue can be overcome by simply giving attention to how animals are "raised" (2020: 31) (a term that euphemizes humans' systematic violence against other animals as a form of parental nurturing). Modern farming practices, she correctly observes, are far from "natural" and damage the environment considerably. Blake (2015) agrees, noting that vegetarianism would be a worthy pursuit for environmental reasons as "raising meat [sic] is tough on the environment" (58). Patterson (2017), too, advises purchasing higher-welfare products, while Bussi (2022) encourages her readers to "make a point of only buying [sic] meat that has been raised in an organic and totally humane way!" in order to "honor life in all its forms" (8). By referencing once living Nonhuman Animals as "meat," it seems unlikely that their "life" is fully acknowledged much less revered. Her insinuations, furthermore, that killing sentient persons for the pleasure of eating them can be done in a "totally humane way!"[2] and that individuals might be classed as "organic" or "not organic" obscure the inherent violence of animal-based agriculture. Similarly, Miernowska (2020) advises incorporating "organic" eggs taken from chickens, presumably because this organic element counters the profound environmental and ethical consequences of animal-based consumption, amplifying the supposed connection to nature through consumption. Labeling schemes, however, have been found to be deeply disingenuous, masking the serious injustices inherent to the production of animal products (Davis 2019, Thibault et al. 2022) and discouraging consumers from reducing their intake in favor of more ethical plant-based alternatives (Bruers 2023).

With fairness to the kitchen witch grimoire, several books do aim to prioritize plant-based foods. Even Chamberlain's (2020) aforementioned *Wiccan Kitchen* is predominantly vegetarian. The nonvegan emphasis on abstaining primarily from "meat," however, protects the inclusion of other products taken from Nonhuman Animals which are equally unjust. In the case of cows' milk, for instance, it is not only the mother cow who suffers but also her many children. Chickens' eggs, too, represent a double sacrifice. Woodward notes that chickens' eggs represent "the hope of life renewed" (2021: 284). This may perhaps be true for humans but certainly not for chickens and roosters. Not only are the chickens themselves mutilated ("debeaked"),[3] genetically manipulated to produce several times the amount of eggs they would naturally and physically tortured (periodically starved and kept in darkness for days at a time to induce reproductive cycles) before being sent to slaughter by the age of one, but for every female chicken who endures this horror, there is a male rooster who was eviscerated alive just after hatching, deemed useless to the egg industry. This holds true whether the breastmilk and eggs were sourced from large industrial operations (which accounts for 99% of animal products available to Westerners) or "happy" local farms where animals are supposedly granted some space and treated with dignity. Intense confinement, whether in battery cages or in "cage-free" "free-range" facilities, creates toxic levels of ammonia and dust, facilitating rapid spread of diseases such as avian flu (Davis 2019).[4]

It is this very resource intensiveness that Damiana (2022) notes is responsible for the associations of prosperity with animal-based foods. The complex and demanding structural oppression and exploitation of other animals, in other words, is recognized as a source of great value, despite kitchen witchcraft's claim of making magic through a harmonious balance with the natural world. The superficiality of this sentiment is further evidenced in Greenleaf's (2016) suggestion that witches avoid using their magical tools for "mundane" (26) tasks such as deboning chicken bodies. Although, on one hand, these animals' deaths are excused as honorable sacrifices, on the other, their "mundane" objectification and consumption illustrates the hollowness of these magical attributes. Unlike Bussi, Murphy-Hiscock's advice to purchase only higher welfare products is purely a means of "self-care," based on the belief that "grass-fed" and "free-pastured beef" is better tasting: "The flavor is truly a revelation" (2018: 94). The personal wellbeing promised by "humane" myths in "meat," dairy, and birds' eggs industries, it seems, is a privilege geared for human consumers, not nonhuman producers. Indeed, welfare marketing intentionally greenwashes animal products to increase sales. Meaningful welfare improvements are usually only implemented if they can improve profits (Wadiwel 2024, Wrenn 2016), but even in these cases, welfare improvements generally lack authenticity as speciesist industries calculate suffering, disease, and death into the regular cost of business. More Nonhuman Animals are thus slated for destruction, and slaughter remains inevitable. Wadiwel (2024) explains that death and severe injury "is not a problem for the value chain unless it threatens the ability of the cargo to realise value within the next phase of production" (145). For this reason, focusing on the "welfare" of Nonhuman Animals does not disrupt the "continued instrumentalization of animal life" (196). Welfare measures, he adds, rarely challenge the intensification of nonhuman confinement. Rather than call for industry-determined measures to reduce suffering, he advises that allies of other animals instead "demand to have lives back" (2024: 197).

As the reliance on hollow "welfare" rhetoric illustrates, cognitive dissonance permeates non-vegan kitchen witchery. Blake, who is sympathetic to vegetarianism but not a vegetarian herself notes, "I am also mindful of the sacrifice of the animal and try to eat with appreciation and gratitude for that sacrifice" (2015: 58). Cunningham is of a similar persuasion, "Life feeds on life. Our bodies cannot survive unless something else gives up its existence to sustain us—whether it's plankton, soybeans or a chicken" (2007: 25). But chickens are, unlike, soybeans and plankton, sentient persons with complex social and emotional lives. They are not "something," they are some*one*. Non-vegan kitchen witch discourse of this kind tellingly absconds humans. A human being is never expected to "give up its existence" for someone else's brief sustenance, certainly not when copious plant alternatives abound. Cunningham also erroneously suggests that eating Nonhuman Animals is required for human health. Not only is this implicitly racist in its pathologization of non-Western foodways and scientifically unsupported, it is certainly not the case that human health depends on the execution of *hundreds of millions* of chickens *every single day* in Western countries alone (Food and Agriculture Organization of the United Nations 2022). This mass slaughter would perhaps not phase Cunningham, who sees it as a necessary sacrifice: "This may seem cruel, but it's not. It's the reality of physical existence," he adds, repeating anthroparchal ideologies that effectively wield "objective" and "natural" frames to dismiss compassionate responses to this wide scale and wholly unnecessary slaughter. Vegetarianism, for Cunningham, is conceptualized primarily as a dietary measure to improve health or psychic abilities, and non-vegetarianism, too, might also achieve these qualities: "Neither position [...] is correct for all" (2007: 27). Nonhuman Animals, who he refers to as "sisters and brothers," are not granted a say in the debate. "Beef," he adds, "represents one of the most protective foods available" (2007: 308). He offers no explanation as to why this would be the case, but it might be surmised that the sacrifice it entails grants the practitioner the slaughtered victim's life force. And, despite his adamant misgivings about processed foods (being unnatural and devitalized), he assures readers that the magical properties of animals' flesh can be obtained by eating frozen pepperoni pizza, Salisbury steak, hamburgers, and other processed "meat" items easily found in the average Western grocery store.

Chamberlain, recall, has considered the ethical conflict in making magic from "meat" but stops short of encouraging witches to go vegetarian. These food ethics are firmly anthropocentric: "What you eat is absolutely your own decision!" (2020: 31). Nonhuman Animals—those whose very lives are at stake—are granted no say in the decision as their own choices are treated as irrelevant. Like Bussi and Murphy-Hiscock, Chamberlain advises sourcing from "farms" where Nonhuman Animals are granted some semblance of "care and respect." But care and respect are incompatible with standard industry practices. *Regardless of production source or scale*, animals condemned as food lack any meaningful legal protection and are subject to genetic manipulation, separation from family units, physical mutilations, stun guns, cut throats, and the degradation of being rendered into a consumable, tradable commodity object. This reality contradicts Chamberlain's warning to readers not to use kitchen spells for manipulating: "no matter how innocent or benevolent the Witch's intentions may be" (2020: 39). Free will, she insists, must be respected, but animals-cum-ingredients are *unavoidably* harmed, and their free will is *unavoidably* undermined. This holds true even in "innocent" magical recipes that nonchalantly include cows' milk, birds' eggs, bees' honey, or arms, legs, bones, or other body parts from nonhumans. It also holds true for "benevolent" spellwork that relies on the bodies of Nonhuman Animals killed with "care and respect." No pig exercised their free will to become the main ingredient in Chamberlain's "Yuletide Cider-Braised Pork Chops with Stewed Apples" (2020: 136). Her Imbolc dish, "Brighid's Mac and Cheese" (2020: 142), likewise, cannot be said to have been made without causing harm. The psychological distress cows and their children experience at the point of separation (usually within 24 hours of the child's birth) (Beaver et al. 2018), the physical harms of incarceration (more than half of dairy cows at any given time will exhibit debilitating infections of the udder due to the conditions of their exploitation)

(Owens et al. 2001), and the horrors of slaughter are *inherent to dairy production*. Most dairy cows are killed before the age of five or six, entering into the food supply as "hamburger." "Veal calves," castoffs of the dairy industry, suffer intentional malnutrition and extreme confinement to maximize the palatability of their small bodies before they are dispatched.[5] The ethics of nonvegan magical cooking, in other words, are decidedly anthropocentric, and, given their reliance on violent entitlement over others, they are decidedly patriarchal as well. Chamberlain describes the kitchen as an altar. If so, it is an altar of blood sacrifice.

If only briefly, Chamberlain at least acknowledges the inconsistency in using animal products for the purposes of positive magic. Most kitchen witches ignore it. *The Witch's Cookbook* (Noir 2022), for instance, simply presents fifty standard recipes drawn from world cuisine refashioned for a witchy aesthetic, most of which contain animal products, with just a sprinkling of witch lore and symbolism offered for some ingredients, such as basil, tomatoes, and honey. There is no explanation for the copious use of animal bodies, breastmilk, and eggs. Madara's *The Witch's Feast* (2021) provides detailed instructions on how to dissect, dismember, and consume the bodies of all sorts of species, including pigeons, with no consideration as to why these practices might be counter to witchcraft principles.

Cunningham (2007) explains the absence of "meat" lore in kitchen witchcraft reflects the historical scarcity of animals' flesh for human consumption (adding that most contemporary practitioners are vegetarian). It is likely the case that most witches intuitively recognize that the magical romance is killed by killing. Bussi, by way of another example, cites the "power and possibilities inherent in herbs, flowers, and other plants" (3) but not in the sentient individuals who are sacrificed for her recipes. To my knowledge, there is no flesh-based companion to Scott Cunningham's (1985) *Encyclopaedia of Magical Herbs*. Witches, in other words, participate in a social construction of history, philosophy, and thealogy that suits modern anthroparchal norms. Murphy-Hiscock's (2017) *The Green Witch*, by way of another example, advises readers to "integrate the power of flowers" (209) and "boost health" with a list of easily procured vegetables (220) but then degrades the magical potential of these healing herbs and plants by diluting them in broths and smoothies comprised of animal flesh. To her credit, some recipes are vegetarian (which is more than can be said of most publications) and some are even vegan, but if the point of kitchen witchery is "eating with intention" to maximize an "assimilation of those energies" (204), it goes without saying that intention is not always inclusive of attention to non-human suffering.

Starhawk actually insists that corpses are *high* in vital life force (2005: 115). Similarly, Murphy-Hiscock is clearer on the magical properties of animal flesh in their *Witches' Book of Self-Care* (2018), citing its "life energy" (94). Perhaps there is some residual life in this flesh—the fear of impending death, the final fight for life. Across the globe, slaughterhouses have begun to phase out straight kill lines in favor of curved kill lines. In the former, victims could more easily see, hear, and smell the killing happening in front of them, and this terror shoots chemicals and hormones throughout their anxious bodies, degrading their flesh for the purposes of human consumption (Ferguson and Warner 2008). The fear of death in the final moments of life literally taints their flesh, such that modern food systems seek to limit their awareness of this impending violence as much as is possible. Could this be the chi or life energy that witches hope to attain through the consumption of sacrificial animals?

At times, authors offer nutritional advice that similarly rests more heavily on anthroparchal ideology than reality. In *Kitchen Witchery: Unlocking the Magick in Everyday Ingredients*, Laurel Woodward promises to help shift the readers' cooking from "a half-hearted attempt into a powerful, fully conscious action that sets energy in motion to nurture, heal, or compel, to manifest your dreams" (2021: 2). While the book is vegetarian and celebrates the healing power of plants, its final chapter introduces products of animal exploitation, namely dairy and birds' eggs. Some witches do more than eat eggs; they also ritualistically massage them over the body to absorb negative energies (Miernowska 2020, Starhawk 1999). For Miernowska, the egg must be from "a chicken that has had a happy, natural life" (2020: 92) to be effective, as the creations of an unhappy bird presumably would not do well to absorb additional unhappiness from humans. For that matter, the healing abilities Woodward and other witches attribute to these products are also suspect; nutritional science is increasingly recognizing the toxic effects of animal products on the human body (Craig et al. 2021). "Eggs are good for you," Woodward assures, as though it were self-evident (Woodward 2021: 284). The scientific support for consuming avian menstruation, however, is unreliable,[6] and the cultural practice is far from universal. Birds' eggs are minimized or absent in many regions of the world, such as Africa, and in many communities, including Hindus, Sikhs, and vegans.

Cunningham (2007) includes an entire chapter on "The Mystic Egg" in his encyclopedia of kitchen witchcraft. "Life was created from a divinely produced egg," he exalts, adding that "eggs sustain human and animal life—much of which hatched from an egg" (201). Yet, Cunningham's kitchen witchcraft calls for the regular sacrifice of these "divine" eggs for spellcraft. Sjöö and Mor (1991) also see the egg as representing the "cosmic mother." If this is the case, does not the consumption of birds' eggs represent cannibalistic matricide? The default approach of increasing power and privilege through ownership, exploitation, and killing is a clear reflection of anthroparchy, and yet, birds' eggs are a popular ingredient in Wiccan workings. The idea of "life-giving mother" (Miernowska 2020: 109) is alluded to in utilizing these Nonhuman Animal products, but most witches remain conspicuously silent on the gratuitous loss of life that cows' milk and chickens' egg production entails for Nonhuman Animal mothers and children. Like Woodward, Cunningham introduces unsubstantiated nutritional claims. For instance, he argues that an animal-based diet is purgative, while veganism is too low in protein (Cunningham 2007). Yet, it is the very excessive intake of protein that is associated with an animal-based diet that contributes to so many chronic health conditions, including gout, heart disease, cancer, and osteoporosis (Delimaris 2013). Animal bodies, furthermore, contain no fiber, and are thus, in actuality, exceedingly more constipating than purgative.

Sociologists have noted that segregation from production sites is a key reason for complicity with speciesist food systems. Most consumers are unaware of what actually transpires in the procurement of "meat," milk, and eggs, allowing industry-manufactured imagery to guide consumers and perpetuate non-vegan consumption. A visit to the industrial facilities where most animals' milk and eggs originate or to the slaughterhouse where all "food" animals are inevitably sacrificed would perhaps deter most witches from assimilating those energies of fear, pain, and suffering in magical practice. Otherwise, a blissful ignorance prevails. Bussi's (2022) *Enchanted Kitchen* encourages readers to "connect to spirit with recipes and rituals." "A kitchen is never just a kitchen," she explains, "it's a place where memories are not only created but also stored and treasured." The average kitchen, however, is a place where the products of extreme violence are stored without second thought to their origin. What makes memories for humans makes nightmares for other animals. Indeed, nonhumans fill the larders of kitchen witches while remaining almost invisible. Bussi dedicates *Enchanted Kitchen* to those past and present who have shared her "kitchen journey," for instance, but the Nonhuman Animals who share that journey as ingredients are unacknowledged. The mundane, disenchanted, and objectified lives of the Nonhuman Animals are rendered marginal as she encourages readers to "celebrate each month and moment of this precious and enchanted life!" (2022: 5).

Honey, Mead, and the Status of Bees

As so much of modern witchcraft relies on natural ingredients or at least presumptions about what ingredients might have been available to practitioners of the olden days, honey is a ubiquitous ingredient. "Honey will sweeten any situation," Damiana (2022: 26) assures readers. Honey certainly features regularly in kitchen witchcraft, but it also sometimes features in herbal work and love magic. Honey's sweetness is thought to impart a metaphorical sweetness onto the practitioner or consumer. Greenleaf suggests incorporating honey into drinks, as it "intensifies the positivity" and "makes it supremely lucky" (2016: 56). Used topically, it is a "miracle salve" (61). Woodward (2021) promotes honey for its indirect plant power, as it contains the essence of a variety of flowers. However, given the considerable violence in extracting honey from beehives, in both commercial and backyard endeavors, the wide variety of other magical sweeteners that Woodward also discusses (from agave nectar to stevia) suggests that plant-based alternatives can achieve similar magical aims without harm to sentient beings. Given the symbolic importance of apples in witchcraft, for example, apple syrup might be a particularly desirable option.

The insistence on using animal-based products in a modern food system that offers countless plant-based alternatives may be indicative of how integral human supremacy remains in kitchen witchcraft. That regular cane sugar and corn-derived syrups tend to be stigmatized in kitchen witchcraft illustrates the fascination with species oppression. Cane sugar and other syrups are also plant-based and natural, but they lack the added layer of speciesist labor exploitation. Cunningham (2007) prioritizes bees' honey as an ancient human food perfect for "purification, health, love, sex, happiness, spirituality, wisdom, weight loss" (153) and preservation, marking it as superior to sugar, which he considers addictive, processed, and lacking in magical power. Maple syrup, however, is considered medicinal. Again, it is the social construction of food as "real," "authentic," and "ancestral" that marks it as superior and magical, rather than its actual chemical makeup.

Conjuring a Vegan Heritage

I have argued thus far that the consumption of Nonhuman Animals and their ingredients for ritual purposes runs counter to the witches' creed of do no harm but likely proliferates as witches seek to legitimate neo-pagan practices with historical claims. Some witches have attempted to align old speciesism with modern anti-speciesist ethics, if inconsistently and with hesitation. Cunningham's *Wicca* makes repeated substitutions for animal-based celebratory foods as far back as 1995. As has been evidenced, Cunningham does not dismiss animal-based food but does suggest for vegetarians that "tofu seems ritually correct" (1995: 143). Cunningham, himself, "isn't strictly vegetarian" (2007: xviii), but he acknowledges that many great magicians have been vegetarian or vegan. Karri Allrich's *Recipes from a Vegetarian Goddess* introduces vegetarianism as a personal "challenge of creating meals without meat" (2000: x) that "enlivened my senses and celebrated the Goddess with pleasure and flavor" (2000: x), insinuating an inherent difficulty and blandness in everyday plant-based eating. Her subsequently published *Cooking by Moonlight* (2003) perhaps seeks to remedy this by including several animal-based recipes. For her, conscious consumption entails healthy eating and eating foods that are "in alignment with the best interests of the environment" (153). Whether or not Nonhuman Animals must suffer to support this consumption is not factored.

The now ready availability of vegan analogues finds them cautiously embraced. Miernowska (2020) encourages plant-based milk, billing it as "Mother Earth's Breast Milk" (81) with its soothing effects. Milky top oats, likewise, drunk in a tea will encourage a feeling of "heart opening and softening as a surge of vitality and energy moves through your body" (81). However, Miernowska does insist that cows can be confined and controlled in such a way as to ensure they are "happy" and "grass-fed," even "connecting" with their human exploiters enough to justify the theft of their breastmilk (2020: 74). Again, these fantasies about the purported happiness and dignity that confinement might provide ignores the inherent violence cows and their children must endure before slaughter at a very young age. Nor does it contend with the ethics of forced impregnation and genetic manipulation introduced to maximize milk production, disrupting bovine family units, and plundering milk from babies. Whatever "connection" Miernowska imagines to justify this theft demonstrates a profound detachment from the reality of animal-based food production.

Alternative plant milks are not mentioned at all in *Cunningham's Encyclopaedia of Wicca in the Kitchen* (2007). The aversion to plant-based milks suggests that it is the fetishization of female exploitation under human supremacy that is thought necessary to attain the magical qualities of milk. For instance, Cunningham rejects cheese alternatives with reference to their processed nature: "Cheese substitutes have no magical value whatsoever. These false cheeses shouldn't be eaten" (212). Cheeses based in fats from nuts such as cashews and coconuts, however, are no less altered than that deriving from dairy, which must be processed to protect shelf life, reduce bacteria and life-threatening pathogens, and contend with the blood and pus lingering within (U.S. Food & Drug Administration 2024).

Haseman's (2023) *The Kitchen Witch's Guide to Healing and Self-Care* offers veganized versions of flesh-based recipes, even suggesting that "meat" and dairy alternatives maintain the same magical properties, but she nonetheless prioritizes animal products as nutritionally superior. Despite identifying as a vegan herself, she notes that even the intentionally vegan recipes she includes can be adjusted to replace animal bodies and excrements to "suit your dietary preferences and health needs" (45). Although her grimoire is intended to promote "healing yourself and your loved ones and healing the earth and all the plants, animals, and rocks who share it" (1), it is ultimately in service of human wants. Robinson also appeals to both vegan and non-vegan cuisine, espousing the more desirable corpse-derived ingredients but also noting that "the real power of the witch in the kitchen is to see and know the healing abilities of the humble" (2022: 23). The fascination with feasting otherwise prevails. Kitchen witch cookbooks seem to burst with animal products, even in the most unnecessary and indulgent ways. For instance, Murphy-Hiscock (2017) and West (2002) include the juices and fats from animal bodies and bones even in basic soup and bread recipes. Exclaims West, "the only person with no cholesterol is a corpse" (2002: 153); vegetarians, by contrast, are "health fiends" (166). Likewise, Madara (2021) fetishizes the historical exploitation of Nonhuman Animals for food as central to community, culture, and spiritual growth for the human species.

Further rituals will need to be identified and celebrated within witchcraft to disrupt the romanticization of Nonhuman Animal sacrifice and flesh-eating. Madara's kitchen grimoire, based as it is on the manipulation of animal flesh for consumption, does identify the art of foraging, which can "bring magic and abundance into your kitchen witchcraft practice" (2021: no page). Some variants of witchcraft draw on a plant-based heritage with a practice of home and community gardening. Starhawk muses,

> Growing at least some food for myself and my friends and family became part of my personal practice. I began to look not just at food but at the

herbs and plants we used in magic in a new way. They were no longer just names gleaned from old books but real characters that I had an ongoing relationship with.

(1999: 8)

Incidentally, the incompatibility of animal flesh with home gardening illustrates just how awkwardly non-veganism sits within plant magic. Murphy-Hiscock's *The Green Witch* (2017), for instance, discourages readers from using "meat" and animal fats in compost as "it will smell dreadful, unbalance the compost you're building, and attract pests" (142), although integrating these very same ingredients directly into the human body is advised elsewhere in the book.

Woodward's *Kitchen Witchery* (2021) and Robinson's *Kitchen Witch* (2022) contain many folk histories of fruits, nuts, fungi, vegetables, and other plants that might be revisited to spare Nonhuman Animals from the cauldron. As does Cunningham's (2007) *Encyclopaedia of Wicca in the Kitchen*. Chestnuts are identified as perfect for Samhain and the dumb supper, as well as love spells. Hazelnuts are noted for their association with wisdom, while peanuts, with African American survival and ingenuity, are useful for money spells. Given their effect on the brain, he advises using walnuts to increase intellect. Coconuts align with lunar symbolism and are thus advanced for their spiritual purposes. Beans and legumes are highlighted for their nutritional value as well as their spiritual associations. Woodward (2021) advises a simmering a cauldron of beans instead of the bone-filled soups other grimoires recommend. Garlic, by way of another example, is well known for its protective qualities (on both physiological and psychic levels) and can easily replace blood, breastmilk, honey, and eggs used for similar purposes. Several kitchen witches also espouse the magical and nutritional benefits of grains, including wheat, barley, buck-wheat, corn, rye, and oats, even linking bread to the divine (Cunningham 2007, Marquis 2015, Woodward 2021). Cunningham (2007) also suggests an exploration of the rich history of plant foods of all kinds, even broccoli, which is thought to be protective. Interestingly, he also highlights soybeans and tofu as protective and useful for honoring spirits of the dead, especially the sacrificial dead. Soy can boost psychic awareness and "induce spirituality" (2007: 95). Vegan witchcraft, then, might even employ tofu (long revered in Asian cultures for its nutritional potency) as a means to honor the countless animal spirits lost to several thousand years of anthroparchal violence, bringing about a spiritualistic reverence for other animals. It is not enough that some authors (Haseman 2023, Robinson 2022, Woodward 2021) offer a handful of accidentally vegan recipes or flesh-based recipes with vegan variations. This effectively marginalizes plant-based consumption and concern for other animals when it should be central given witchcraft's principle of doing no harm.

Beyond the wealth of plant food lore that might contribute to kitchen witchcraft, the growing body of vegan nutritional science can add evidenced potency to recipes. Here, vegan witchcraft might also be understood as a type of protection magic for both human and nonhuman animals. Modern Western science places much emphasis on dealing with medical problems *after* they arise (Collard 1988). Medications, therapies, and other prescriptions may enrich the healthcare industry but divert attention and resources from more sustainable lifestyle choices and fuel the heinous vivisection industry. An emphasis on veganism would thus align witchcraft with its core interest in protection work. Although veganism cannot prevent or cure every ailment, it might also further reduce reliance on pharmaceuticals, almost all of which have been produced through vivisection. These plant-based approaches Kheel describes as "non-invasive forms of healing [...] which have been practiced by women healers for thousands of years" and "do not rely on painful experiments to prove their validity" (1990: 5). Vegan witchcraft may also introduce new mythologies, uplifting, for example, the properties of fruit, nuts, and vegetables now known to be superfoods or revisiting the diversity of plant-based global diets that are quickly vanishing under the Western colonial animal-based agricultural regime.

Veganism is often unfairly mischaracterized as a diet of restriction and austerity, flavorless, boring, and either devoid of nutrition or so saturated with nutrition that its consumption is a chore. But food, for vegans, is an important point of cultural celebration, and it can be delicious, even voluptuous. With food intentionally grown or purchased to avoid harming other animals, its consumption becomes a political act that encourages the eater to relish compassion and celebrate life. Vegan food is not only laden with the abundant flavors of plants but laden with the essence of solidarity with other animals and resistance against speciesism, colonialism, climate change, pandemics, and diet-related diseases. Vegan food, for some, is pursued as a healthy, nutrient-dense diet, but for many vegans, it is all about decadence and pleasure-seeking (Bertella 2020). Food is key to anti-speciesist living, and it can be joyful, serving as an important counterpoint to the psychological burden of grappling with systemic violence against other animals (Simons et al. 2021). Veganism's intentional decadence is one aspect of eating that finds parallel with modern witchcraft. As witchcraft is framed, to some extent, as a rejection of restricting religious practices, it tends to encourage eating for pleasure. The "body as a temple" principle that dictates many formal religions with regard to dietary restrictions finds less audience within luxury-seeking witchcraft. Several leading witches have encouraged healthy eating as a means to support wellbeing, but this is not to be compared with the expectations of fasting, food taboos, and guilty indulgence that is typical of institutionalized religions. Allrich (2000) reminds readers that "the Goddess gently urges us to make time for the simple pleasures in life; to enjoy her seasons, her abundance" (xi), but there is nothing to say veganism is incomparable with this important pagan principle.

Conclusion

As with green witchcraft, kitchen witchcraft prioritizes the use of plants and herbs but more specifically takes interest in the alchemy of cooking and food preparation as a measure of care and healing for oneself and others. Madara describes kitchen witchcraft as "guided always by intuition, curiosity and a sensual engagement with the world" (2021: no page), denoting an attentiveness to, and degree of flexibility and appreciation for pleasure. Recipes serve as spells, and ingredients and cooking techniques become conduits of magic. The preparation and digestion of food truly is magical: material ingredients are gathered, sometimes cooked, dressed, eaten, and, thanks to a complex interplay of unseen organic and cellular activity, soon transformed into usable energy and measurable vitality. In this context, this chapter has argued that veganism might inform kitchen witchcraft, as it also celebrates the use of plants, herbs, spices, and other natural ingredients for their ability to transfigure matter for personal or communal wellbeing. By incorporating animal ingredients, however, kitchen witchcraft fails to fully realize the energetic potential of gastronomy. Not only is "meat" greatly underrepresented in kitchen witch lore and myth given its minimal use in premodern cultures, but modern nutritional science has exposed its overall toxic effect on human bodies. The incommensurate attention kitchen witchcraft grants to breastmilk, eggs, and nectar sourced from other animals, meanwhile, overwhelmingly masks the inherent exploitation and systemic violence the production and procurement of these ingredients entail. Exploitation and violence are rejected in modern witchcraft as unethical, but speciesism tends to be exempted in the pursuit of the elusive ancestor's feast, ripe with high-cost, high-resource foods and ingredients that Nonhuman Animal products exemplify.

As kitchen witchery demonstrates, the witchcraft community takes an inconsistent position on veganism. Its appreciation of plant magic assures some degree of accommodation, but its fascination with the mythologized ancestral ways of early human societies has protected speciesist foodways and some degree of anti-vegan stigma. Western kitchen witchcraft most frequently employs the *actual* bodies and killing of other animals when engaging sympathetic magic through cooking. Dead matter makes for dead magic. Veganism, research now confirms, supports human health and can even reverse the effects of many physical and mental ailments. By comparison, meat and dairy have toxic effects on the human body. Killing Nonhuman Animals is killing human witches. The consequences for vulnerable workers in Nonhuman Animal agriculture, incidentally, also warrants mention. "Meat-packing," for instance, is one of the world's most dangerous industries, with extremely high rates of employee turnover and injury. In the West, these workers are disproportionately immigrants, often non-English speaking, undocumented, and racially otherized (Lee 2022). The "fishing" industry is also known for its systemic enslavement of vulnerable peoples from the Global South (Wadiwel 2024).

Vegan feminism is well aware of these harmful intersections between humans and nonhumans who languish in entanglement to produce animal protein. It has critiqued the interplay of gender, class, race, and species oppression in food rituals, noting that women in Western cultures are often seen as consumable objects in similar ways to other animals, while women's domestic drudgery in food preparation is often exacerbated by the expectation that they provide copious amounts of animal products (often at the patriarch's insistence) for family meals. Kitchen witchcraft today offers little to no critique of women's oppression in food preparation, exalting gender essentialist tropes about women's capacity to nurture through food and ignoring the exploitation shared with other animals, who often serve as that food. Nor is there a critique of the Westernization of animal-based diets, which present "meat," nonhuman breastmilk, and birds' eggs as normal, natural, and expected leading ingredients in the human diet, despite their minimal to non-existent presence in the diets of colonized peoples of the world.

The regular description of Nonhuman Animals as "meat," meals, and ingredients, furthermore, is indicative of capitalism's influence on even the most pagan of witches. That so many attempt to negotiate this speciesist objectification with their claims of respecting Nonhuman Animals and the environment with appeals to higher "welfare" products only reiterates the fetishization of animal flesh in modern witchcraft. Vegan witchcraft instead places faith in the power of plants, a scientifically supported healing practice that is better aligned with ancestral diets and more inclusive of the global majority. It rejects dead animal-derived food as unethical, unhealthy, and environmentally destructive, and thereby devoid of magic and counter to witchcraft's desire for connectiveness and global recovery.

Notes

1 Vegan diets are sometimes flagged as insufficient due to low levels of vitamin B12, however modern agricultural practices have significantly reduced its bioavailability in non-animal-based foods such that even "livestock" feed is supplemented with B12. B12 deficiency in the modern diet, incidentally, is not restricted to vegans, and even today a variety of plant-based foods offer bioavailable B12 (Marques de Brito et al. 2023).
2 Although, from a vegan feminist perspective, any unnecessary killing is incompatible with the concept of "humanness," it is also the case that the colloquial understanding of humane slaughter is divorced from the true experiences of Nonhuman Animals, who are doomed to die for human food. Humane rearing practices, statistically rare in a largely industrialized food system, stop short of the slaughterhouse. Nonhumans are well documented as being aware of and fearful of their impending death, often trembling, producing tears, frothing at the mouth, and attempting to escape. This is not the exception, it is the norm. Given the speed of the kill lines, many animals are not fully stunned (or even stunned at all) before they are slaughtered; some even manage to remain conscious at the time of butchering. When pregnant dairy cows are sent to slaughter, it is not unusual for still living calves to be pulled from their dead mother's body during butchering. For other species, such as chickens and pigs, it is increasingly common for farmers to use electricity and carbon monoxide as methods of execution; the former is also known to be inconsistent in killing all victims on the kill line before butchering given the fast-paced, high turnover of bodies; the latter taking several minutes to cause death, which is not pain-free. In halal and kosher slaughtering practices, stunning is prohibited on grounds of religious purity, and it takes several minutes for fully conscious victims to bleed out (bound and chained to keep them relatively stationary as they writhe in fright and pain) and finally expire (RSPCA n.d.).

3 A standard process for poultry of all species to reduce stress-induced cannibalism and self-mutilation, debeaking entails cutting the nerve-dense and highly sensitive tip of the beak using a hot blade. Because the procedure is conducted on thousands of birds at a time at high speeds, cuts may be imprecise such that many victims will lose most of their beaks, sometimes impacting their nostrils, tongues, and ability to eat and breathe.

4 As of this writing, no birds imprisoned in the UK food industry are allowed outdoor access due to regular bouts of avian flu that threaten public health.

5 In India, the dairy industry is much newer, with additional horrors inflicted on parent and child (Narayanan 2023). Because Indian cow breeds have not yet been fully genetically manipulated to serve human needs, the infant will need to be kept nearby to trigger their mother to produce milk, but the infant will be denied this food, often starving to death. Farmers sometimes keep the bodies or heads of the infant nearby to continue to physiologically trigger the grieving mother to produce milk.

6 Chickens' eggs are extremely high in cholesterol and have a detrimental effect on the human body. Many studies, however, obscure this toxicity through biased analysis. Speciesist industries are able to manipulate knowledge production by funding scientific research. By way of an example, a study in the journal of *Nutrients* titled, "Eggs: Healthy or Risky? A Review of Evidence from High Quality Studies on Hen's Eggs" purports to objectively explore leading journals to understand the health consequences of eggs, yet overwhelmingly touts eggs as high in vitamins and "high-quality protein" (Myers and Ruxton 2023). The study was funded by the British Egg Industry Council and one of the two authors serves on the Council's Nutrition Advisory Group. The authors provide only six sentences explaining the study's methodology.

References

Adams, C. 2015. *The Sexual Politics of Meat*. New York: Continuum.

Allrich, K. 2000. *Recipes from a Vegetarian Goddess*. St. Paul: Llewellyn.

Allrich, K. 2003. *Cooking by Moonlight*. St. Paul: Llewellyn.

Andrews, T. 1993. *Animal Speak*. Woodbury: Llewellyn.

Balcombe, J. 2017. *What a Fish Knows*. London: Oneworld.

Ballard, H. 2021. *Roots, Branches & Spirits*. Woodbury: Llewellyn.

Beaver, A., R. Meagher, M. von Keyserlingk, and D. Weary. 2018. "A Systematic Review of the Effects of Early Separation on Dairy Cow and Calf Health." *Journal of Dairy Science* 102 (7): 5784–5810.

Bertella, G. 2020. "The Vegan Food Experience." *Societies* 10 (4): 95.

Blake, D. 2015. *Everyday Witchcraft*. Woodbury: Llewellyn.

Buckland, R. 2002. *Complete Book of Witchcraft*. Woodbury: Llewellyn.

Budapest, Z. 1986. *The Holy Book of Women's Mysteries*. Oakland: Consolidated Printers.

Bussi, G. 2022. *Enchanted Kitchen*. Woodbury: Llewellyn.

Bruers, S. 2023. "Animal-Welfare-Labelled Meat is Not a Stepping Stone to Animal-free Diets." *Journal of Environmental Economics and Policy*. Online first.

Carolan, M. 2016. *The Sociology of Food and Agriculture*. London: Routledge.

Chamberlain, L. 2020. *Wiccan Kitchen*. New York: Sterling Ethos.

Collard, A. 1988. *Rape of the Wild*. London: The Women's Press.

Craig, W., A. Mangels, U. Fresán, K. Marsh, F. Miles, A. Saunders, E. Haddad, C. Heskey, P. Johnston, E. Larson-Meyer, and M. Orlic. 2021. "The Safe and Effective Use of Plant-Based Diets with Guidelines for Health Professionals." *Nutrients* 13 (11): 4144.

Culinary Magic. n.d. "About." Retrieved October 10, 2023, from: https://culinarymagic.com/about/.

Cunningham, S. 1985. *Encyclopaedia of Magical Herbs*. St. Paul: Llewellyn.

Cunningham, S. 1995. *Wicca*. St. Paul: Llewellyn.

Cunningham, S. 2007. *Cunningham's Encyclopaedia of Wicca in the Kitchen*. Woodbury: Llewellyn.

Damiana, A. 2022. "Magical Snacks." pp. 23–27, in *Llewellyn's Witches' Datebook 2023*, L. Heineman (ed.). Woodbury: Llewellyn.

Davis, K. 2019. *For the Birds*. New York: Lantern Books.

Daw, M., C. Roe, and C. Cooper. 2023. "How Fasting and Vegetarianism is Perceived to Support PSI among Adepts." *The Journal of Transpersonal Psychology* 55 (1): 111–133.

Deckha, M. 2012. "Toward a Postcolonial, Posthumanist Feminist Theory." *Hypatia* 27 (3): 527–545.

Deckha, M. 2020. "Veganism, Dairy, and Decolonization." *Journal of Human Rights and the Environment* 11 (2): 244–267.

Delimaris, I. 2013. "Adverse Effects Associated with Protein Intake above the Recommended Dietary Allowance for Adults." *International Scholarly Research Notices* 2013 (1): 126929.

Dukes, R. 2019. *The Abramelin Diaries*. London: Aeon Books.

Ferguson, D. and R. Warner. 2008. "Have We Underestimated the Impact of Pre-Slaughter Stress on Meat Quality in Ruminants." *Meat Science* 80 (1): 12–19.

Food and Agriculture Organization of the United Nations. 2022. "FAOSTAT." Retrieved July 9, 2024, from: https://www.fao.org/faostat.

Green, M. 2002. *A Witch Alone*. London: HarperCollins.

Green, O. 2024. "Witchy Wisdom." Retrieved May 22, 2024, from: https://www.you tube.com/watch?v=AUWGGo4hTkE&ab_channel=OwlvineGreen.

Greenleaf, C. 2016. *The Book of Kitchen Witchery*. London: CICO Books.

Grimassi, R. 2000. *Wiccan Magick*. St. Paul: Llewellyn.

Grimassi, R. 2021. *The Witch's Familiar*. Woodbury: Llewellyn.

Hall, N. 2023. *Path of the Moonlight Hedge*. Woodbury: Llewellyn.

Haseman, M. 2023. *The Kitchen Witch's Guide to Healing and Self-Care*. Oakland: Rockridge Press.

Kheel, M. 1990. "If Women and Nature were Heard." *Feminists for Animal Rights Newsletter* 5 (3–4): 5–8.

Lee, C. 2022. "Racist Animal Agriculture." *City University of New York Law Review* 25 (2): 199–240.

Leek, S. 1973. *The Complete Art of Witchcraft*. New York: New American Library.

Madara, M. 2021. *The Witch's Feast*. London: Nourish.

Marques de Brito, B., V. Menezes Campos, F. Neves, L. Ramos, and L. Tomita. 2023. "Vitamin B12 Sources in Non-Animal Foods: A Systematic Review." *Critical Reviews in Food Science and Nutrition* 63 (26): 7853–7867.

Marquis, M. 2015. *Lughnasadh*. Woodbury: Llewellyn.

McKay, C. 2003. "Food & Magic." *Reclaiming Quarterly* 89 (Winter): 16–19.

Miernowska, M. 2020. *The Witch's Herbal Apothecary*. Beverly: Quarto.

Murphy-Hiscock, A. 2017. *The Green Witch*. Avon: Adams Media.

Murphy-Hiscock, A. 2018. *The Witches' Book of Self-Care*. London: Adams Media.

Myers, M. and C. Ruxton. 2023. "Eggs: Healthy or Risky? A Review of Evidence from High Quality Studies on Hen's Eggs." *Nutrients* 15 (12): 2657.

Narayanan, Y. 2023. *Mother Cow, Mother India: A Multispecies Politics of Dairy in India*. Redwood City: Stanford University Press.

Newmeyer, J. 1986. "Advice for Cat Owners." *Reclaiming Quarterly* 23 (Summer): 31.

Nibert, D. 2003. "Humans and Other Animals: Sociology's Moral and Intellectual Challenge." *International Journal of Sociology and Social Policy* 23 (3): 5–25.

Noir, F. 2022. *The Witch's Cookbook*. New York: Rock Point.

Owens, W., S. Nickerson, R. Boddie, G. Tomita, and C. Ray. 2001. "Prevalence of Mastitis in Dairy Heifers and Effectiveness of Antibiotic Therapy." *Journal of Dairy Science* 84 (4): 814–817.

Patterson, R. 2017. *Animal Magic*. Hants: John Hunt.

Petti, A., B. Palmieri, M. Vadala, and C. Laurino. 2017. "Vegetarianism and Veganism." *Progress in Nutrition* 19 (3): 229–242.

Robinson, S. 2022. *Kitchen Witch*. Shanagarry: Womancraft Publishing.

Robinson, S. and L. Pearce. 2023. *The Kitchen Witch Companion*. Shanagarry: Womancraft Publishing.

RSPCA. n.d. "End Non-Stun Slaughter for Farm Animals." Retrieved July 15, 2024, from: https://www.rspca.org.uk/getinvolved/campaign/slaughter.

Simons, J., C. Vierboom, J. Klink-Lehmann, I. Härlen, and M. Hartmann. 2021. "Vegetarianism/Veganism." *Sustainability* 13 (7): 3618.

Sjöö, M. and B. Mor. 1991. *The Great Cosmic Mother*. San Francisco: HarperSanFrancisco.

Spencer, C. 1993. *The Heretic's Feast*. London: Fourth Estate.

Starhawk. 1997. *Dreaming the Dark*. Boston: Beacon Press.

Starhawk. 1999. *The Spiral Dance*. Third Edition. New York: HarperCollins.

Starhawk. 2005. *The Earth Path*. New York: HarperCollins.

Telesco, P. 2000. *A Kitchen Witch's Cookbook*. St. Paul: Llewellyn.

Thibault, M., S. Pailler, and D. Fruend. 2022. "Why Are They Buying It? United States Consumers' Intentions When Purchasing Meat, Eggs, and Dairy with Welfare-Related Labels." *Food Ethics* 7 (12). Online.

U.S. Food & Drug Administration. 2024. "The Dangers of Raw Milk." Retrieved September 14, 2024, from: https://www.fda.gov/food/buy-store-serve-safe-food/dangers-raw-milk-unpasteurized-milk-can-pose-serious-health-risk.

Wadiwel, D. 2024. *Animals and Capital*. Edinburgh: Edinburgh University Press.

West, K. 2002. *The Real Witches' Kitchen*. London: Thorsons.

Whitehurst, T. 2015. *Holistic Energy Magic*. Woodbury: Llewellyn.

Whitehurst, T. 2017. *Magical Housekeeping*. Woodbury: Llewellyn.

Whitehurst, T. 2018. *You Are Magical*. Woodbury: Llewellyn.

Wolfe, D. 2004. "The Raw Food Revolution." pp. 134–139, in *Pop! Goes the Witch*, F. Horne (Ed.). New York: The Disinformation Company.

Woodard, V. 2014. *The Delectable Negro*. New York: NYU Press.

Woodward, L. 2021. *Kitchen Witchery*. Woodbury: Llewellyn.

Wrenn, C. 2016. *A Rational Approach to Animal Rights*. London: Palgrave.

Wrenn, C. 2017. "Skeptics and the 'White Stuff': Promotion of Cows' Milk and Other Nonhuman Animal Products in the Skeptic Community as Normative Whiteness." *Relations* 5 (1): 73–81.

5

SABBATS AND SPECIESISM

Introduction

Witchcraft adopts a cyclical worldview counter to the linear history that dominates modern Western life. As was explored in a previous chapter, this perspective reflects witchcraft's alignment with ecosystems and natural flows. Certain points along this turning are flagged for festive observation and contemplation and are known as sabbats, which form the witch's "wheel of the year." Traditionally, the wheel of the year turns along seasonal changes and, by association, also the agricultural rhythms linked to these seasons. The sabbats Lughnasadh, Mabon, and Samhain, for instance, represent the three major harvest points of late summer through end of autumn. This wheel is praised in Wiccan thealogy as it "prepares us to give way gracefully to new life," as Starhawk (1999: 53) explains. This turning serves as a reminder of how birth and death, waxing and waning are endless spirals in temporal existence: "Each is to be welcomed in its proper time and season, because life is a process of constant change" (Starhawk 1999: 53). Lunar phases, known as esbats, and other lunar events are also followed. Many witches celebrate the moon's orbit as a more immediate reminder of the cyclical and sometimes "shadowed" manner of existence.

Sabbats and esbats may be aligned to solar, lunar, and seasonal changes, but, as this chapter will demonstrate, they are also rooted in archaic speciesist practices. This poses a number of contradictions in Wiccan thealogy and witchcraft philosophy. As has been the case in green witchcraft and kitchen witchcraft, ideations of premodern life have ingratiated speciesism in modern practice. Attempts to honor or replicate ancient human societies to legitimize contemporary witchcraft finds Nonhuman Animals slaughtered for feasting tables, exploited for their eggs, or harassed for festival amusements. Lady Sabrina's (2001) recommendations reflect stereotypical seasonal associations such as

DOI: 10.4324/9781032649801-5

gooses, ducks, turkeys, and "roast beef" in the winter months, lambs' bodies, "ham," and cows' milk for spring, and salmons, pigs, and "game" hens for early summer. Plants, flowers, and grains may also be used but are often over-shadowed by Nonhuman Animals, given their perceived luxuriousness and superiority in quality. The dinnerplate, for many witches' sabbats, becomes the altar of animal sacrifice. Vegan feminism has argued that anthroparchy aggrandizes itself by supporting life for the community through killing, vio-lence, and death (Luke 2007), particularly, as explored in Chapter 3 on green witchcraft, in exalts of "the hunt." Transfiguring Nonhuman Animals from living persons into objectified victual by arrow, spear, bullet, or bolt gun serves an androcentric, human supremacist hero tale, a patriarchal mythology of con-quest (Kheel 2007). Sabbats seem to draw on this, celebrating birth, life, and prosperity by also celebrating death, killing, and inequality. Kitchen witchcraft, too, has been shown to rely heavily on patriarchal Nonhuman Animal-based agriculture. Vegan witchcraft, then, envisions how sabbats might employ a more feminist approach to the seasonal, cyclic celebration of cosmic turnings and nature's renewal. It is, after all, more than possible to support human life without directly taking the life of sentient others. This chapter subsequently examines sabbats, esbats, and ritual work more broadly to suggest where areas of anthroparchal influence might be reclaimed.

This pursuit will be worthwhile given that ritual work is a key aspect of both group-level and individual witchcraft, drawing together psychological and phy-sical elements of the practice (Barrett 2000). Salomonsen (2002) notes this to be especially true of feminist witchcraft, which offers much needed affirmation in a society that otherwise demeans and disempowers feminized groups. Indeed, Starhawk (1997) says of ritual: "They are the events that bind a culture toge-ther, that create a heart, a center, for a people" (155), allowing each practi-tioner to familiarize themselves with the "power-from-within" (155). Within veganism, too, ritual is important for resilience in a violently anti-vegan world. Psychologists, for instance, have noted that coming together in large numbers "can act as an identity resource for stigmatized, moralized minority-group members to connect with one another, strategize, and affirm their moral values and social action efforts" (Prosser et al. 2024: 19). Thus, this chapter con-tributes to vegan religious studies, with an emphasis on the importance of life-affirming feminist spirituality in defying and circumventing life-denying andro-centric religious institutions.

Solar Sabbats

Imbolc

Celebrated around the first of February, the pagan holiday of Imbolc marks the turning point from deep winter to spring's edge in the Northern Hemisphere. Imbolc was historically a point of celebration as domesticated animals were nearing the season of birthing. As such, dairy is perhaps the most ubiquitous association with this early spring festival (Greenleaf 2016). This connection is amplified by Imbolc's alignment with Ireland's Saint Bridget's Day, Bridget being the saint of healing, hospitality, and nonhuman breastmilk. Modern eco-feminists, witches, and feminist pagans often frame this breastmilk as symbolic of nurturance, a "mystical gift" (Woodward 2021: 101). Cunningham agrees, adding that "foods appropriate to eat on this day include those from the dairy, since Imbolc marks the festival of calving" (2003: 131).

Imbolc is traditionally aligned with exploitation of sheeps, and today this relationship is romanticized as taking place in a peaceful rural idyll. The reality is anything but romantic, however. All ovine inhabitants of the "idyll" will meet a violent end, and many of them are separated from their mothers and sent on a harrowing journey to slaughter at just a few weeks old, given the popularity of "lambchops" and "leg of lamb" (RSPCA n.d.b). The peaceful scene of the pasture is far from the horror of the finishing floor.

The pasture itself is a site of considerable suffering. Mother sheeps are genetically manipulated to produce multiple children to maximize the surplus value to be exploited from their labor, leading to high mortality rates for both mother and children. Pregnancies coerced deep in the winter to meet spring market demands for babies' flesh, furthermore, leave newborn lambs vulnerable to freezing weather. As a result, almost one in five British lambs do not survive to slaughter (Viva! n. d.). All lambs are subject to "tail docking." The severing of their tail is accomplished with a knife, hot iron, or a rubber band, which causes slow necrosis, and anesthesia is not offered. To increase their market weight, improve the palatability of their flesh, and reduce their capacity to resist the violence they endure in the trade, male lambs have a similar procedure inflicted on their genitals.

Even in "wool" production, suffering is high; these sheeps also undergo manipulated pregnancies, early removal from their mothers, and unanesthetized mutilations. The "live export" trade, furthermore, relies heavily on the production of sheeps' hair. Once "wool" industry victims become burdensome and less productive with age, they are crammed onto transport ships to countries where they can be slaughtered for food and religious purposes. With animals exposed to extreme heat or cold, overcrowding, accumulated filth, poor air circulation, fear, and stress, conditions are so horrific on these multi-level ships that death counts are high. These ships occasionally wreck as well, with animals trapped below deck or flung into open sea where they die by drowning. With pandemics (most of which have zoonotic origins) now a regularity, sometimes these ships will be denied port, leaving animals to suffer on board for weeks until they die of thirst or heat exhaustion. In these cases, Nonhuman Animals back up in their home countries as well, prompting hasty destruction. After Brexit and COVID-19, for instance, Irish dairy farmers experienced a "calf tsunami" as the domestic dairy industry expanded and international markets shrunk. Many infant boys were shot in the head by farmers a day or two after birth as farmers could not cope with their care as they awaited transportation to offshore slaughterhouses (Kevany and Busby 2020). Male babies are the inevitable "byproduct" from the systematic exploitation of female bodies and always meet with a violent end.

Modern witchcraft ignores these unsavory realities of "meat," "dairy" and birds' eggs production, drawing instead on delusions of peaceful, consenting relationships with other animals. For instance, an Imbolc ritual shared by Elizabeth Barrette (2014) invites practitioners to "celebrate the day by giving thanks for all the things that sheep have given us," including "fleece for sweaters and milk for cheese" with an "Imbolc prayer." The process of domestication itself, however, troubles the possibility of consent, and domestication by its very nature manipulates the minds and bodies of other animals to facilitate human mastery. Domesticated sheeps are born, live, and die at the whim of human desires. Vegan feminism sees domestication as an anthroparchal system of oppression that intentionally undercuts the agency of Nonhuman Animals, locks them in bondage through physical and cognitive manipulations and architectural incarceration, and replicates anthropocentric hierarchal arrangements (Cudworth 2011, Mason 1993). Regardless of whether this domestication takes place in backyards, rural pastures, or factory farms, it entails violence and oppression. This is no gift; it is theft.

The modern nature of Nonhuman Animal agriculture has not only rendered insensible the horrors inflicted on Nonhuman Animals, but it has also rationalized speciesist exploitation such that nonhuman bodies and excretions are readily available and artificially affordable for most. As explored in the previous chapter, the ubiquitousness of animal-based foods has undoubtedly influenced witches' dietary preferences, shaping the celebration of sabbats in turn. Dairy and other forms of animals' flesh in early agrarian societies would have been scarce, and were, in some cases, intentionally omitted through the rest of the winter months; this practice would be adapted into the Christian practice of Lent. Despite this modern emphasis on abundance and feasting, Imbolc was historically a time of purification, often calling for fasting. Fresh foods were scant and stored foods would be running low. Fasting may have taken on a spiritual, ritualistic quality as a measure to regulate food stores. Practitioners originally forwent any flesh, dairy, or eggs. Later, Lent laws would be relaxed, and fishes and other animals' products might be allowed. Today, few practice plant-based winter fasting, as Nonhuman Animal products are now ever-abundant with intensive genetic manipulation and industrialized agricultural practices.

Modern witches seem a bit unclear about this history. *The Real Witches' Kitchen*, by way of an example, notes that "fresh food would not have been plentiful at this festival" (80) but nonetheless suggests that "lamb is ideal for this feast" (West 2002: 81). Likewise, *The Witches Feast* (Brooks 2023) offers a vegetarian stew recipe to celebrate Imbolc in an attempt at historical accuracy, but it eagerly advocates roasting an "herby leg of lamb" for March's spring equinox, as this "delicious and impressive looking feast [...] makes the most of the meat that would have traditionally been available at this time of year" (57).

Imbolc, then, seems to be considered a celebratory time for drinking the breastmilk of pregnant mothers who are preparing to give birth to their babies, while equinox entails consuming the babies themselves.

It seems odd that the patriarchal domination inherent to domestication, reproductive manipulation, and blood sacrifice would remain so central to ecofeminist spirituality today. However, while it is true that speciesist traditions remain prevalent in many ecofeminist spiritual paths, being creative feminist practices, there are no set requirements for ritual observance. This suggests, to some extent, a degree of capriciousness and ample room for retooling for multispecies inclusivity. Bridget is not just associated with the birthing of new lambs and other animals destined for use and slaughter but midwifery more generally, as well as the hope and warmth that burning flames and a strengthening sun provide in the darkness (Bitel 2004). After retreating and resting in the winter months and cleansing body and home, might new rituals for celebrating rebirth and renewal be developed beyond speciesist practice?

The Irish government, for instance, declared St. Bridget's Day, February 1st, a national holiday in 2018. A corollary to the more equinox-aligned St. Patrick's Day, which follows in March, St. Bridget's Day honors the major feminist achievements in recent Irish history. But advocates for the holiday emphasize the holiday's importance in celebrating healing in an era of climate devastation. As the Director of Woman Spirit Ireland explained in an announcement of the new saint's day: "In a post-Covid world, we will be able to reflect further on her role, asking how the integration of nature, culture and technology can serve to heal our wounds and the vulnerable earth" (Condren 2022). Bridget, in other words, has come to embody an ecofeminist worker of magic, and this might easily replace the exploitation of sheeps and cows in a vegan Imbolc.

Ostara

While Imbolc heralds the coming of light and warmth, Ostara marks the spring equinox and the beginning of the growing season. With mammalian oestrous as its lingual origin, Ostara, like Imbolc, is often associated with the birth of new generations of "livestock." For witches, the bodies of these newborn harbingers of spring are often eaten to celebrate this turning of the wheel. West (2002), for instance, writes that "lamb is very appropriate, as is humanely raised [sic] veal" (85). Indeed, for many witches like West, the Ostara season calls for child sacrifice. Historically, this child sacrifice would have included the killing of fetuses in using hens' eggs, as the fertility of the Ostara season is most popularly symbolized with other-than-human eggs. Today, however, most eggs are unfertilized and remain symbolic in their representation of "rebirth and renewal" (Robinson 2022: 201). Squire (2022) explains that eggshells were historically thought vehicles for witches and fairies. She recommends collecting and powdering them for use in protection and fertility spells. Murphy-Hiscock (2018), likewise, suggests ritual work with eggs to take advantage of the "abundant, fertile energy of nature" for "productive, creative energy" (89), ignoring the questionable naturalness of apes consuming the ovary outputs of other species, the vast majority of whom endure genetic manipulation, forced molting, debeaking, lack of stimulation, ammonia-laden air, an inability to nest or roost, and extreme levels of stress, leading to the spread of zoonotic disease, hemorrhages, broken bones, premature death, and even trauma-induced cannibalism.

Some authors advise "free range" eggs to avoid absorbing the energy of bird suffering, likely unaware that suffering is inherent to egg production for human consumption, regardless of source. All industrially-raised hens, after a short life in either a battery cage or an industrial barn, go to slaughter. The egg industry is also known to be especially exploitative of human laborers, many of whom are women of color (Ducey 2018). "Free-range" schemes include many of these standard practices and have been described as intentionally misleading to extract greater profit from concerned customers (Scrinis et al. 2017, Swanson 2013). Even "backyard hens" suffer the bodily exertion of constant egg production, a genetic manipulation that is neither natural nor healthy for their small bodies. Indeed, it consistently leads to eventual reproductive collapse. Backyard hens who wane in production are vulnerable to abandonment or slaughter. Rescues and sanctuaries have only enough space for a few individuals cast aside from backyard operations, much less those rescued from industrial ones. Even the most kindly treated of chickens (an infinitesimally small fraction of the billions of chickens exploited by humans every year) remain under human control. They, too, have been genetically manipulated to serve humans, and their labor is not their own (Davis 2019). This is not working with nature; this is working *over* nature.

Cunningham (2007) muses that Ostara is "a time of joyous celebration, for the killing months of winter were over" (37), but clearly this is not the case for all. Nonetheless, his observation that Ostara marks a time of moving past death and toward life could be an important aspect for vegan witchcraft to revisit. Veganism encourages mindfulness about one's ethical and consumptive relationship with the world, in order to commemorate life and seek balance with nature. Rather than marking the equinox with the taking of others' eggs, perhaps Ostara could be used to rededicate one's commitment to the vegan path. Indeed, the imagery of seeds, seedlings, and vitality are heavily utilized in vegan narratives and symbolism.[1] Although eggs are centered as a traditional food for the Ostara sabbat feast, hot cross buns and seeded cakes are also recommended and may be plant-based. Cunningham (2007) also suggests incorporating edible flowers, for instance, which are just as representative of a budding spring as birds' eggs. West (2002) suggests the nettle and dandelion that proliferate during the Ostara season in the Northern Hemisphere might be edible symbols of this springtime. Greenleaf (2016) prioritizes beans, not even making mention of birds' eggs, while Squire (2022) suggests nuts, which also symbolize nurturing energy necessary for birth and growth, albeit plant-based.[2] Wheat, which is symbolically associated with the summer harvest, might provide another alternative. "Wheat holds magickal energy for abundance, fertility, prosperity, and protection," Woodward (2021) explains, as it contains bran, germ, and endosperm, the nutrient-rich ingredients for life and reproduction, not unlike that of an egg. Supporting the healthy reproduction of birds for their own sake is another alternative, including the provision of fresh food and water for free-living species. These traditions seem more in line with the affirmation of life that Ostara is meant to represent.

The making of this food is as magically important as the eating of it. Because Ostara marks the official start of spring in the Northern Hemisphere, it is an appropriate time to prepare the garden for a new season of growth. For vegans, this can be a bit tricky, as most commercial potting soils and fertilizers are composites of slaughterhouse renderings, chicken litter, and other byproducts of speciesist systems. Although vegan alternatives are commercially available, it is also possible for some witches to simply use their own eggs. Miernowska's *The Witch's Herbal Apothecary* (2020), for instance, suggests "bleeding on the earth" with human menses. This ritual, however, does not otherwise surface in the leading witchcraft discourse, despite being vegan, free, and an easily available means of fertilizing the soil. The failure to incorporate unused human eggs in Ostara rituals suggests that it is the domination of other animals—the extraction of their "gifts"—that creates a sense of magic. Human menstruation, stigmatized by its association with women, nature, and animality, thus goes untapped in favor of more romanticized avian ovulation.

Bealtaine

Marking the beginning of summer in the North, Bealtaine is a major sabbat that observes the returning sun, plant-life, and fresh fruits and vegetables. In Irish, Bealtaine refers to the fire (*tine*) of the Celtic god Beal.[3] There is a fire element to all four major sabbats,[4] but the fire on the eve of May 1st is perhaps the most magnificent, as Bealtaine was an important time for protecting "livestock." Cows might be made to jump over the May Day fires, or they and their living quarters might be decorated with protective plants and herbs to maximize fertility and keep the evil eye or dangerous fae away (Buckland 2002). Witches, recall, were often accused of interfering with "livestock" as well. In modern witchcraft, killing and eating animals is, predictably, often advised, as is the case in West's *The Real Witches' Kitchen* (2002), which condemns pigs for this purpose. As many sheeps, cows, and other animals were giving birth in April and May, wealth could be extracted from the breastmilk and offspring they produced. Perhaps for this reason, Cunningham (2007) advises incorporating dairy into May Day festivities. Bees, too, are often included in Bealtaine celebrations, as mead, a fermented honey drink, is regularly used (Greenleaf 2016), and, to a lesser extent, wine, too, is used (Cunningham 2007). Bealtaine may not incorporate speciesism as deeply as Imbolc or Ostara, but it continues the romanticization of speciesism in "livestock" exploitation and animal-based foods and drink.

A time of union, handfasting, and the start of the summer season with its high fertility, Bealtaine also marks a time where the "masculine" and "feminine" energies of the Earth are thought to merge as the feminine darker months wane with the return of the sun. There are certainly many ecofeminist possibilities in recognizing the fruits of female labor and the destabilization of gender polarities in this cross-quarter point in early May. Indeed, this is the season of the Green Man, or the Jack in the Green, a mythic embodiment of the nonhuman natural world. Religious scholars have identified this figure as potentially effective for mobilizing modern environmental activism (Whitehead and Letcher 2023). If Bealtaine is also a time for "protecting" farmed Nonhuman Animals from witches, this history might be reframed for antispeciesist activism as well. Vegan witches do indeed aim to interfere with speciesist agriculture, not to spoil farmers' stocks but to liberate their victims. Subsequently, the first of May might incorporate rituals of protection for farmed Nonhuman Animals, working to protect them from the real threat to their wellbeing: *farmers*.

Litha and Lughnasadh

The summer months are less violent times in the witches' wheel of the year, given the focus on growing crops and flourishing vegetation. In the Northern Hemisphere, Litha (Old English for "midsummer") marks the summer equinox, the longest day of the year. Although kitchen witches often suggest eating the bodies of other animals barbequed or grilled on open fires, this early summer celebration is often enjoyed with more fruits and vegetables than other sabbats (West 2002). Cunningham (2007) invites practitioners to harness the sun's power by consuming "flaming foods" (38). With the sun at its full energy and plant life thriving, many witches prioritize herbs for drying in the sun, to create sun-infused oils and teas, or to hang in the home as a measure of protection. Free-living nonhumans can also be supported at this time, with offerings of food, fresh water, and native flowers and other plants.

The second harvest festival in the pagan year, Lughnasadh (which translates to "August" in Gaelic and refers to the Celtic god Lugh) is often celebrated by honoring the masculine power of the sun and the abundance of grain. Most often, this is expressed through baking. Cunningham (2007) draws attention to sunflowers, which are thought to symbolize the sun's energy and the abundance of plant-based foods as well as protection, success, and luck. He advises gathering their seeds at sunset, eating them, and making a wish. Sunflowers, incidentally, have become a global symbol of environmentalism and veganism, only amplifying their magical properties. Another Lughnasadh appropriate spell entails visualizing intentions over a bowl of sunflower seeds representing the "energies of the sun" (98). Cunningham also promotes the use of grains, breads, and berries as appropriate kitchen magic for this season. Indeed, food historians and archaeologists find that the medieval diet in Britain was dominated by grains and cereals, since access to animal protein was largely determined by wealth and status (Moffett 2006, Schofield 2006). Nonetheless, witches often manage to incorporate speciesism into this plant-based celebration. West (2002), for instance, speaks of the "merciful" abundance of rabbits, who may be drawn out of the fields for killing and eating as a "free source of food" that "would not have been wasted" (96). Her kitchen witch cookbook instructs practitioners to cook their flesh until tender, except for babies, whose flesh will still be supple. The flavor of their corpses, she adds, can be enhanced by stewing or braising. Rabbits, of course, are not the only species at risk. Cows, sheeps, and pigs are also recommended by West as sacrifices for the witch's feast.

In Ireland, free-living goats also come under assault. The Puck Fair is a rare example of an ancient Lughnasadh celebration that has persisted into modern times (Mulvihill 2014). Each August, a male goat is captured and hoisted atop a platform for three days of festivities. The Puck Fair overlaps with the Celtic harvest festival and reflects traditional worship of the horned god, but, like many persisting Irish traditions, it also has colonial roots. A version of the festival has been held in County Kerry since the Middle Ages, but the formal Puck Fair that began in the 17th century was made possible by the patronage of the British monarchy, primarily for the purpose of collecting tolls on the Non-human Animals sold therein. Recently, activists have called for an end to the capturing and hoisting of goats, but because the goats are believed to be "royally treated," the cruelty involved is generally overlooked given the traditional values the practice represents. The Puck Fair itself is a complex of rituals that bond the community and reproduce hierarchies of species, class, and gender (Wrenn 2021). This point is particularly relevant given the traumatic legacy of British colonization, which animalized the Irish, devasted Irish culture, and encouraged the cultural conservativism in Ireland well into the 20th century.

Mabon

Celebrated at the time of the autumn equinox, Mabon is a celebration of the second of three agricultural harvest festivals. Not only is it a time for humans to harvest apples, pears, fruits, nuts, fungi, and other stuffs, but many free-living Nonhuman Animals will be stocking up in preparation for the winter months as well, particularly those who are preparing for hibernation. In this way, Mabon is a jointly celebrated festive season with significance across the species barrier, although Nonhuman Animals are often slated for "harvest" themselves. In the British Isles, Mabon transitioned into the Christianized version, Michaelmas, and was celebrated over the corpse of a goose. Green (2002) recounts a particularly horrific torture in Britain whereby gooses would have their feet tarred in order to toughen them for a death march to market for feasting at the end of September. West (2002), too, sees gooses as the ideal victims for autumn festivities, as they would have traditionally been fattened on the cleared fields "until they were large enough to feed the family" but still small enough that their bodies should not require hot water basting (100). They can be "simply roasted on a rack over a roasting tin (boiler tray) to catch any fat which drops" (100), she surmises. As many emigrated from the British Isles and other parts of Europe to the Americas, Canada's Thanksgiving celebration in late September formed a loose translation of these agrarian festival practices. Held a month later in the United States, in late November, many of the same sentiments would also translate into American Thanksgiving. Food traditionally gathered and served on this holiday include North American contributions such as pumpkins, potatoes, and, of course, the bodies of native turkeys, who would replace Michaelmas gooses.

There are many ways that Mabon may be modified for multispecies celebration. In the United States, Mabon adopts many Native American food traditions. Cunningham (2007), for instance, suggests working with the hardy and nutrient-dense "three sisters" crops: corn, squash, and beans. Many Indigenous foodways were historically heavily plant-based, in fact, but the Western colonizer's ideological penchant for anthroparchal oppression has tended to magnify histories of "the hunt" (Robinson 2024a). This trend, as explored in a previous chapter, thrives in witchcraft today. Vegetables and grains, however, have their place in autumnal celebration, as does the sharing of foodstuffs, not just at the feasting table but in the wider community. Witches often encourage donating to food banks, for instance, although Nonhuman Animals are too often forgotten in these acts of generosity. Donations of shelf-stable food for companion animals would also be welcomed by needy recipients, as financial hardship is a primary reason why Nonhuman Animals are surrendered at "shelters." Supplies would be welcomed by charities accommodating farmed species as well, given that they provide a very thinly spread safety net to the few individuals lucky enough to avoid the slaughterhouse. Indeed, a vegan Mabon might look to the experiences of the most vulnerable nonhumans as a point of inspiration for new, multispecies ritual practice. Many farmed animal sanctuaries, such as Farm Sanctuary in Watkins Glen, New York, reclaim these celebrations of speciesism by offering Thanksgiving for turkeys events in which the public is invited to join sanctuary staff in feeding turkeys a grand buffet of fruits and vegetables.

Samhain

The last of the year's harvest festivals, Samhain (meaning "November" in Gaelic) is not just the most prominent festival in the witch's calendar but perhaps the most relevant for vegan witchcraft. Greenleaf (2016) marks it as a time to "let your 'wild side' out, to be free and more connected to the ancient ways" (133). What constitutes these "ancient ways" differs according to interpretation. Greenleaf presumably refers to a shaking loose of civilization's domesticating effect, but many others see it as linked to violence. While Lughnasadh celebrates the harvesting of grain and Mabon the harvesting of fruits and nuts, Samhain, the day of the dead, signifies the harvesting of Nonhuman Animals condemned as "food" or "stock." Lady Sabrina notes that Samhain is the time for killing most of the herd for winter supplies, creating a distinctly ominous air: "Slaughter, barren earth, and decreasing daylight made the concept of death an ever-present reality" (2001: 117). West (2002) adds that Nonhuman Animals not thought to survive the winter (presumably sick, old, disabled, or otherwise vulnerable) would also be slated for slaughter, as well as those who were simply thought too expensive to keep alive. West frames these as mercy killings rather than systematic violence against "unproductive" or "burdensome" individuals who are especially marginalized in an increasingly capitalistic society. She rationalizes that the leaner months of winter meant that pigs, cows, and other animals constituted more mouths to feed, making it more prudent to turn those mouths into food, a perspective that could be seen as practical from an anthroparchal perspective or dismissive and cruel from a vegan feminist one. Buckland (2002), too, describes this third "harvest" as a culling of weaker animals, taking this history to mean that the sabbat is subsequently well suited to rituals that aid the witch in releasing weaknesses. As might be expected, this mass slaughter is interpreted as an invitation to feast on the bodies of Nonhuman Animals. West (2002) emphasizes that eating other animals on Samhain is in continuation of traditional European practices and a means to honor "our ancestors" (71). Sometimes the very blood of these slain animals would be baked into cakes and puddings (Franklin 1997). Cunningham assures readers that this association is only symbolic (2003: 67), but the violence it symbolizes is ideologically aligned with persistent speciesism in modern society.

Samhain truly is a festival of death, one in which witches and pagans are expected to remember loved ones and ancestors who have passed on. In honoring ancestors, festivals of the dead reach back across an ambiguous number of generations, but few, if any, seriously consider the full extent of the human practitioner's ancestry. Vegan witchcraft would remind us that humans, having evolved from primates, are apes. Preceding this primate lineage, humans have evolutionary ties to all manner of pre-humanoid species, including small mammals, fishes, and even microorganisms. In addition to Nonhuman Animals, the Earth itself is an ancestor, providing the first elementary ingredients (carbon, hydrogen, oxygen, and so on) for what would become sentient life. Trillions of Nonhuman Animals over more than four billion years of Earth's existence have thus contributed to human flourishment. The human supremacy of Samhain celebrations, then, misaligns with a complex lineage of interconnectivity in human evolution.

If Samhain is a time to reflect on death, for that matter, it is also a time to reflect on injustice. Weinstein (2020) takes this as an opportunity to remember the violence of the burning times and a powerful time for hexing the patriarchy or individual perpetrators of misogynistic acts, for instance, while Starhawk makes space for grief in her San Franscico Samhain events, given the city's tragic association with the AIDS epidemic. For Budapest, this occasion calls for retaliation spellwork, as Samhain is "the night of the revengeful Mother, who is the fierce protector of her sisters when aroused" (1986: 90). Samhain, falling as it does on the eve of World Vegan Day, might serve as a space for communally acknowledging the grief associated with the global violence on Nonhuman Animals. Indeed, The Vegan Society chose November 1[st5] as the day to celebrate veganism, as it aligns with All Saint's Day, the day to remember the persecution of Christians and the saints who had entered heaven. The vegan version of All Saint's Day, falling the day after the Day of the Dead, could celebrate the promise of life following death, or a more peaceful multispecies society that could be achieved after the destruction of speciesism. Samhain, in *vegan* witchcraft, should be a time to honor ancestors but also recognize that "harvest time" has been a period of intense violence across the ages. Just as the mass killing of witches has been cause for somber remembrance, so too should Nonhuman Animals who have been harassed, killed, and "sacrificed" for entertainment, pleasurable consumption, religious bargaining for a deity's favor, scientific advancement, and so on.

Recall that there is a ritual importance to food and feasting, particularly given its nurturing and revitalizing properties and its ability to bond and heal. The witches' new year takes advantage of all of these qualities. Cunningham (2007) draws attention to various root crops, pomegranates, grains, wine, cider, and other plant-based offerings from the harvest, but pumpkins are perhaps the most famous of all Samhain foods. These squashes sustained many Indigenous Americans as a sacred staple. Rich in vitamins and protein and highly versatile, pumpkins have also become an important element of vegan cuisine. In Celtic lore, however, carved and lit with candles, pumpkins (as well as turnips and cabbages) were used to bring light into the darkness and ward away evil. For witches, pumpkins also symbolize protection but also abundance, harvest, and transformation (Woodward 2021). Robinson (2022) records the use of nuts and apples for these qualities. For witches and vegans alike, these autumnal foodstuffs have long been cherished for their lifegiving qualities, offering energy and nutritional support, particularly in the needier months of autumn.

Samhain is also a day for divination. Traditionally, this might have included blood sacrifice, but today it is more frequently practiced with the sharing of harvest bounties. The "dumb supper," for example, is a traditional meal ritual that offers a place at the table for the spirits of those passed over. Sometimes it is advised to leave these portions outside as offerings for faeries, spirits, or free-living animals (Cunningham 2007). A vegan Samhain might set a place for the trillions of Nonhuman Animals lost that year (and all the trillions whose lives were taken by humans in preceding years), ensuring that some of the portions provided are appropriate for free-living animals, who may be offered the meal at the end of the evening. Historically, "soul cakes" were also made and distributed to those in need (as well as passing spirits). Easily veganized, these might serve a similar purpose. The sharing of soul cakes and dumb suppers both make space for and draw attention to the dead, offering ritualistic compassion and acknowledgment. Given the overwhelming invisibility of Nonhuman Animals in a speciesist society, especially those killed for food, Samhain seems an especially potent moment for remembering the nonhuman dead and honoring multispecies community.

Yule

Following the mass sacrifices of Samhain, the winter solstice season is comparatively dormant. A time of relative scarcity, however, would mean great difficulty and persecution for Nonhuman Animals, being the most vulnerable to dwindling food supplies and harsh weather. This season has traditionally served as one final burst of sacrificial activity. In Europe, a number of stone henges have been constructed to align with this solstice, including the famous Stonehenge and Avebury sites in Southern England. To attract thousands of prehistoric peoples to the region, the winter solstice was celebrated with several days of feasting. Although these spaces can be psychically powerful for modern visitors who feel a connection across the millennia to ancestors who organized their lives around celestial rhythms, these are highly sterilized spaces today. When in use, they would have been sites of incredible violence against Nonhuman Animals. Thousands of Nonhuman Animal skeletons have been found at Stonehenge and Avebury, especially those of pigs, who appear to have been marched to the sites from afar and ritually slaughtered for the festivities (Madgwick et al. 2019).

Today, many winter solstice traditions are less harmful to other animals, as observers are more inclined to mull wine and decorate the yule tree with sacred foods formed into magic-enhancing shapes (Cunningham 2007). Wassailing, an old English practice of blessing "livestock," pastures, orchards, and other agricultural spaces, has been revitalized in recent years and could celebrate a positive relationship with nature and other animals. It must be considered, however, that wassailing is not typically engaged for the benefit of those being blessed, but rather for those who are doing the blessing, given its purpose of increasing agricultural fertility. Vegan wassailing might alter this narrative, blessing imprisoned Nonhuman Animals in hopes for their consequent liberation or blessing animals residing at sanctuaries to symbolically support their continued healing. Indeed, winter solstice is a time for contemplating the return of the light and would also suit the contemplation of peace on Earth, particularly given its correspondence to holy days of peace across the world.

Yule is thought to rest deep in the "womb time" of the Wiccan calendar, making it a point of feminist reflection as well. Robinson (2022) notes this might be a time for witches to convene for celebration, and, indeed, this might also be a day for acknowledging the feminized labor exploited from other animals and celebrating cows, chickens, and other nonhuman mothers.[6] This would mark a month of feminine observance in the return to Imbolc, or Bridget's day, and the burgeoning rejuvenation of humans, other animals, and nature. Budapest describes her coven's winter solstice celebration as including a "period of humming that builds up to a birth scream," a ritual that reminds participants that "we are reborn along with Lucina"[7] (1986: 74). Her coven has similarly adapted other sabbats to feminist interests. As the Yule season slides into Imbolc, a period often used for Wiccan initiation, Budapest marks this period as a reawakening of women's knowledge and wisdom. Here, women figuratively come into the light, resisting patriarchal attempts to block women from education and enlightenment. Vegan witchcraft would subsequently honor these months of darkness by resting, revisiting feminist theory, and supporting free-living animals who, in the Northern Hemisphere, will be tried by the hardships of winter. Indeed, supporting life in a season that has historically served as an occasion for death is a revolutionary act.

Lunar Esbats

The seasonal wheel turns around the sun over 365 days, but the thirteen turns of the lunar wheel in that time are more immediate influences in the witches' calendar. In modern witchcraft, the moon is considered as important as the sun and is subsequently incorporated in all manner of rituals. Indeed, Lady Sabrina suggests that "Wicca is a lunar-based magical system" (2001: 97), the idea being that humans are affected by its phases. Full moons, for instance, represent ideas and projects come to fruition. At its most powerful, it is believed to influence emotions, even "lunacy." The moon card in the classic Rider-Waite tarot deck depicts these effects with an illustration of a dog and a wolf drawn to the moon's gaze. They are joined by a lobster (who represents intuition) drawn up from tidal waters (which symbolize emotion and liminality). For witches, this attraction to the moon is thought evidence of humanity's base animality, and for vegan feminists, it is this very animality that is transformative in undermining socially constructed, segregating anthroparchal hierarchies. Vegan witchcraft, then, might look to the moon as a symbolic reminder of interspecies connectiveness, feminine wisdom, the power of emotion, cyclical nature, and the possibility of lightness and new beginnings in the darkest of times.

Another intersection between humanity, femininity, animality, and the cosmic might be found in menstrual cycles. Menstruating humans characteristically share the same number of days in their cycle with that of the moon, and the moon's cycle was thought to influence reproduction in earlier times (Helfrich-Förster et al. 2021, Sjöö and Mor 1991). Whether or not there is a biological connection, it is nevertheless true that the moon (and stars) had considerable meaning for many ancient cultures, as many of them developed sophisticated systems to track the cosmos. Some stone henges, such as the Standing Stones of Calanais in Scotland, are aligned to the moon's path, rather than the sun's. Today, belief in the moon's influence has been diminished as mere astrology in Western society. This disassociation between humanity and the "magic" of the cosmos reflects the rationalization of society that transpired after the Enlightenment period and solidified in the industrial age (Sjöö and Mor 1991). This was more than an effort to secularize human life, however; it was also a means of extracting humans from the natural world. Reconnecting with humanity's ancient connection to the moon, subsequently, is not just a reimagining of old spiritual practices. It is an embracement of human *animality* and a recognition that the human experience is just as embodied and natural as it is cerebral and cultural.

Familiar work is subsequently revisited in lunar esbats, reinforcing the interconnectivity of women, more-than-human animals, and mysterious nature. Rachel Patterson, for instance, advises the incorporation of "power animal" representations in her *Moon Magic* (2014). Rather than engage the intersectional possibilities of moon magic, however, species are anthropocentrically spotlighted based on special significance to humans. The intersectional failure of moon magic is also found in the mythology of the lunar calendar. Not unlike the solar wheel of the year, each moon cycle is associated with "hunting" and "domesticating" Nonhuman Animals. For instance, Lady Sabrina (2001) explains that the October Blood Moon "marks the season of hunting and the slaughter of the animals for winter food and clothing. Blood is the force of life. Now is the time for thanksgiving, rest, and reflection" (103). Valiente (1962), too, suggests that animal-based agriculture was aligned to the moon, dictating times to force "livestock" breeding or to castrate them. Thus, lunar cycles are not symbolically guaranteed to liberate, despite the exaltation of human animality and connection to the natural world. The feminine power of the moon, rather than serving as a point of feminist resistance and solidarity with other animals, remains subsumed under anthroparchal oppression.

Kitchen witchcraft based on lunar phases proves just as conflicting. Madara (2021) suggests the consumption of particular foods based on the phase of the moon. The arrival of the half moon, for instance, is thought a time to seek balance. She suggests eating herbs and other relaxing foods known to increase intuition, including the bodies of chickens and ducks. The days of a waning moon are thought to be the optimal time for banishing, grounding, and purification. As such, Madara (2021) suggests consuming the roasted bodies of Nonhuman Animals. For the waxing moon, a time for building, planning, and attracting, she suggests eating the bodies of other animals in cured form. However, Madara suggests vegetarian fare for the full moon, a peak time of manifestation, cleansing, and love, perhaps due to its feminine association. Indeed, as many witches follow the pagan practice of planting and harvesting plants during particular cycles of the moon to maximize fertility for certain plant species (Valiente 1962), this seems an opportunity for a vegan alternative to working with foods by the moon. Because the full moon has also historically been seen as a point at which women could transfigure into other animals such as hares, it could also be a time to honor shared animality.[8] Valiente (1962) adds that moon magic is central to healing work and positive magic. As such, there exists considerable potential to break free of patriarchal moon mythology with vegan witchcraft in extending this magical intention beyond the human species.

Veganizing Ritual

Although the exploitation, death, and consumption of other animals features heavily in the modern reinterpretation of the pagan year, not all authors apply modern dietary norms to traditional practices. Greenleaf (2016), for instance, does not mention slaughter or the consumption of animals' flesh in their seasonal book on kitchen witchery. Indeed, for Greenleaf, the magic is not found in the foods and ingredients used across the sabbats but in the associated celebration and rituals. Because modern witchcraft greatly values a do-it-yourself approach to mythological and thealogical interpretations, spellwork, and rituals (Clifton 2006), veganism might readily be incorporated. Robinson's *Kitchen Witch* (2022) while not vegan illustrates the importance of practical flexibility. She presents many medieval seasonal folkways and traditional witchcrafts but repurposes many of them for modern utility. She considers that this may erode their authenticity or magical potency but argues that revisions allow practitioners to "bring them back into lived experience" (2022: 227), and, as Wiccan thealogy reminds us, "change happens and will continue to happen" (227). Witches need not be bound to the past and have the capacity for self-realization and manifestation. Robinson asks, "With this power, we have a choice—which kind of witch do we want to be?" (233).

Writes Charlene Spretnak (1993), "Goddess spirituality is the perceptual shift from the death-based sense of existence that underlies patriarchal culture to a regeneration-based awareness, an embrace of life as a cycle of creative rebirths, a dynamic participation in the processes of infinity" (273). To fully embrace the essence of this spirituality, the assault on other animals systematized by patriarchy's death-based sense of existence will need to be disconnected from the feminist emphasis on regeneration. As it stands, expectations of life regenerated are too often used as an excuse to kill. Morningstar (2005) emphasizes that this forward-thinking and creative witchcraft must include consideration of other animals. "The Wiccan heart moves out to all sentient life" she surmises, "and so animals are very much a part of any Wiccan healing picture" (205). As such, she offers a number of spells for healing Nonhuman Animals, including spells that counter depression, trauma, timidity, and compromised immunity.

Sociologists, too, have studied spiritual practice as a powerful means of community support in the face of considerable inequality. Perhaps the most well-known analysis of this religious function comes from Karl Marx, who noted its drugging effect, a necessary escape in an otherwise extremely alienating society (Lobkowicz 1964). Marx, an atheist, viewed religion with some suspicion, believing it had the potential to distract and dissuade from egalitarian possibilities. Indeed, religion plays conflicting roles in modern society, both inflaming inequality with its tendency to bulwark the power of the dominant class *and* facilitating a sense of solidarity across differences in the service of social justice. To the latter point, sociologists have observed that activist groups can negotiate identities that run counter to even the most conservative religious norms, drawing on religious insights for the development of movement goals and claimsmaking to resonate with a larger body of potential participants (Coley 2020). This identity negotiation may also be necessary for vegan campaigning, as it attacks one of the most fundamental elements of human religiosity, that being the human supremacist expectation of environmental stewardship even in pagan and Wiccan religions, which despite deep ecological rhetoric continue to prioritize the interests of the human species and presume human dominion.

All major religions are flexible to some degree as is necessary to remain relevant, but witchcraft and Wicca are explicit in the importance of change. "Ritual that is alive does not become frozen in form," Starhawk advises (1987: 99). It is vital for weaving culture, she further explains, and thus must remain flexible. Change is recognized as inherent in universal workings and thereby must also be accommodated rather than resisted in individual practice. Barrett (2000), for instance, make clear that the power of ritual can and should be manipulated to suit modern needs. Feminist witches, as has been shown, have tailored rituals to empower women, heal women, and even counter the emotional turmoil of sexual assault. Indeed, this variant of witchcraft actively encourages creativity in devising and revising rituals as needed (Eller 1995). "When done with care and consciousness," Barrett assures, "ritual is a powerful tool for personal and social transformation" (2000: 199). Removing speciesism from pagan rituals should not undermine their authenticity; all sorts of horrible acts of violence against animals have been practiced in the spirit of the season only to be abandoned as attitudes about other animals have changed. Many in the goddess tradition, such as Sjöö and Mor (1991), see this as evidence of the nonlinear aspects of cosmic time. If witches seek to challenge linear patriarchal thinking, assuming that life in the recent past is preferable or superior simply because of its location in time, the practice becomes stagnant and closed to change. Vegan feminism, however, also informs a vegan witchcraft that finds solace and celebration in rituals, nature-working, and the turning of the seasons. Taking time throughout the year to observe nature and connect with other animals can be revitalizing, while oppressive traditions can be reclaimed and reworked to repair systemic harms. The wheel need not turn on the exploitation of Nonhuman Animals.

Sex Magic

There are, of course, other cycles of the natural world that have relevance to humans. Feminist witchcraft has focused on the cycle of human birth, life, and death, for instance. Marion Weinstein's (1991) wheel makes no mention of Nonhuman Animals, instead referring to broader cycles of life, sex magic, fertility, and reproduction. Leek (1975) notes that grains, vegetables, and fruits in their recurrent and ample abundance symbolized the fertile union of male and female. Vegan witchcraft might lean toward this sex magic, focusing instead on *human* cycles of life rather than that of other animals, making love not meat.

Sex magic can be a source of life itself should it result in pregnancy, but in its most basic practice, procreative or not, it can offer participants access to deeper consciousness (Greenwood 2000). Shuttle and Redgrove (1978), for instance, identify the period following coitus as one of psychic intensification. They also suggest an alignment with the menstrual cycle as "an opportunity of contacting natural energies" (162). Sex magic is by no means limited to heterosexual relations. Vegan feminist Greta Gaard (1997) finds considerable political relevance in the erotic element of ecofeminism, particularly given the connection between queer oppression and witchcraft persecution. "Women accused of witchcraft were accused not only for their gender but for their perceived sexuality and erotic practices" (132), she argues, just as Indigenous persons were persecuted by colonizers and homosexuals by the Church for their supposed deviant sexual practices. Starhawk also champions erotic energy as a sacred, joyful practice linking humans to the natural world, conscious that "control of sexuality [...] is a cornerstone of the structures of domination" (1987: 25).

Plants offer inspiration as well. Starhawk proposes an Earth path, one that encourages the practitioner to become intimately knowledgeable of their own home and its surroundings; this concerns "understanding the mythological and practical significance of every hill and stream and valley, knowing the uses of the herbs and the medicinal properties of the trees and shrubs, and being responsible for the area's spiritual and ecological health" (2005: 5). This not only improves the witch's eco-literacy but profoundly counters the disconnection that patriarchy and modernity have imposed between "civilized" life and the natural world. Although she advocates stewardship and domestication, sliding into patriarchal elements of control and entitlement, this Earth walking might easily be veganized, creating a psychological connection with nature by simply spending time in it, consciously. "Once we have learned to hear," Starhawk observes, "then we can begin to understand. And only after we understand do we begin to speak, to intervene" (2005: 12).

Starhawk (1997) especially emphasizes the magic of sexuality in raising power, energy, and connection. Eroticism and pleasure, she adds, are fundamental to a life well lived and are not to be marginalized or dismissed. Indeed, if "denial of feeling replaces erotic celebration," as Starhawk observes (1987: 51), sex magic has the power to reawaken. Sollée (2017) regards sex magic as a powerful means of reclaiming women's power, solitary practice included. Of course, sensuality comes in many forms, as the asexual community might attest. Sex magic, Sjöö and Mor explain, is practiced "for the sake of ecstatic self-transcendence, a sexual-spiritual fusion of the human with the cosmic All" (1991: 75), and this can be achieved not just by orgasm but by controlled breathing, dancing, and other rhythmic movement. Salomonsen (2002) offers many creative possibilities as well: "spiritual union is sought in mundane life, in passion, sensuality, and relationship—through being fully human" (287). Indeed, vegan witchcraft rooted in erotic pleasure would frustrate negative stereotypes that pit veganism as abstinent and joyless. It would also lend support to expressions of sexuality that exist beyond the confines of patriarchal desires and compulsory heterosexuality.

Some caution is necessary, however, in witchcraft's articulation of free love, as sensual indulgence has so often incorporated the unearned privileges of speciesism. By way of an example, many witchcraft guidebooks advise ritual bathing for the purposes of self-care, merging mind and body, and preparing for spellwork. Herbs, essential oils, and salts are ideal for special occasion baths, but even here Nonhuman Animals are integrated for human benefit. By way of an example, popular witchcraft writer Murphy-Hiscock (2017, 2018) encourages readers to add cows' milk for its skin softening properties. Certainly, human breastmilk might be added instead, but many would likely find this option unappealing. This begs the question as to why soaking in the breastmilk of another species is considered the height of luxury, and perhaps the answer lies in the resource intensiveness of its procurement, the human supremacist desire to elevate humans through the consumption of other animals, and the symbolic association between Nonhuman Animals and nature. Cows' milk, despite its nefarious origins, is thought to provide "nourishment, longevity, and healing energy" (Murphy-Hiscock 2018: 117). Plant milks are even more accessible, of course, but are thought to lack comparable qualities. Murphy-Hiscock explicitly diminishes vegan alternatives as they supposedly "won't have the same physical effects" (2018: 117). However, they suggest readers looking for an alternative might slather themselves in bees' honey to tap into its powers of "immortality, healing, happiness, beauty, and abundance" (2018: 119). Animal products thus come to represent sensuality and indulgence, and it is this pleasurable consumption, vegan feminism has argued, that obscures underlying systems of oppression (Adams 2003).

Ritual Work

Even vegan sex magic would maintain anthropocentrism in practice,[9] and multispecies witchcraft that serves both human *and* nonhuman animals will also be necessary to tap into the many positive aspects of ritual work. Ritual is perhaps one of the most fundamental human (and nonhuman) experiences, especially for social species. It is important for meaning making and group solidarity. Ritual reframes the everyday to provide useful insight. Anthropologist Catherine Bell (2009) describes ritual as the co-creative marrying of thought and action, requiring symbolic play and interpretation to create an object or event that is distinct from the mundane. For witches, ritual is important for honoring creativity, connecting with the natural elements, and making magic real through symbolic interpretation of the everyday: poetry and rhyme, plants and herbs, shared food, dance, and more. It can be countercultural, furthermore, in its manufacture of an alternate symbolic lifeworld.

Veganism has its own rituals based on liberating or caring for Nonhuman Animals, preparing and sharing food, and connecting with ancestors (who, for the global majority, ate primarily plant-based diets) by consuming traditional foods (Sanchez 1993). Sarah Pike (2017) has also identified ritual in environmental and anti-speciesist mobilizations, as they "interrupt the everyday, taken-for-granted world" (132) and transform sites of protest "into spaces of resistance and confrontation" (133). Vegan witchcraft might conjoin these shared elements of ritual by veganizing ritual ingredients and incorporating multispecies narratives. Pike notes in her ethnographic work that consciously engaged spirituality and ritualism have even been embraced by secular activists, who benefit from the shared action, collective identity, and emotional resilience they can provide.

Whitehurst is perhaps the most prolific pro-animal spellcrafter from whom vegan witchcraft might find inspiration. Though not vegan herself, she regularly includes spells for other animals in her texts. For instance, she offers a chapter on "Magic for Our Animal Friends" in *Holistic Energy Magic* (2015), which includes a blessing for Nonhuman Animals and the Earth, a spell for finding lost companion animals, and "A Blessing for the Animals Who Suffer at the Hands of Humans" (2015: 199). The latter guides the practitioner in asking for forgiveness on behalf of humanity, conveying comfort and love to suffering animals in "labs, slaughterhouses, circuses, amusement parks, and everywhere else" (2015: 200), and sending a "beam of [anti-speciesist] awakening" to humanity:

> I invoke divine comfort and love for all animals currently suffering at the hands of Humans. God, Goddess, All That Is, please intervene on behalf of all suffering animals, bringing them as much peace, joy, comfort, and love as possible. Thank you.
>
> *(Whitehurst 2015: 201)*

As was explored in Chapter 2, whether or not to physically include Nonhuman Animals in this pro-animal witchcraft will need to be carefully considered. Roderick (1994) offers several rules for this purpose. Nonhuman Animals should only be included if they can consent to do so. They should not be restricted or caged to force their inclusion, the author explains, and they must have freedom of movement. Loud drums and loose incense or candles should be avoided, as should dangerous herbs, plants, and essential oils. Roderick also advises the practitioner remain sensitive to their body language to ensure continued consent, comfort, and safety. He offers quite a few rituals designed to aid companion animals or to include them, even a ritual of dedication to induct and consecrate them as magical subjects in their own right. "One of the usual functions of shamans and witches," they clarify, "is the blessing of animals" and "any animal in the life of a magical worker should be blessed and protected" (1994: 129).

The same consideration will need to be given to the tools used in the craft. Practitioners often use a variety of items to facilitate rituals, such as altar candles, purifying salt, incense, small statues of sacred deities or special images, chalices, a cauldron (for working with fire, candles, or herbs), flowers or other natural items collected from outside, and directional instruments such as wands, athames, or swords. Given the emphasis on the natural connection in ritual work, many tools are animal in origin, actively sought and intentionally incorporated. Valiente's (1978) *Witchcraft for Tomorrow*, for instance, advises using preserved skin and hair from other animals in protection work. She decorates her altar with horns, hooves, and bones from Nonhuman Animal corpses.

Cunningham and Harrington (2001) also advise using the foraged bones of other animals for the altar. These practices draw on pagan totemism whereby the body parts of other animals are thought to be charged with those powers thought characteristic of their species. Patterson (2017a), for instance, explains that bones are a "good way of connecting with the spirit of the animal and working with those energies" (77). This can even include the bones of animals killed and eaten for Sunday dinner, as Patterson recommends, given their ability to add a magical boost to rituals. Antlers, skulls, and shells are also frequently utilized, and this tends to be excused if they are naturally sourced. It is generally not contemplated that the incorporation of these body parts might inflame the objectification and lowered status of Nonhuman Animals, although some comprehension of this oppressiveness does register for some. For example, Weinstein (1991) suggests blessing these items to release any "negative influences" (21). Indeed, she seems rather unconvinced that using body parts in ritual work is appropriate at all. For instance, she argues it is only a stereotype intended to link witches to "barbarism" (2020: 81), and these exploitations "have nothing whatever to do with Witches, who categorically revere all nature" (81). Body parts and sacrifice, she insists, have no magical effect and are linked to witchcraft primarily by those who wish to denounce it. As examined in Chapter 3, however, Weinstein's position is hardly definitive. The utilization of "roadkill" is consistently advised in the discourse. Recall that many, like Andrews, view it as a "tremendous honoring of the life of the animal and of nature" (1993: 221), but this overlooks the carnage imposed on Nonhuman Animals due to human activities and anthropocentric infrastructure.

Nonhuman Animals are also harmed in less conspicuous ways in everyday witchcraft. Candles are perhaps the most ubiquitous, and although most are often made of cheaper non-animal ingredients such as paraffin wax in modern times, those made of bees' wax tend to be coveted given the perceived closeness to nature. Cunningham and Harrington (2001) explain that natural ingredients should be used whenever possible to maximize their available power, as artificial analogs are devoid of energy. For candles, they are specific that bees must be exploited, as beeswax "has the longest history and, as the product of bees, is intimately linked with nature" (92). Certainly, many other natural ingredients can create a candle, but they seem to lack the same allure or practicality as bees' wax. Cunningham and Harrington, for instance, suggest the possibility of crafting candles from bayberry wax as was done in the American colonies, but it is less efficient and bayberries are difficult to source. Soy, a commonly available alternative, is arguably just as natural, but its mundanity likely renders it less attractive.

Feathers, too, are regularly featured in ritual work. Cunningham and Harrington (2001) do advise foraging for feathers rather than purchasing them, but so too do they suggest visiting "zoos" to take advantage of imprisoned birds. In fact, Andrews (1993) offers an entire chapter on the sacred uses and meanings of birds' feathers in *Animal Speak*. He recommends using feathers from totem birds, presumably by foraging, though doing so could disturb them (and may even be illegal). Drawing heavily on Native American spiritualities, he suggests creating a feather headdress for shamanic work but also using feathers in everyday fashion.[10] Down feathers are prescribed for managing empathy, given their closeness to the body of birds, presumably allowing the practitioner to understand the boundary of themselves and of others. Down feathers involve considerable suffering for birds, who are often plucked multiple times across their short lifetimes before eventual slaughter (RSPCA n.d.a). Andrews, however, does not discuss how these feathers might be procured.

Although animal parts seem to dominate many witchcraft sabbats and rituals, they are rarely explicitly required. Many witches insist that no tools whatsoever are really required to practice. Writes Miernowska (2020): "A Witch truly only needs their body, breath, and connection to Spirit to perform rituals of healing, magick, and transformation" (19). Many witches draw specifically on the power of the elements in their ritual work, which can refer to real or imagined beings, weather, and energy associated with the four directions. On the altar, the elements can also be called up through earth, air, water, fire, and sometimes spirit (or creative energy). For many witches, especially Wiccans, earth may be represented by salt, air by incense, water by purified water, sacred well water, or wine, and fire by candle flame. Spirit or energy is more loosely interpreted according to the practitioner, sometimes represented with crystals given their complex molecular makeup and supposed vibrational energy; others may use sacred symbols such as a spiral or pentacle (the pentacle with its five points is itself an embodiment of the five elements). Fundamentally, then, the basic tools of witchcraft are by default vegan; the roots of ritual are not incompatible with a vegan witchcraft.[11]

Cakes and Wine

I have already examined feasting as a central theme to witchcraft in a previous chapter, but everyday ritual work frequently incorporates food given its capacity to soothe and recharge. Starhawk reflects, "I often start groups with a potluck dinner, so that everyone can share a very tangible form of energy: food" (1999: 66). Sharing food and drink, she adds, grounds ritual energy-raising. Vegans are not unfamiliar with the power of food in group work. Vegan protest often incorporates food-sharing to build strong social networks and entice non-vegans to participate; they offer a tangible and embodied means of enacting the future that vegans envision. The rituals of eating, for witches, Wiccans, vegans, and others, are "intended to provoke some sort of awareness and intentionality" (Brumberg-Kraus 2024). The previous chapter explored these provocations at length, but it is worth noting that even the simplest seasonal sabbats often entail ritualistic consumption. This centrality of ritual consumption will of course have ramifications for Nonhuman Animals, who are too often considered ritual consumables. Indeed, consumption, vegan feminism has argued, remains fundamental to the othering of Nonhuman Animals, given its tendency to prioritize the human consumer and objectify the nonhumans consumed (Adams 2003).

Many witches' sabbats and spell casting call for cakes and wine as libation, both being items of indulgence in both agrarian and modern societies. Cakes today often contain copious amounts of animal products, as birds' eggs are usually used to bind ingredients and cows' butter used to frost. Until only recently, vegan cakes were not widely commercially available, necessitating that they be made at home with specialty vegan cookbooks or, for vegans living in major metropolitan areas, obtained from obscure specialty shops. Subsequently, a subcultural fascination with vegan cake rippled through the vegan community in the early 2000s, culminating in bestselling books from pioneering vegan chefs such as *Vegan Cupcakes Take Over the World* (Moskowitz and Romero 2006) and *Ms. Cupcake: The Naughtiest Vegan Cakes in Town* (Morgan 2013). In fact, cupcakes would become such a ubiquitous element of vegan culture that many grassroots organizations began offering a "cupcake for a conversation" at campaigning events. It seems plausible that the vegan cupcake might serve a similarly political yet pleasurable role in vegan witchcraft rituals.

Wine is fundamentally a vegan drink being as it is supposed to be nothing more than fermented grape juice. Unfortunately, in the modern wine industry, standards regarding clarity of the liquid and long shipping distances have encouraged many vineyards to introduce foreign ingredients to improve the appearance and shelf life of the product. One commonly found ingredient is isinglass, a viscous substance obtained from the bladders of certain fishes such as sturgeons. Gelatine may also be introduced and is compiled of various slaughterhouse by-products including bones and hooves. These additions add no flavor; they are simply introduced for aesthetic clarity. As of this writing, vegan wine is rather difficult to source in the United States but is far more normalized in the United Kingdom. In any case, the incorporation of alcohol has been resisted by some witches, who see it as perpetuating dependency. In the case of group ritual, it is also thought to unnecessarily exclude participants who struggle with addiction (Starhawk 1999). Herbal teas and fruit juices have been suggested instead, given their similar connection to the land and harvest. The accommodation of non-alcoholic alternatives thus provides an enticing example of ritual flexibility already in practice. If witchcraft is open to replacing ritual ingredients that could cause harm to some humans, it seems plausible that the same might be extended to other animals. This requires more than simply substituting nonvegan wine for apple juice; it also necessitates a negotiation of flesh-based meals, bees' wax-based candles, birds' feathers, and anthroparchal myths that also serve witchcraft's addiction to speciesism.

Conclusion

This chapter has explored the traditions, myths, and rituals associated with major sabbats in Western witchcraft that aim to affirm women and other marginalized groups in a modern culture largely detached from the natural world. Indeed, these cycles of birth, death, and regeneration are central to the witches' thealogy and most fundamentally align with life-affirming ecological and agrarian happenings such as new growth in springtime and harvest in the late summer. Unfortunately, many speciesist traditions associated with these points of the year (stealing breastmilk from cows and ewes in the spring, for instance, and slaughtering in the autumn) go without critique despite their contrariness to witchcraft's commitment to life-affirming and nature-based alternatives to patriarchal relations. In Western cultures, there are holidays for presidents, civil rights leaders, union workers, veterans, and saints. Witchcraft is one of the only spiritual practices that regularly celebrates Nonhuman Animals, who have also sacrificed (if nonconsensually) for humanity's wellbeing. *Vegan* witchcraft, however, celebrates this sacrifice by recognizing their personhood and working toward a liberatory future where sacrifice is no longer called for. The exaltation of sacrifice and heroism, as vegan feminism reminds, often serves a hierarchical worldview and generally disadvantages marginalized groups. While ritual is so important for individual affirmation and group solidarity, Nonhuman Animals remain largely excluded except as consumable goods. Sympathetic to these oversights, vegan witchcraft seeks to restore a nonlinear, nonhierarchical, nonbinaried, and inclusive recognition of solar, lunar, and social change. In doing so, it advocates creation, adaptability, and pleasure-seeking in support of bountiful and equitable living. The lunar cycle, in particular, with its association with femininity, animality, and alternativity, might serve as powerful inspiration for vegan shadow magic, challenging the speciesist, masculinized qualities of the solar cycle.

Thus, this chapter has also considered how veganism can inform contemporary pagan practice, reflecting on the sociological relevance of religiosity and ritual to create more inclusive traditions that resist rather than replicate anthroparchal systems of oppression. Vegan witchcraft is thus conjured by recrafting the wheel of the year, creating species-inclusive and sustainable sabbat celebrations, rites of multispecies solidarity and nonhuman appreciation, and toolkits, grimoires, and apothecaries that are free of animal body parts and excrements. Vegan witchcraft is presented not simply as a witchcraft that, whether physically or symbolically, *uses* the environment as is so often the case in mainstream witchcraft. Instead, it is one that identifies a shared experience across species boundaries, inviting Nonhuman Animals—and nature itself—into the witch's coven to transfigure an unjust world into one where all are granted dignity, rights, and compassion.

Notes

1 The logos of the American and Australian vegan societies as well as several vegan packaging labels resemble a sprouting plant in the shape of the letter "v"; the UK Vegan Society's logo is a sunflower.
2 Not all nuts are harvested by sustainable or ethical means, however. Many cashews are produced by very poor women in the Global South, and the caustic chemicals associated with the plant burn and disfigure their fingers and hands. Almonds, meanwhile, have been flagged as a particularly unsustainable crop given the considerable amount of water needed to produce them. The industrial exploitation of bees is an essential part of the almond industry as well. Although bees rely on almond blossoms as a nutritious food source, bees in the agricultural system are artificially managed and frequently trucked to sites. This process is extremely stressful, with a high fatality rate. It also displaces native pollinator populations. Of course, choosing only perfectly cruelty-free food can be difficult to achieve, and nuts are an important source of calories and nutrition in a vegan diet, but, generally, aiming for locally produced foods that are certified fair-trade can reduce the negative impact.
3 Outside of Ireland, this is anglicized as *Beltane*.
4 Candle fire in Imbolc, bon fire for Bealtaine, sun fire for Lughnasadh, and hearth fire for Samhain.
5 World Vegan Day and World Vegan Month are also said to be held in November to commemorate the first issue of *The Vegan* authored by Donald Watson, on November 24, 1944 (The Vegan Society 1994).
6 Much of the merrymaking of the Yule season has only been possible with the invisible preparatory labor of women. In Ireland, *Nollaig na mBan* ("Christmas for women") is still celebrated two weeks after Christmas, allowing women a day of respite from the exhausting work of carrying the festivities for their families and community.
7 A reference to Diana, goddess of childbirth.
8 The crescent shape of the waxing and waning moon could be linked to the symbolism of horned animals so revered in British witchcraft or even the lucky horseshoe (Valiente 1962). This symbolism could offer another opportunity to honor the special connection between humans and other animals.
9 Vegan feminism strongly opposes bestiality, but some vegan feminist scholars have considered that zoophilia, the loving of animals and intimate cohabitation with other animals, is both valid and transformative (Rudy 2012).
10 Margaret Robinson (2024b) notes that her own L'nuwey tribe treats feathers as sacred objects that should not be put on casual display and should not be bought and sold.
11 Although many witches prefer to work with incense made of herbs and resin, some rolled incense does contain animal ingredients in the binding material. Given the environmental and human rights violations associated with crystal-mining, vegan practitioners will want to seek ethically-sourced products or substitute with a more readily available (and considerably cheaper) rock they find outside, keeping in mind that many state and national parks and sacred sites the world over forbid collecting and foraging.

References

Adams, C. 2003. *The Pornography of Meat*. London: The Continuum International.
Andrews, T. 1993. *Animal Speak*. Woodbury: Llewellyn.
Barrett, R. 2000. "The Power of Ritual." pp. 185–200, in *Daughters of the Goddess*, W. Griffin (Ed.). Oxford: AltaMira Press.

Barrette, E. 2014. "Imbolc Prayer." Retrieved April 19, 2025, from: https://www.lle wellyn.com/spell.php?spell_id=5472.

Bell, C. 2009. *Ritual Theory, Ritual Practice*. New York: Oxford University Press.

Bitel, L. 2004. "'Hail Brigit!': Gender, Authority and Worship in Early Ireland." pp. 1–14, in *Irish Women's History*, A. Hayes and D. Urquhart (Eds.). Portland: Irish Academic Press.

Brooks, L. 2023. *The Witches Feast*. Salpe Publishing.

Brumberg-Kraus, J. 2024. "Food and Religious Rituals." *Oxford Encyclopedia of Food Studies*. Retrieved August 12, 2024, from: https://oxfordre.com/foodstudies/view/10.1093/acrefore/9780197762530.001.0001/acrefore-9780197762530-e-21.

Buckland, R. 2002. *Complete Book of Witchcraft*. Woodbury: Llewellyn.

Budapest, Z. 1986. *The Holy Book of Women's Mysteries*. Oakland: Consolidated Printers.

Clifton, C. 2006. *Her Hidden Children*. Oxford: Alta Mira Press.

Coley, J. 2020. "Reframing, Reconciling, and Individualizing." *Sociology of Religion* 81 (1): 45–67.

Condren, M. 2022. "Why the Time is Right to Choose Brigid, Saint or Goddess, to Be An Icon For Women." Retrieved February 3, 2022, from: https://www.irishtimes.com/opinion/why-the-time-is-right-to-choose-brigid-saint-or-goddess-to-be-an-icon-for-women-1.4789132?.

Cudworth, E. 2011. *Social Lives with Other Animals*. London: Palgrave.

Cunningham, S. 2003. *Wicca*. Woodbury: Llewellyn.

Cunningham, S. 2007. *Cunningham's Encyclopaedia of Wicca in the Kitchen*. Woodbury: Llewellyn.

Cunningham, S. and D. Harrington. 2001. *Spell Crafts*. St. Paul: Llewellyn.

Davis, K. 2019. *For the Birds*. New York: Lantern.

Ducey, K. 2018. "The Chicken-Industrial Complex and Elite White Men." pp. 1–17, in *Animal Oppression and Capitalism*, D. Nibert (Ed.). Santa Barbara: Preager.

Eller, C. 1995. *Living in the Lap of the Goddess*. Boston: Beacon Press.

Franklin, A. 1997. *Familiars*. Berks: Capall Bann.

Gaard, G. 1997. "Toward a Queer Ecofeminism." *Hypatia* 12 (1): 114–137.

Green, M. 2002. *A Witch Alone*. London: HarperCollins.

Greenleaf, C. 2016. *The Book of Kitchen Witchery*. London: CICO Books.

Greenwood, S. 2000. *Magic, Witchcraft and the Otherworld*. Oxford: Berg.

Helfrich-Förster, C., S. Monecke, I. Spiousas, T. Hovestadt, O. Mitesser, and T. Wehr. 2021. "Women Temporarily Syncronize Their Menstrual Cycles with the Luminance and Gravimetric Cycles of the Moon." *Science Advances* 7 (5).

Kevany, S. and M. Busby. 2020. "It Would be Kinder to Shoot Them": Ireland's Cales Set for Live Export." Retrieved July 15, 2024, from: https://www.theguardian.com/environment/2020/jan/20/it-would-be-kinder-to-shoot-them-irelands-calves-set-for-live-export.

Kheel, M. 2007. *Nature Ethics*. Landham: Rowman & Littlefield.

Lady Sabrina. 2001. *The Beliefs, Rites, and Rituals of the Wiccan Religion*. Franklin Lakes: New Page Books.

Leek, S. 1975. *The Complete Art of Witchcraft*. London: Leslie Frewin.

Lobkowicz, N. 1964. "Karl Marx's Attitude toward Religion." *The Review of Politics* 26 (3): 319–352.

Luke, B. 2007. *Brutal*. Champaign: University of Illinois Press.

Madara, M. 2021. *The Witch's Feast*. London: Nourish.

Madgwick, R., A. Lamb, H. Sloane, A. Nederbragt, U. Albarella, M. Pearson, and J. Evans. 2019. "Multi-isotope Analysis Reveals that Feasts in the Stonehenge Environs and Across Wessex Drew People and Animals from Throughout Britain." *Science Advances* 5 (3): eaau6078.

Mason, J. 1993. *An Unnatural Order*. New York: Simon & Schuster.

Miernowska, M. 2020. *The Witch's Herbal Apothecary*. Beverly: Quarto.

Moffett, L. 2006. "The Archaeology of Medieval Plant Foods." pp. 41–55, in *Food and Medieval England*, C. Woolgar, D. Serjeantson, and T. Waldron (Eds.). Oxford: Oxford University Press.

Morgan, M. 2013. *Ms. Cupcake*. London: Square Peg.

Morningstar, S. 2005. *The Art of Wiccan Healing*. London: Hay House.

Moskowitz, I. and T. Romero. 2006. *Vegan Cupcakes Take Over the World*. Boston: Da Capo Press.

Mulvihill, J. 2014. *The Puck Fair*. Killarney: Killarney Printing.

Murphy-Hiscock, A. 2017. *The Green Witch*. Avon: Adams Media.

Murphy-Hiscock, A. 2018. *The Witches' Book of Self-Care*. London: Adams Media.

Patterson, R. 2014. *Moon Magic*. Hants: John Hunt.

Patterson, R. 2017a. *Witchcraft into the Wilds*. Winchester: Moon Books.

Patterson, R. 2017b. *Animal Magic*. Hants: John Hunt.

Pike, S. 2017. *For the Wild*. Oakland: University of California Press.

Prosser, A., S. O'Neill, L. Witmarsh, J. Bolderdijk, T. Kurz, and L. Blackwood. 2024. "Overcoming (Vegan) Burnout." *Political Psychology*. Online first.

Robinson, M . 2024a. "Indigenous Veganism." pp. 295–313, in *The Plant-Based and Vegan Handbook*, Y. Athanassakis, R. Larue, and W. O'Donohue (Eds.). London: Springer.

Robinson, M. 2024b. "L'nuwey Views of Animal: Personhood and Their Implications." pp. 25–35, in *Animals and Religion*, D. Aftandilian, B. Ambros, and A. Gross (Eds.). London: Routledge.

Robinson, S. 2022. *Kitchen Witch*. Shanagarry: Womancraft Publishing.

Roderick, T. 1994. *The Once Unknown Familiar*. St. Paul: Llewellyn.

RSPCA. n.d.a. "What are the Animal Welfare Concerns with the Production of Down (Feathers)?" Retrieved May 14, 2024, from: https://kb.rspca.org.au/knowledge-base/what-are-the-animal-welfare-concerns-with-the-production-of-down-feathers/.

RSPCA. n.d.b. "Sheep Welfare." Retrieved July 15, 2024, from: https://www.rspca.org.uk/adviceandwelfare/farm/sheep.

Rudy, K. 2012. "LGBTQ...Z?" *Hypatia* 27 (3): 601–615.

Salomonsen, J. 2002. *Enchanted Feminism*. London: Routledge.

Sanchez, C. 1993. "Animal, Vegetable and Mineral – The Sacred Connection." pp. 207–228, in *Ecofeminism and the Sacred*, C. Adams (Ed.). New York: Continuum.

Schofield, P. 2006. "Medieval Diet and Demography." pp. 239–253, in *Food and Medieval England*, C. Woolgar, D. Serjeantson, and T. Waldron (Eds.). Oxford: Oxford University Press.

Scrinis, G., C. Parker, and R. Carey. 2017. "The Caged Chicken or the Free-Range Egg?" *Journal of Agricultural and Environmental Ethics* 30: 783–808.

Shuttle, P. and Redgrove, P. 1978. *The Wise Wound*. London: Marion Boyars.

Sjöö, M. and B. Mor. 1991. *The Great Cosmic Mother*. San Francisco: HarperSanFrancisco.

Sollée, K. 2017. *Witches, Sluts, Feminists*. Berkeley: ThreeL Media.

Spretnak, C. 1993. "Earthbody and Personal Body as Sacred." pp. 261–280, in *Ecofeminism and the Sacred*, C. Adams (Ed.). New York: Continuum.

Squire, L. 2022. *Earth Magick*. Brighton: Leaping Hare Press.

Starhawk. 1987. *Truth or Dare*. New York: HarperCollins.

Starhawk. 1997. *Dreaming the Dark*. Brown: Beacon Press.

Starhawk. 1999. *The Spiral Dance*. Third edition. New York: HarperOne.

Starhawk. 2005. *The Earth Path*. New York: HarperCollins.

Swanson, M. 2013. "How 'Humane' Labels Harm Chickens." pp. 204–222, in *Confronting Animal Exploitation*, K. Socha and S. Blum (Eds.). Jefferson: McFarland & Company.

The Vegan Society. 1994. "World Vegan Day." *The Vegan* 10 (2): 4.

Valiente, D. 1962. *Where Witchcraft Lives*. London: The Aquarian Press.

Valiente, D. 1978. *Witchcraft for Tomorrow*. London: Robert Hale Limited.

Viva!. n.d. "How Sheep and Lambs are Farmed and Killed." Retrieved July 15, 2024, from: https://viva.org.uk/animals/sheep-lambs/#:~:text=Lambs%20are%20sent%20to%20slaughter,of%20their%20natural%20life%20expectancy.

Weinstein, M. 1991. *Earth Magic*. Custer: Phoenix Publishing.

Weinstein, M. 2020. *Positive Magic*. Newburyport: Weiser Books.

West, K. 2002. *The Real Witches' Kitchen*. London: Thorsons.

Whitehead, A. and A. Letcher. 2023. "'We'll All Dance Each Springtime with Jack-in-the-Green': The 'Green Man Complex' in Contemporary British Culture." *Journal for the Study of Religion, Nature and Culture* 17 (2): 228–252.

Whitehurst, T. 2015. *Holistic Energy Magic*. Woodbury: Llewellyn.

Woodward, L. 2021. *Kitchen Witchery*. Woodbury: Llewellyn.

Wrenn, C. 2021. *Animals in Irish Society*. New York: SUNY Press.

6

SPELLWORK FOR A VEGAN WORLD

Introduction

This book has argued that veganism is relevant to magical practice for two key reasons. First, as already discussed, it more accurately aligns the witch with the core values of witchcraft, these being respectful connection and collaboration with nature. Second, as this chapter will explore, veganism encourages an emphasis on the communal elements of witchcraft. As Weinstein muses, witchcraft binds individuals to one another and the universe beyond, "Even though we use our magic to enrich our own lives and those of our loved ones, let us also remember that the ancient role of the witch was to help the community" (1991: 68). Indeed, community service for "unequivocal peace and safety on our home planet" (1991: 69), she insists, is a key facet of practicing witchcraft. Witchcraft, in other words, is in the business of social change.

In *Revolutionary Witchcraft*, Sarah Lyons insists that witchcraft is itself a form of activism because it "requires a living relationship with the land," "emphasizes femininity," predates capitalism, resists dogma, and "resists nihilism and alienation" (2019: 1). Magic, she reminds readers, "is about realizing we can change the world" and also "about realizing we actually change reality all the time, every day, without noticing it" (2019: 2). The material world has considerable influence over humanity, she explains, but this relationship is reciprocal given the influence that humans, too, contribute. Starhawk's definition of magic supports this interpretation, identifying it as "the art of evoking power-from-within" and "the art of liberation" (1987: 6). "To practice magic," she adds, "is to bear the responsibility for having a vision, for we work magic by envisioning what we want to create, clearing the obstacles in our way, and then directing energy through that vision" (1987: 8).

Consistent with vegan feminist theory, this chapter thus presents vegan witchcraft as a practice of anti-oppression, one that explicitly recognizes the

DOI: 10.4324/9781032649801-6

domineering effects of anthroparchal capitalism. It emphasizes that an intersectional lens must be applied to fully theorize and thealogize inequalities that persist today, but it also calls for an intersectional collaboration in resisting these inequalities. To that end, hierarchies must be confronted and the assumption that revolution can be achieved in the marketplace should also be contested. As will be shown, however, debates over equality, diversity, and inclusion indicate that witchcraft's values of interconnectedness and resistance to domination may largely refer to self-interests. This chapter examines politics of choice feminism to illustrate the consequences of self-focused emancipatory politics in witchcraft, namely the capitalist corruption of collective justice work whereby women's liberation is conflated with the freedom to consume and to exhibit a reclaimed identity through purchasing choices. Capitalism is argued to complicate modern witchcraft beyond its feminist leanings, however, given the detrimental influence it wields over human relationships with the Earth and each other.

Witchcraft has thus faced significant political limitations, but it maintains a powerful ethic of resistance and inclusiveness. Witchcraft itself can be understood as a form of activism for this reason. As this chapter will outline, there is indeed a robust history of feminist and environmental activism in the community. Given this substantive engagement with social change politics, this chapter revisits the exclusion of Nonhuman Animals from this magical activism, arguing its comparable relevance to witchcraft and the transformative potential that solidarity with other animals allows. If it is accepted that a plant-based diet and a comradery with other animals are fundamental to human heritage, then it should follow that rejecting the anthroparchal domination of other animals has positive implications for humans as well.

Witchcraft as a Social Movement

Can witchcraft be understood as a social movement? Lyons' position is certainly a common one. Its commitment to agency and change makes it difficult to dismiss as simply a mere belief system, but it should not be presumed that all witches will lean left. "One could not escape the conclusion that Neo-Paganism and the Craft are adaptable to almost any stance on politics" Adler observes, and "the differences were often extreme" (2006: 403). Secular variants of witchcraft could at least be understood as a cultural movement, but the consistent themes of feminist resistance, environmental intervention, and general intent to effect change suggest an underlying political motivation. The rise of witchcraft, recall, corresponded with the counterculture of the 1960s (Clifton 2006), such that many activist elements are prominent in the craft. Adler (2006) records that the political element of witchcraft did not actually come to dominate until the 21st century, particularly its environmentalist component. Greenwood (2000), however, charges that witchcraft and morality have *always* been entangled, especially in light of historical justifications for witchcraft persecution.

Social movement theorists might also disagree on how best to categorize witchcraft. Social movements are notoriously difficult to define (Diani 1992), but at minimum a movement must demonstrate a sustained effort to address social problems and an intention to motivate participation and resonate with the public. It must be contentious, furthermore, and subsequently should not rely on institutional methods of social change (such as voting or lobbying). Witchcraft is certainly contentious and extrainstitutional, but its lack of agreement on what constitutes a social problem and how to address it coupled with its disinterest in recruitment means that achieving a sense of shared identity and solidarity needed to motivate collective action is difficult. For that matter, witches do not all agree on whether or not they should be political, what their politics should be, or what tactics are most appropriate. Explains Cunningham, "Wicca doesn't seek new members. This has been a major stumbling block for those wishing to learn its rites and ways of magic. Wicca doesn't solicit" (1995: xv). He seems wary to "trumpet Wicca as the salvation of our planet" (xv) but concedes that Wicca, as a nature-revering religion, could counter serious systemic injustices, including the threats of war. Cunningham also says of Wicca that "concern and love for our planet play major roles in Wicca" (1995: 5), whereby "the power is in the hands of every practitioner," suggesting that apathy and inaction are not conducive to its practice. His understanding of magic as a "method whereby individuals under none but self-determined predestination take control of their lives" (1995: 20) certainly reflects the ethos of many social movements, comprised as they are of individuals who rebel against social systems that instill control to manipulate societal destiny. Vanderbeck agrees, suggesting that "magic is about harnessing the natural energy that's all around us and within us. Instead of powering the lights, magic powers our dreams and aspirations. It's the energy of imagination, inspiration, and intuition" (2020: 7). This, surely, is the stuff movements are made of.

As previously discussed, the desire to influence others is treated with considerable suspicion in witchcraft philosophy. Yet, activist witchcraft seeks to do just that. If this manipulation is in the service of the greater good as is certainly the case with veganism, might vegan witchcraft make space for this type of wishful encouragement? Witchcraft, after all, is "the work of transformation" (Weinstein 1991: 84), as it focuses on shifting that of the psychic or psychological realm into the material realm. Indeed, manifestation is the primary means of transformative work, accomplished through concentration, belief, and intentional language. For Weinstein, this work not only has ramifications for the material world but for the witch herself, who can become positively transformed through service. Yet, when the power of the individual is married with that of others, the potency of that power only increases. "Shared perception in a group," she notes, "is a powerful way to create just about anything" (1991: 96). Eller (1995) finds a paradox here, noting that many witches embrace the craft for solidarity, empowerment, and community, but this same identity invites persecution given wider sexist norms. How to negotiate a stigmatizing identity and still maintain community is, incidentally, a problem typical of many social movements, including feminism (Moore and Stathi 2020), gay rights (Taylor and Raeburn 1995), and, of course, veganism (Markowski and Roxburgh 2019). It will be up to initiates to wield this resistance to their advantage.

Lyons (2019) maintains that "witchcraft is a verb" (8), and it is "inseparable from politics" having "always contested with political power" (9). Be it left, right, or center, witchcraft cannot escape its underlying interest in creating change, but its position on Nonhuman Animal rights is ambiguous. As I have demonstrated across past chapters, modern witchcraft purports to align with nature and respect other animals, but speciesism remains a consistent feature in theory and practice. Lyons is no exception. Although Lyons' introductory book speaks to social justice for African Americans, Native Americans, trans persons, and even the environment, she does not extend her "revolutionary witchcraft" to Nonhuman Animals. There is room for expansion, however, and the basic tenets of Lyons' witchcraft activism can be repurposed for multispecies magic. For one, Lyons places a consistent emphasis on the importance of connecting to nature and finding power there. They also highlight the importance of allyship with other groups, regardless of their distinctive experiences.

Unfortunately, these are the same principles that have been advanced by many of the 20th-century feminist witches, and none have, as of yet, extended them to other species, with the exception of a few preferred free-living species. Not all 21st-century witch activists remain bound by anthropocentric concerns, however, offering possibilities for multispecies ambitions. David Salisbury's *Witchcraft Activism* (2019), for instance, offers ample advice for affecting social change at the community level and beyond, incorporating the principles of magic and witchcraft to heighten the power and sense of efficacy as does Lyons. Unlike Lyons, however, Salisbury includes other animals as potential beneficiaries of this collective magic-making.

In any case, it is clear that a more comprehensive ideological shift will need to take place to properly include other animals in the witch's political agenda. MacCormack (2020) is perhaps the strongest advocate for a multispecies approach, suggesting that secular spirituality has potential to undermine human supremacy. MacCormack envisions this as manifested in a respectful balance between humans and other species in a non-hierarchical societal structure that resists oppression. This occulture, it is suggested, is a radical reimagination of global cohabitation that rejects the notion of divine entitlement and offers "an entirely adaptable creative mode of activism" that is "absolutely driven by commitment to and compassion for alterity" (2020: 103).

There is a tendency for practitioners to engage the occult for purposes of self-improvement, personal gain, and other egoistical aims, but, to an extent, this is important for overcoming centuries of enforced and internalized helplessness. For women to acknowledge their self-worth and step into their own power is an important point of resistance to patriarchy. Yet, feminism has also succumbed to capitalistic, consumer-driven individualism, falsely equating feminism with purchasing power and "personal choice" (Zeisler 2016). Feminism loses its potency when it is reduced from a collective of conscious collaborators to individualized consumers. This consumerist undermining of political solidarity has been well examined in sociology. Writing in the mid-20th century, sociologist Marcuse (1972) warned of the disenchanting, disempowering, and destructive nature of a technological, bureaucratic society. For Marcuse, this allowed for the proliferation of vacuous marketing and consumerism, and, as a consequence, the average citizen's reduced ability to think critically and to resist inequality. An ahuman occulture could resist this tendency toward disempowerment, but to successfully accomplish this it must avoid the self-serving, individualism that permeates modern witchcraft. MacCormack muses: "Loss of self is a key aspect of occulture's pleasure" (2020: 106).

It is possible that the environmental focus of witchcraft could effectively resist individualism, as it is inherently broader in its area of concern. Environmentalism is thought by many to be integral to the practice. Morningstar (2005) observes that the love of Earth must be integrated into practice, as does Miernowska (2020), who notes: "A Witch is an ally and lover of the Earth who works within the cycles of nature" (21). Leek agrees, advocating a degree of action and personal sacrifice in this allyship:

> Part of the work for witches in the future will be to help in all forms of ecology, in order that good can triumph over evils such as the grave unharmonious states of sickness which pollute the air, water, and countryside.
>
> *(1975: 56)*

This, she emphasizes, is necessary not necessarily for nature's sake but to advance human evolution. To that end, attention to environmental pollution can bring greater attention to internal pollution and imbalance. "We, as members of the Old Religion, acknowledging nature as part of our religion, can only be appalled at the terrible state the ecology is in today" (56), she insists. Andrews (1993), who specializes in shamanic work with other animals, suggests that readers boycott products that come from free-living animals, pick up litter, plant trees, pressure policymakers for nature protection, and educate others about the plight of Nonhuman Animals, "wild" ones at least. In *Wicca*, Cunningham (1995) also encourages environmentalism. To underscore its importance to pagan practice, he charges, "If you're [...] asking yourself what this has to do with Wicca, set this book down and put it away. Or, reread it" (89). Leek muses of witchcraft, "we do not think in terms of a future Utopia, but of means to make life here, *now*, more attractive and harmonious" (1975: 196).

The American feminist witches, of course, have made environmentalism perhaps as central to their practice as their feminism. Like Andrews, Blake recommends several ways that witches might serve the Earth, such as buying organic, buying second hand, saving water, picking litter, and donating to environmental organizations. Not being able to remedy complicated issues of climate change and environmental degradation should not be an excuse to do nothing, she insists: "As Pagans, I believe we have a responsibility to be mindful of the planet we live on and of how we treat its gifts—earth, air, fire, and water among them" (2015: 57). Caring for other animals is included in this stewardship for Blake, who suggests adopting Nonhuman Animals and volunteering in rescue centers. Starhawk centers environmentalism in the very definition of the witch:

> To be a Witch, to practice magic, we can't simply honor nature's cycles in the abstract. [...] It is also a vital base for any work we do to heal the earth and transform the social and political systems that are assaulting her daily.
>
> *(2005: 5)*

Indeed, witchcraft characteristically pairs intention with action. As Adams (1993) reminds us, ecofeminism has been critiqued as hiding in the supernatural and ignoring the real inequalities that require real action to undermine: "We do not dematerialize the sacred or despiritualize matter" (1993: 4). Witches, for the most part, appear to adhere to this principle of complementary spiritual *and* material engagement.

British witchcraft was once regarded as less obligated to the environment, but this is no longer the case. Maxine Sanders has identified this as a defining change of 21st-century British practice:

> I think the Craft has to start taking generally more responsibility for the Mother Earth. We're constantly going on about, 'You know we love, we work with mother nature, we work with the cycles.' Well put your money where your mouth is. Get to work.
>
> *(Sanders 2017)*

Her Temple of the Mother, she recalls, would visit sacred sites to pick up litter—clear up after other practitioners who had left behind rubbish from their rituals. Her group also regularly planted trees and cleared streams. Valiente (1978) echoes this attention to nature with a caution to take care with outdoor ritual fires that could, improperly attended, get out of control and cause harm to the environment and Nonhuman Animals living there. She, too, was wary of climate change, advocating for "peaceful co-existence" (1978: 133). Humans, she suggests, are in a unique position to orchestrate this, witches in particular: "Witches, even more than most people, should be concerned with the preservation of our countryside" (1978: 124). Leek agrees change will be needed:

> Many people are beginning to face facts in their own lives, and consciously seeking to adapt themselves, to fit into a better environmental scene. It will be the first battle, on a huge scale, of mind over matter. Until now, man [sic] survived by deliberately adapting the environment to himself rather

than himself to it. Many people ... have found latent sparks within themselves, components of spirituality—as weapons against pollution.

(1973: 203)

Environmentalism, in other words, is foundational to witchcraft and its commitment to healing. "Now that we know what the problem is, and the diagnosis is clear, we can begin to think in terms of a solution," Leek charges (1973: 204). She is not alone. Many modern witches are clear that healing cannot just transpire at the individual or even at the community level; it must encompass the globe.

A History of Feminist Witchcraft

Feminism, like environmentalism, proliferates in American and British witchcraft, providing further evidence of its association with activism. Eller (1995) observes that the connection comes easily for many: "The journey some women took from secular feminism to feminist spirituality was direct and simple: feminism precipitated such deep and comprehensive changes in consciousness that it already functioned as a spirituality" (42). Although these are major elements in ecofeminism, some feminists see spirituality as a diversion from political goals (Russell 1985). Yet, spirituality can also reshape how marginalized persons see their place in the world, offering them a sense of self-worth and empowerment. Furthermore, it has the capacity to shape culture as a means of reclaiming their power and improving their status. Starhawk sees women in particular as creative forces, makers of culture, and sustainers of civilization (1999). Indeed, for some women of second wave feminism, witchcraft offered an exciting alternative to the oppressive patriarchal institutions that dominate spiritual and political life (Salomonsen 2002).

In working to override Judeo-Christian patriarchal traditions, for that matter, feminist witchcraft is inherently activist. Paganism had worked to resurrect old religions, but this feminist approach, which drew on emerging women-centered research in the humanities and social sciences, attempted to create a new religion instead, one that centered a goddess and feminine creative potential. Paganism and British witchcraft had not always been welcoming of feminist ideas, sometimes finding them too political (Gallagher 2000), but American feminist witches, namely those associated with Starhawk and Budapest, were not bound to these traditions, crediting instead their own personal revelations and feminist politics. Witchcraft ritual offered a means of affirmation, empowering women and creating a "break away from the hegemonic sociological worldview that sexual asymmetry is trans-historical and universal" (Salomonsen 2002: 35). Feminist witchcraft became "a form of resistance to mainstream patriarchal culture," Greenwood adds (2000: 129), healing and raising consciousness: "domination has been internalized through a psychotherapeutic reclamation of a sense of wholeness" (Greenwood 2000: 129).

American feminist witches may have been most strongly associated with this anti-patriarchal agenda, but pagan British witchcraft would eventually adopt a feminist element as well. Valiente's (1978) *Witchcraft for Tomorrow*, for instance, is quite radical in its promulgation of female empowerment, gender equality, and sexual liberation.

That said, it should not be assumed that feminism automatically manifests in witchcraft. The aforementioned Crowley was a notorious misogynist and abuser of women (Valiente 1978), supposedly responsible for psychologically traumatizing women to the point that they required institutionalization or even took their own lives, a sordid history that the current witchcraft community (its men in particular) rarely acknowledges (Jencson 1998). Jencson (1998) has subsequently uncovered continued veins of misogyny and sexual predation in witchcraft, years after Crowley's death. Men, she warns, have sometimes infiltrated goddess worshiping communities as a means of pursuing their own sexual pleasure. Given the community's promotion of sexual freedom and essentialist ideas of ideal femininity, this manipulation is perhaps not so difficult to accomplish. Because quite a few women who turn to witchcraft do so as a measure of escape from repressive and conservative religious communities, furthermore, they may be particularly vulnerable to becoming sex objects and victims of assault. Witchcraft's commitment to sexual liberation, in other words, can also invite sexual predation. Jencson fears that persistent, unchecked ideologies of hegemonic masculinity in the craft ultimately restrict the free and safe expression of women practitioners, as there remains "little use for the Wise Old Crone, the Lesbian, or the Virgin aspects of the feminist Goddess" (1998: 256).

While it is an obvious corruption of the intentions of modern witchcraft, the lack of reflexivity creates a vulnerability for women and other feminized practitioners. This includes Nonhuman Animals. Crowley, by way of an example, was also reported to have practiced bestiality (Jencson 1998). The sexual objectification and exploitation of feminized persons, even if those persons are nonhuman, will certainly undermine any meaningful attempt to achieve women's autonomy and true sexual freedom. The patriarchal degradation of Nonhuman Animals has historically entailed negative implications for women, as they are similarly categorized in anthroparchal culture (Kheel 2007). This risk arguably persists in even the most feminist covens should a clear anti-speciesist stance not be adopted.

Without a clear anti-hierarchical stance, furthermore, the potential for men to dominate in leadership and celebrity is great. This intention to avoid replicating oppressive conditions was one of the core motivations for Kheel's (1985) development of an all-female, consensus-operated vegan feminist collective. Although witchcraft has historically been understood as women's practice, as with many social and cultural movements, the establishment of witchcraft in the 20th century has been largely credited to male leaders. This, too, increases the likelihood of sexism and sexual abuse. Alex Sanders, founder of one of the leading British denominations in the 1960s, is primarily remembered for his partnership with the aforementioned Maxine, but his legacy is ethically troubling. A biography written in his lifetime recounts extremely predatory behavior toward young women, including his wife (20 years his junior) (Johns 1969). Maxine's recollection supports this (Sanders 2017) but adds that his great love for press attention also drew criticism from the witch community, concerned as it was that his egoism ran counter to the healing emphasis of the practice and could invite unnecessary ridicule or danger. As an illustration, one documentary finds him interrogated about the ethics of including a 6-year-old girl in a sky-clad ritual (What Witches Do 2021). The interviewer certainly had reason to be concerned, as Alex concedes that some covens "deflower virgin daughters" on altars. Thus, witchcraft today may be interpreted as an inclusive and female empowering practice, but it has a history of male dominance, female vulnerability, and, in some cases, sexual predation and assault. This patriarchal toxicity would invariably prove prohibitive to the inclusion of other animals, given their categorical association with other women as vegan feminism advanced.

Progenitors of the 19th Century

Fortunately, many witches have understood these intersections, if only implicitly, for some time. Anti-speciesism, feminism, and veganism developed in response to many major societal shifts transpiring at the time in Western societies, including a rapidly increasing wealth gap, urbanization, an industrializing food system, and increasingly powerful institutions of rationality, namely science and medicine. These changes disturbed centuries of social traditions, agrarianism, religiosity, affiliation with natural spaces, and environmental integrity. The disruption also created opportunities for organized resistance in an effort to stymie the more oppressive consequences of modernity and wrest the wave of change for the creation of a more equitable and peaceful society. Not all of these efforts were political in the traditional sense. One consequence of the rapid social change and dramatic increase in scientific knowledge was a renewed interest in the occult. With so many elements of life, nature, and universe suddenly demystified, it seemed that even the metaphysical might also be understood and utilized for social progress. This trend would create the seedbed of modern witchcraft, inspiring the likes of Crowley and Gardner, who sought to wield occultism in the creation of hedonistic lifestyles, but what is less remembered are the efforts of female occultists who believed in the possibility of supernatural resistance to social injustice. Quite a few early feminists were spiritualists or otherwise involved in the occult (Salisbury 2019, Sollée 2017).

This feminist spiritualism sometimes included challenges to speciesism. Juliet Severance, a feminist, abolitionist, and labor organizer, for example, was also a student of psychic healing and advanced vegetarianism for its nutritive and healing properties (Wisconsin Historical Society n.d.). Anna Kingsford, Britain's first qualified female medical doctor, was especially horrified by the burgeoning vivisection industry in the 19th century. Women were disadvantaged by their societal exclusion when protesting men's scientific violence against other animals, but Kingsford's medical training granted her unique access, insider knowledge, and proof that a degree could be earned without harming other animals. She also used her medical training to research the suitability of plant-based eating, contributing to the newly establishing science of nutrition. When science and medicine proved ineffectual in her liberation campaign, she turned to the psychic realm to combat vivisectionists (Ferguson 2022). Kingsford is remembered as one of the first vegetarian feminists, bravely resisting anthroparchal violence in an era that offered little platform to women, but I would suggest that she also be remembered as one of the first vegetarian *witches*, though she might have chosen another moniker. Kingsford reserved the witch identity for her enemies, reframing vivisectionists from objective, calm, scientists to fiendish sorcerers engaged in evil magic who would meet karmic retribution in their next life. She believed that nonhuman victims would have access to an afterlife as well, and this offered some solace and a point of potential communication. Kingsford (1889) regularly worked with Nonhuman Animals on the metaphysical level, claiming that they approached her in séances. These, along with regular dream visions from other animals, informed her path to vegetarianism, and this vegetarianism, in turn, she believed increased her psychic receptivity.

Born thirty years after Kingsford (who died at the age of 41), Lizzy Lind-af-Hageby, a vegetarian and suffragette leader born in Sweden, believed herself psychically bound to her progenitor and also underwent the arduous task of obtaining a medical degree at the turn of the 20th century (Phillimore 1964). She and her partner Leisa Schartau documented their observations of gratuitous vivisection in the highly influential book *Shambles of Science* (Lind-af-Hageby and Schartau 1904), and the two would go on to found the Animals Defense and Anti-Vivisection Society, a long-lived British charity that fought for all manner of anti-speciesist campaigns. Decades before the repeal of the Witchcraft Act, she was also an advocate for spiritualism, incensed by the close-mindedness and gender bias the law exhibited: "There are lawyers, politicians, and physicians who tell 'fortunes' and practice 'witchcraft' of their own brand, decidedly more harmful and disruptive than the visions of the unlettered clairvoyant" (Lind-af-Hageby 1917: 57). Lind-af-Hageby looked to the development of other animals and the science of evolution as inspiration for honing psychic powers and advancing a utopian future: "Nature is unexhausted. Desire and experience are ever creating new forms, new organs. [...] Mind is not arrested by formal obstacles. It builds, destroys, and rebuilds" (1917: 74).

Susan B. Anthony Coven No. 1

Although Kingsford and Lind-af-Hageby may not have identified as witches, the same concentrated intention for ending patriarchal violence and enacting justice through metaphysical means would be taken up by second wave feminists in California a century later. Budapest's (1986) Susan B. Anthony Coven No. 1 exemplifies this new feminist witchcraft-cum-religion. Formed in the early 1970s, No. 1 was loosely influenced by the spiritualist interests and generally inspirational nature of the first wave forebearers and other covens named after similarly powerful women in history springing up elsewhere in the United States. And it was decidedly activist based: "We believe that we are part of a changing universal consciousness that has long been feared and prophesized by the patriarchs," claims Budapest (1986: 1). At the time of *The Feminist Book of Lights and Shadows* publication in 1976, the coven had expanded from its original six witches to include over 200 members. Witchcraft and goddess worship became a radical means of reclaiming feminine power. The goddess-consciousness promoted by Budapest's coven is premised on the defeat of patriarchy and a potential return of the modern world to a "workable, long-lasting, peaceful period" (1986: 12). Indeed, the hierarchical, domineering patriarchal system is thought to hamper human potential, necessitating feminist intervention: "We believe that female control of the death (male) principle yields hummin [sic] evolution" (1). "By developing our spirituality, our mythology, and our rituals, we are going to give birth to new kinds of jobs, needs, inspirations, arts, and inventions" (1976: 6), she continues. A rejection of tradition and a prioritization of creativity is central to Californian feminist witchcraft and a major distinction from 20th-century British variations (Eller 1995). This creativity is both individual and communal as Budapest summarizes: "We gave birth to society long ago and we can remake tomorrow's society by remaking ourselves" (1976: 6).

The spells cast by Coven No. 1 have a distinctive feminist flair, advising on how to magically improve educational attainment, home ownership, employment success, and financial success and deal with harassment and assault. They reach beyond women's issues to assist with the release of political prisoners. One can imagine the psychological effect of a hex against particularly violent men that concludes with the practitioner sticking pins into a doll's genital area. "May patriarchy fall," the spell concludes (Budapest 1986: 58). The Coven's manifesto clarifies its explicit activist aims. Budapest and her ilk tackled many oppressions associated with patriarchy, including environmentalism, rape, child abuse, and abortion. Ritual practice and thealogy, in other words, are not sufficient to manifest the world they envision; there must also be action. Here, witchcraft serves as an important source of power and encouragement for its practitioners, as well as a vision for what could be possible: "To reclaim our souls is the next step in achieving the goals of the movement, after taking back our bodies. We now have to turn the very weapons of culture-making that defeated us gradually, against our oppressors" (Budapest 1986: 18). Indeed, Budapest rejects "cupcakeism" and "turning the other cheek." "This is for Judeo-Cristians," she explains, "not witches" (1976: 84). "Vent your righteous anger magically; send it where it belongs!" (52). These feminist witches understood that casting spells and making magic was a powerful act. Budapest notes that spellcasting is thought a willful undertaking, and rightfully so, as it encourages women to collaborate with nature: "A woman is part of the natural order. Her directed willpower is part of nature" (1986: 31).

The Reclaiming

While the Susan B. Anthony Coven No. 1 was based in Southern California, further north in the San Francisco Bay area, Starhawk's community had coalesced into what would be named The Reclaiming. Based in the goddess tradition, it served as a spiritual support system and a feminist source of empowerment. Starhawk's coven drew perhaps more explicitly on the burgeoning mid-century science of social justice to highlight strategies for community-building and solidarity, active listening, consciousness raising, creative brainstorming, free exchange of feelings and emotions, and reflexivity (Starhawk 1997). The Reclaiming as a center was formed in 1979, prioritizing feminism, environmental direct action, and collaboration with other leftist political groups. Many, if not most, of its membership identified as queer. The Reclaiming dissolved in 1997.[1] According to Jone Salomonsen (2002), this was due to a number of reasons, including the anarchist leadership style (which accommodated a wide diversity of directions), disagreement over whether or not to use witchcraft for profit, and concerns that feminism was becoming overshadowed by other political interests.

The Reclaiming may be defunct, but it remains very relevant in 21st-century witchcraft, and Starhawk, at the time of this writing, remains highly active in leading permaculture training programs and online community rituals. Salomonsen sees Starhawk's witchcraft as being like that of Budapest's—that is, more emancipatory. To this point, Salomonsen observes that Starhawk and many others associated with The Reclaiming emphasized intentional living, reflecting their Jewish and Christian cultural backgrounds. Indeed, quite a few members of The Reclaiming were Jewish; many also continued going to church or temple as witches. Rather than magical power being an "inherent gift" that some witches tout, The Reclaiming instead emphasized "a moral responsibility for the well-being of the world" (Salomonsen 2002: 109). Accountability was expected for those thought to harm the community, a particular draw for women from toxic religious backgrounds. The "power over" mentality that dominates mainstream Western society was itself interrogated by The Reclaiming. Not even women were exempt from this analysis, and reflexivity was invited as an opportunity for personal growth. Oppressive behavior was believed controllable rather than naturally occurring and unavoidable. Personal and community development, likewise, was emphasized, as was the possibility of a healing feminist alternative rebirth and social reintegration through a process of "surrender, love and connection" (Salomonsen 2002: 275). Initiation rituals were used to create new meanings in the everyday, "relinking humans with their source of being, with their fellow humans, with the natural elements, with their Deep Self," and their "body and spirit" (276).

The Reclaiming prioritized the attainment of peace and practices non-violence. As such, it has been actively involved in "all forms of justice," including environmental and social (Starhawk 1999: 6). Witches, Starhawk reports, "have accrued a proud record of involvement in feminist issues, gay liberation, and antinuclear, antiwar, and environmental campaigns" (1999: 7). Despite this wide breadth of campaigning, engagement with the Nonhuman Animal rights movement is conspicuously absent. The coven's deep entanglement with politics of race, nationality, gender, sexuality, environmental integrity, nuclear development, homelessness, war, imperialism, class, and more paired with a near disregard for Nonhuman Animal liberation is striking. Only a short two-page story on Food Not Bombs and a brief reference to its vegetarian policy is included in The Reclaiming newsletter, for instance (Smith 1997).

W.I.T.C.H.

Although less organized and enduring than the covens of Budapest and Star-hawk, W.I.T.C.H. also warrants mention, given its explicit formation for the purposes of protest. As was true of Coven No. 1 and The Reclaiming, "these first feminist Witches did not gather to worship nature" exclaims Eller, "but to crush the patriarchy" (2000: 34). Based in the spectacle of witchcraft imagery and rhetoric rather than that of religion, Eller (1995) credits W.I.T.C.H. for resurrecting witch tropes and politicizing them in the feminist framework. Indeed, the martyrdom that witches of yesteryear represented offered ripe analogy in modern feminist causes.

In the 1960s, activists strategically took on the guise of witches, formulating spells and hexes to creatively campaign for all manner of leftist causes (Sollée 2017). The acronym began as standing for the Women's International Terrorist Conspiracy from Hell, but this would change as needed to inform other campaigns. W.I.T.C.H. formed as a critical response to the radical feminists who wished to remain single issue, reaching beyond pure feminist causes to recognize linked oppressions between women and other marginalized groups. The witch archetype represented one of the most powerful tropes of female deviance, and embodying it as free and powerful women was potent activism. W.I.T.C.H. was not the only feminist group to utilize witchcraft for the demonstrative purposes of protest. Indeed, Adler (2006) recounts that a primary appeal of W.I.T.C.H. was its accessibility to all manner of protesters. Adopting the persona of witchcraft rendered participant actions inherently political, and these benefited from the incorporation of ritual. In one Youth International Party gathering in Washington D.C., for example, a group of some 36,000 attempted to levitate the Pentagon in protest of the Vietnam War. The building may have stayed put, but the spectacle of thousands of deeply intentioned protesters certainly created an impact.

Politics of Inclusion

The craft's alignment with collective action reflects the idea that greater power can be raised through the collaboration of individuals. The social element of group work can elevate the real or perceived effects of spells and rituals. Indeed, given the cultural and activist elements to witchcraft discussed above, a witch never truly practices alone, being always within the sphere of social influences. Many witches, whether activist or not, find community through social channels, be they in-person moots or online TikTok communities. Social movement theory has emphasized these kinds of community—be they historical, contemporary, virtual, or material—as fundamental to the wellbeing and resilience of adherents (Jasper et al. 2015). Collectives facing institutional discrimination and stigmatization in the political environment may be especially prone to forming a sense of shared identity and belonging (Lobbedez and Buchter 2023). Indeed, radical inclusion has become a cherished value in modern witchcraft.

Practicing witches today may not face the stake, but they do face social ostracization, job discrimination, and harassment. The exclusivity and relative clandestinity of coven work, however, has proved difficult for mobilizing beyond existing networks, particularly as witchcraft is not a proselytizing religion or practice (Russell 1985). Initiation rituals, too, may be explicitly worded to maximize inclusivity but can find difficulty in prioritizing group solidarity while also remaining open to newcomers. This identity dilemma is well documented by social movement scholars (McGarry and Jasper 2015) but is likely all the more conflictual for the witchcraft community given its ardent individualism.

Even so, inclusiveness remains central to witchcraft. Younger women and older women especially benefit in being granted more respect and space than is often allowed in mainstream society. This extends to sexual identity as well. Monteagut summarizes, "The witch breaks the boundaries of gender and sexuality and empowers those on the margins who have historically been oppressed by mainstream religions. The witch kept me safe when I didn't have any other way to express my queerness" (2021: 151). Gay activist Arthur Evans (1978) saw magic as a birthright today denied to humans, given the crushing oppression of colonization, patriarchy, and capitalism, identifying the ways in which heterosexism finds roots in the burning times and reclaiming witchcraft for gay resilience and resistance. Christopher Penczak (2004) adds that "'all acts of love' are acts of worship to the Goddess. Sexual preference [does] not matter" (236). In fact, their ownership of witchcraft served their homosexual acceptance, lifting them from the "spiral of doubt and fear" (Penczak 2004: 238). Doreen Valiente, too, was in support of gay rights (*Wicca Magazine* n.d.). Based in San Francisco, The Reclaiming was especially motivated to accommodate.

Just as often, however, modern witchcraft spaces are active facilitators of that discrimination. Homosexuality, for instance, has been a major point of debate in the witchcraft community throughout the 20th century, albeit less so today (Coombes 2004). Leek (1975) worries that, despite their empathetic strengths, the capacity of homosexual people to rise in the ranks of witchcraft leadership is limited. Witchcraft, she surmises, could be an important respite from rampant persecution in patriarchal religions. When asked her position, Maxine Sanders (2017) argues that sexuality and gender are irrelevant, though she, like Leek, suspects that homosexual men are more sensitive to their magical power than their heterosexual counterparts.

Challenging Binaries

Some have been less accommodating. Z. Budapest was reported to have turned away several trans women from a woman-only workshop, for instance (Salisbury 2019). Even Starhawk (1999) takes a liberal view to organizational inclusion styles, suggesting that covens can remain open to all genders or, if needed, restrict access to particular genders or sexes. Her primary concern is to allow leadership without establishing hierarchies that squash autonomy. Although the reality of men's violence and tendency to dominate group events means that having women-only spaces is important, the active exclusion of those who do not fit squarely in the biological or stereotypical definition of a "woman" undermines feminist politics of care and compassion.

This is not only a measure of reactive feminism. Cis men, too, have protected these constructed binaries. Grimassi (2001) celebrates pagan androcentrism and is skeptical of feminist efforts to undermine it. "Despite the modern opinions of certain political groups," he writes of feminism, "true men do not as a whole consciously oppress or abuse women" (2001: 236). For Grimassi, it is "natural for men to compete and maintain social leadership roles stemming from ancient drive that first formed the Hunter/Warrior cults" (236). This "natural" dominance and aggression, he further argues, makes pornography consumption acceptable.[2] Presumably this extends to an entitled access to women in the everyday, since men, according to Grimassi, are supposedly unique in their requirement for visual stimulation. By framing these requirements and behaviors as deviant, he concludes, it is feminism that is truly at fault for men's sexual disfunction and abuse. Essentialist tropes that link entire groups of people to imagined, unsubstantiated historic identities, in other words, have proved just as problematic for women and queer folks as they have for other animals.

The binaries protected by Budapest and Grimassi are culturally specific and tend to reflect Western norms. Greater fluidity is recognized by many Indigenous cultures (Monteagut 2021), and, increasingly, the utility of the gender binary itself has been questioned (Coombes 2004). Starhawk (1999) has more recently renounced a rigid adherence to male and female polarities as unnecessary in witchcraft. Certainly, many important leaders in 20th- and 21st-century witchcraft have eschewed heteronormative gender expectations as well. Indeed, many have been gay or bi/pansexual, including Alex Sanders, Starhawk, Scott Cunningham, and Z. Budapest. The Reclaiming, recall, was also disproportionately lesbian (Adler 2006, Eller 1995), while the gay community, particularly in the New York City area, also integrated magical practice into its early activism (Adler 2006, Salisbury 2019). Selena Fox, who identifies as queer and gender non-conforming, offers trans-inclusive ceremonies at her Circle Sanctuary and on social media platforms, even founding the Gay Liberation group (now the Lambdas Society) at her alma mater William & Mary in 1969 (Fox 2019).

Binaries are not only unnecessary but can easily render invisible anyone who does not fall into the cis-gendered framework. Magic happens within *and* without binaries. Recall that circular organizational styles are preferred in witchcraft to combat the tendency toward binaries in Western society and ensure a "mutual bond of love and trust which transcends individual prejudice and dissolves any sense of incongruity or reserve brought in from the desacralized cosmos" (Jones and Matthews 1990: 35). Starhawk adds: "There is no hierarchical authority, no Dalai Lama, no Pope. The structure of Witchcraft is cellular, based on small circles whose members hare a deep commitment to each other and the Craft" (1999: 59). Leadership will inevitably be required, of course, but this leadership should be taken with great responsibility and be based on the contributions of others in the group and shared: "The more influence we have in our communities, the more responsibility we have" (Starhawk 1999: 268). Unchecked anthropocentrism, however, offers no responsibility to other animals, who are rarely, if ever, included in this consensus-making, especially if they are labelled as food. Witchcraft that does not confront its maintenance of the species boundary cannot be said to be free of hierarchical authority.

Behringer (2002) suggests social Gaianism as a means of living beyond binaries. There are many structures that permeate nature, she adds, and they might inspire more suitable types of social relationships. Branches of a tree, for instance, suggest functional hierarchies, whereby all parts of the whole serve a particular function. Nonhuman Animals are presumably placed lower than humans in this metaphorical tree given her rejection of vegetarianism. Sociologists have noted that this functional idealism tends to obscure power more generally, naturalizing socially constructed roles for groups (Davis and Moore 1945). Gender roles, which disproportionately burden women with housework and childcare and men with paid work and political engagement in the public sphere, for instance, have been promoted and replicated with this functionalist logic. The inequality in power, resources, and quality of life that results thus escapes critique, given a presumption of efficiency and a presumption that women's drudgery and men's prowess are innate. Human relations with other animals interpreted within this functionalist logic lend Nonhuman Animals to fill the "natural" function of feeding, clothing, and entertaining humans. Thus, ideological interpretations of "nature" can buttress even the most egregiously unequal social roles.

The spiral structure promoted by Starhawk is perhaps more useful here, as it erodes hierarchies, beginnings, endings, and inequalities. Circular formations, she notes, are more democratic, and "everyone will have a chance to look into each other's eyes" (2005: 194). Indeed, circles are regularly found in ancient pagan art and architecture, indicating the importance this formation would have had for community (Jones and Matthews 1990). If only Nonhuman Animals were seen and recognized she and other witches might look into their eyes as well. Unfortunately, only a handful of nonhuman species—primarily those romanticized as charismatic wildlife—are socially perceived.

Advancing Justice

The invisibility of racial difference, too, misaligns with anti-hierarchical, anti-authoritarian values. White-centrism and settler-colonialist ideations have been critiqued in modern witchcraft, particularly that of the 20th century (Eller 1995). Indeed, most, if not all, of the foundational texts on Western witchcraft are authored by white women and often appropriate from Indigenous cultures. People of color have also noted their feelings of discomfort or experiences of outright exclusion from witchcraft communities (Karade 2004). For instance, Alexis Nikole Nelson (also known as "The Black Forager"), a vegan social media influencer specializing in wildcrafting, has been open about the importance of her work in normalizing Black participation. It is not simply that foraging and plant magic are white-dominated subcultures, for indeed, Indigenous peoples of the Americas and the African diaspora have their own historical relationship with gathering plants for sustenance, healing, and spiritual practice (Monteagut 2021). Wild spaces also offered important shelter for Indigenous and enslaved peoples eluding bondage. That said, wild spaces could also be dangerous for people of color, as the ambiguousness and anonymity of these spaces meant that all manner of white supremacist harassment and violence could take place within them without repercussion. Racial segregation of outdoor recreational areas also prohibited people of color from entering a number of natural spaces. To this day, African Americans have much lower attendance rates in America's National Parks. Environmental groups and recreational organizations have been thusly criticized for constructing nature through a white European lens and failing to acknowledge variations in experiences and needs with regard to the environment (Finney 2014).

More fundamentally, the colonial separation of people from land, which entailed the disruption of traditional foodways and environmental knowledge, would create long-lasting vulnerabilities. People of color are subsequently engaged in their own projects of reclaiming. Monteagut (2021) describes the witchcraft practiced by people of color in the West as deeply entangled with the legacies of colonialism, perseverance, resistance, and healing. White-identified and white-presenting witches alike, she suggests, would do well to face "the shadow" of racism and colonialism, and thus acknowledge the ways in which they benefit from this shadow, which serves as an ally to those who carry the cost (2021: 197). For Riley (1993), the wide diversity of precolonial African belief systems and African women's leadership in the Global South could serve as inspiration. Riley also advises supporting Afrocentric ecowomanism as a form of resistance, empowerment, and sustainable living.

Vegan witchcraft will need to consider this and more, as race has often shaped the relationship between women and other animals. Women of color have historically been animalized in distinctive, arguably more potent ways than white women (Jackson 2020). For many women of color, there is understandably a vested interest in owning their humanity and staying well clear of animality (Ko 2019). Honoring shared animality across species may prove difficult in a white supremacist society that has historically couched racism in speciesist constructions. Until animality itself is uplifted as a measure of celebration and shared identity, it will continue to thwart intersectional efforts in witchcraft. Many white-identified witches are aware of these racial politics and do earnestly work with sensitivity and respect, Starhawk being one: "We need to notice ways in which our community fails to reflect the diversity around us and ask if we are subtly excluding people," she warns, "We need to ask: What are the interests of the most oppressed in this situation, and how can we serve them?" (1999: 261). Her anthropocentric focus, however, ensures exclusion, not just for Nonhuman Animals but for the human groups whose oppression is bound to their association with other animals. A radically expanded circle of compassion will be necessary, not only to disempower racism but to demystify humanity to reclaim animality for all. This may require a change of perspective, one that destabilizes the role of antagonism in advocacy. "What if revolution is not a fight?" Monteagut asks (2021: 163), championing the value of integrating the traditions of immigrant and Indigenous people of color into activism. A diverse witchcraft community, she underscores, might yield a more peaceful and no less powerful form of resistance, a strategy she envisions as "an opening to more and more love" (163).

Although a radical reclaiming of animality will be necessary to move beyond many structures of oppression, there are some ways that mainstream Western witchcraft will need to address inequalities in racial representation. Save for Valiente's brief (and unexplained) membership in white nationalist groups in the mid-20th century (*Wicca Magazine* n.d.), popular witchcraft discourse has tended to be more implicit than overt in its racism, centering white women practitioners despite the long legacy of witchcraft for resilience and resistance in communities of color. The persistence of witchcraft in non-Western countries (particularly those in Africa as well as India and Papua New Guinea), furthermore, warrants little mention, though its persecution involves the terrorization and sometimes killing of hundreds of vulnerable humans and other animals each year (United Nations 2020). This will be a fruitful endeavor not only for uplifting excluded practitioners, but the practice itself would benefit from acknowledging the diversity of crafts and wisdoms as they relate to inequality and social change. Difference, as Black feminist Audre Lorde (2017) has emphasized, should be a point of strength, not weakness.

Vegan Witchcraft as Anti-Capitalism

The difficulties with binaries, hierarchies, and equality in the Western witchcraft community are not unlike that experienced in conventional feminist circles. The feminist movement's struggle to manage identity politics and inclusivity, furthermore, has been complicated by the perils of capitalist co-optation. Witchcraft, too, has faced this quandary. From its 20th-century inception, witches have debated the monetization of its ceremonies, rituals, spells, and magical miscellanea. Craft leaders in the 20th century have been very explicit on the rejection of charging for a witch's services beyond that which is needed to cover time and labor (Starhawk 1999). Lyons (2019) suggests that the threat of capitalist co-optation is an extension of wider processes of privatization and commodification that created the feelings of disenchantment and alienation that draw practitioners to witchcraft in the first place. Feminist witchcraft, as Starhawk and Budapest have envisioned it, is pleasure-seeking—prioritizing feasting and lovemaking—and celebratory. As I explored in Chapter 5, it is easy to see how this might slide into pleasurable consumption as well. Yet consumer culture, they argue, can run counter to the core beliefs of witchcraft. Indeed, Adler (2006) identifies this resistance to profit as one key distinction witchcraft holds among other religions. Change is thought to come from within, from community, and from freely available natural elements. But, as Sollée notes, "hex sells" (2017: 131). For witches of color, this encroaching consumerism can pose additional complications, as providing spiritual products and tools can be an important source of income in a society that economically discriminates against them. However, given the long history of colonial exploitation, white consumerism of non-white spirituality risks objectifying witches of color and perpetuating colonial pathways in harmful ways (Monteagut 2021).

Berger and Ezzy's (2007) study of teenage witches in the United States, Britain, and Australia has noted that witchcraft as a "new religious movement" is unique in its self-centeredness. This, they suggest, reflects the utilization of witchcraft as an identity marker. Development of the self, of course, is a key element of the teenage experience, but individualism dominates in witchcraft regardless of age. By the late 1970s, the idea of witchcraft as a sort of secret society that requires initiation and group work began to be replaced with the idea of the "lone witch" (Davies 2021). For this reason, understanding witchcraft as anything more than a personal or loosely connected secular or spiritual practice or a consciously grouped social movement may be difficult. "Witch" offers an identity status, but identity in the postmodern West is highly individualistic, being manufactured through capitalist consumption more often than a sense of solidary to others. The alienating nature of capitalism tends to prohibit collaborative interest in challenging capitalism, encouraging self-interestedness and deliberately masking the oppressive relationships that proliferate in capitalist production that might disturb this individualistic orientation. Subsequently, the reduction of witchcraft to identity, Sollée explains, obscures its potential for collective resistance and large-scale social change.

The covens of 20th-century witchcraft have been all but replaced by solitary witches in sequestered practice who supplement the diminished communal aspects of the witch identity through heavy consumption. The witches' market is infinite with its offerings of crystals, books, oracle cards, tarot decks, incense, candles, herbs, jewelry, and more. This disconnection could be disempowering, undermining the witchcraft community's potential to disrupt the stigma and discrimination placed on witches, women, and nature. It also obscures those harmed in the capitalist system, a system that increasingly dictates the witch's identity and its expression. The extraction, production, and circulation of witchcraft paraphernalia, notably crystals and white sage, is linked to considerable environmental degradation in areas that are disproportionately inhabited by communities of color. Crystals, in particular, are often mined in *tonnes* by child laborers in the Global South earning a pittance in dangerous conditions as a means of sustaining their families living in deeply impoverished conditions. It also utilizes the exploitation of Nonhuman Animals, who are made to cart heavy materials where landslides and mine collapses are common (DW Documentary 2023). In fact, many witchcraft products rely on the exploitation of workers in the developing world (Sollée 2017). Neither has veganism escaped the spell of late-stage capitalism and its encroachment into all aspects of social life (Sexton et al. 2022). As veganism is increasingly conflated with personal identity and fixates on exciting new products, food services, restaurants, holidays, weddings, and other things for sale, humanity's obligation to uplift Nonhuman Animals is rendered invisible (Wrenn 2024). Mainstreaming witchcraft and veganism has been very much facilitated through the open market, but this has come with the trade-off of diluting them of their ethical and spiritual foundations.

A Witch Alone

Individualism is a concern in this larger context of capitalist co-optation because it discourages collaboration, cooperation, and consensus. Individualism serves capitalism in disrupting solidarity and prioritizing self-interested consumer behavior, but it has also been celebrated for championing personal freedom and facilitating human rights. For groups that have been historically marginalized by social institutions and suppressed with expectations of conformity, individualism has been an important expression of modern independence. Witchcraft is popular with many precisely *because* it accommodates individualism. "Wiccans are taught to think for themselves," explains Lady Sabrina, and to "take responsibility for their lives" (2001: 13). Eller (1995) also emphasizes this element as central to the Californian feminist branch of witchcraft, which prioritizes consciousness raising and inner journeying, noting the influence of therapeutic groups such as Alcoholic Anonymous that aid in helping individuals to cope with trauma. Indeed, feminist witchcraft became a sort of do-it-yourself accessible therapy, whereby the individual does not just worship the divine but comes to understand themselves as divine as well (Adler 2006, Griffin 2000).

Yet, individualism renders community building difficult. As I have shown, witchcraft ultimately prioritizes self-directedness and personal agency; moral actions are not strictly ordered as is the case in institutionalized religions (Greenwood 2000). Here, also, there are parallels with veganism. There are many more individuals who adopt the vegan identity than there are activists. Indeed, sometimes even the vegan identity does not align with vegan practice, as more people today adopt aspects of veganism or vegetarianism as a means of accessing the associated morality (Wrenn 2020). Here, too, witches may benefit from "facing the shadow" of speciesism, deliberately acknowledging the ways in which humans benefit from the oppression of Nonhuman Animals and choosing to serve as their allies rather than their consumers. Vegan witchcraft must subsequently contend with the depoliticizing aspects of individualism, consumerism, and capitalist co-optation, a potentially difficult task given the great popularity of choice feminism and pop witchcraft, which encourage the uncritical consumption of endless products, even those based on killing or exploitation of other animals.

Both witchcraft and veganism have struggled to advance alternative lifestyles without succumbing to a consumption-oriented expression. YouTube influencer HearthWitch heavily promotes new products on her channel and operates her own online shop but is nonetheless careful to remind her audience that amassing a large collection of witchcraft sundries is completely unnecessary:

> You do not need a massive library of books or a collection of magical items to be a successful practitioner. Witchcraft is not about the books that you own, it's not about the things that you have, it's about you, your connection to the energy and your practice.
>
> *(HearthWitch 2024)*

The vegan movement, similarly, has fought hard against the stereotype that veganism primarily entails buying expensive "meat" and dairy analogues. While convenient and highly processed "alternative proteins" that realistically resemble the body parts or excretions of other animals can be more expensive than their animal-based counterparts (for a variety of systemic reasons that do not reflect the true cost of production), plant foods, with their greater affordability and efficiency in production, have formed the bulk of the global diet for the majority of the world's peoples for many thousands of years. An Oxford study, in fact, has identified that a vegan diet on average costs just a third of that exacted by "meat"-based diets (Springman et al. 2021). Consumerism, therefore, can significantly detract from the political possibilities of collective action and must be carefully considered.

Magical Thinking

Despite the peculiarities of witchcraft as an especially individualist, somewhat consumerist, and sometimes religious practice, there are many fundamental ways in which it remains complementary to social justice activism. Witchcraft aids in establishing intent (through meditation, candle burning, and so on) and creates a sense of self-efficacy with practices such as breathwork, chanting, and movement. For Salisbury (2019), magic offers a sense of protection, confidence, and strength. Setting intention and envisioning alternatives is the basis of modern magic. For Whitehurst, its manifestation capabilities can be raised by employing "vibrant visualization" (2015: 14), bringing the future into the present consciousness, bridging "the gap between what you desire and what is," and making it "highly likely that it will flow into your life experience" (2015: 11). For Starhawk (1999), magic is reclaiming culture, practicing agency by manifesting the ideal world. Eller (2000), too, emphasizes that witchcraft practiced as a spirituality can encourage an imagination for utopian possibilities and socialize practitioners into political engagement.

Within the Nonhuman Animal rights movement, too, professional advocates often allege that believing a vegan world is possible constitutes magical thinking. Because the movement (like many movements) is male-dominated and caters to rationality and rational organizational structures, emotion and imagination are subject to denigration and dismissal (Wrenn 2019). Here witchcraft may be especially helpful. Lyons summarizes: "Small steps can be necessary to reach our goals, but sometimes we are sold small steps to keep us from imagining bigger ones. Besides, even if our steps must sometimes be incremental, why can't our dreams be big?" (2019: 59). Ultimately, magical thinking is liberatory thinking. Activists might avoid this magical framework as a matter of respectability politics, but Starhawk counters that doing so is self-defeating: "when we [...] cease to care if people see us as woo-woo, suddenly we can think about anything. We expand the range of our inquiry beyond the categories already fixed in our minds" (2005: 27). It is the "constriction of our imagination," she argues, that normalizes and sustains an unjust world. Magical thinking entails a conscious acknowledgment of how socialization and mental schemas can shape perceptions and realities. As Lyons describes it, "the art of dreaming—of dreaming big—and pulling things out of the realm of imagination and into this world is what good magic is all about" (2019: 60).

Witchcraft, then, is symbolic ritualism that socializes practitioners as capable, building resilience. It is not only the non-magical but also the magical community that will benefit from more magical thinking. As impossible as it may seem to build a society that is not dependent on speciesism, imagining it as possible is the first and most important step. Spells made by individual witches and covens may not create immediate change, but they are recognized as psychologically important for changing attitudes and subsequently the propensity to change. As was seen in the chapter on familiars, shapeshifting is often advised as a means to gain another perspective. Starhawk (1999), too, advises meditative shapeshifting, for purposes of inclusiveness, creating empathy, and bringing other animals into the circle. Indeed, her own taken name came from one such dream vision. Vegan witchcraft might adopt this mindful shapeshifting to develop empathy with other animals and improve inclusivity. Setting an intention to disrupt suffering will be key. Budapest identifies pain as a "primordial evil" and encourages witches to "actively interfere with avoidable, meaningless pain, wherever and however possible" (Sophia 1986: 118). Eating and exploiting other animals, particularly in the wealthy West, seems one of the most fundamental variants of meaningless pain that might easily be interfered upon by way of veganism. The interconnectedness that veganism promotes not only reduces the primordial evil of pain but the patriarchal wickedness of conflict as well.

Further gleanings might be taken from Starhawk and Budapest, despite their apologetic stances on speciesism. As discussed previously, feminist witchcraft is unique in making space for grief, an inevitable emotion that burdens all social justice activists. Communal grief work, Starhawk advises, is helpful for consciousness raising, finding solidarity, and discussing painful emotions and memories that may not have other venues for expression (2005). Incorporating ritualistic measures of closure can build resilience and replenish activists' minds and bodies. Using magic to support vegan transition will also be important. Budapest also offers spellwork for purification following sexual assault, which entails bathing in cleansing herbs and other soothing and restorative measures. Budapest explains, "To reclaim our souls is the next step in achieving the goals of the movement, after taking back our bodies" (1976: 107). Might this also be adapted to those who are seeking a transition to veganism? Vegan witchcraft will also require a reclaiming of plant power. Many witches, recall, see plants as allies, especially those who walk the green witch or kitchen witch path. Starhawk (2005) advises entering into deep communication with plants to achieve these connections. Veganism, however, advises deep communication with all plants *and* animals, as nonhuman species can act as allies, too. Vegan witchcraft is energized through plant-based consumption, a practice that supports the physical health of adherents but also fulfills them emotionally, as vegan food is an important source of pleasure and joy in a world of normalized and widespread violence against other animals.

To this end, ancestor working may also prove useful for remembering the considerable injustice done to nonhumans and making space for both humans and other animals to find peace and cope with the legacy of tragic death. Mallorie Vaudoise (2020) suggests incorporating forgiveness as some means of coping with ancestral trauma, even creating memorial art to cope with grief. "The process of forgiveness can manifest in a renewed commitment to truth-telling and activism" (34), she advises. W.I.T.C.H., the aforementioned feminist protest group from the 1960s, capitalized on the heightened energy of Halloween and altered the meaning of its acronym to align with its campaign intentions. Might vegan witchcraft try the same? As Sollée (2017) observes, powerful women today continue to be derided, dismissed, and harassed as witches. Perhaps there is room for vegan feminism to reclaim this misogynistic archetype, with particular reference to the cultural connection forged between women and other animals. This magical thinking will also be grounded in the material. Art, imagery, and even music, she suggests, can be used to advance social justice and undermine sexism, countering the misogynistic spectacles of witchcraft trials and executions and the persecution of women and other marginalized groups that persists today. Creating rituals for honoring Nonhuman Animals and managing the intense emotions tied to veganism and ant-speciesist activism with the use of creative endeavors will be an important element for a new vegan witchcraft.[3]

There is evidence that some witches are incorporating these practices in their anti-speciesist efforts. In the early 1990s, for instance, the *Feminists for Animal Rights Newsletter* announced the formation of a new sister group in New York, Witches for Animal Rights. Witches for Animal Rights (1994) rallies fellow witches by imploring them to "save the world with your fork" (15). Feminists for Animal Rights (1994) explains that "members worship the God-dess by promoting the wellbeing of her nonhuman animals" (16), suggesting that interested readers contact the Morningstar Coven in McDonough, New York. Witches for Animal Rights also surfaces in the record as a performing group in "No RIO," an anti-gentrification guerrilla project in New York City that provided space and platform for radical artists and activists (Forte 1989). Likewise, in the 2010s, The Protego Foundation formed from a group of Harry Potter fans who contextualize their anti-speciesist activism in the magical crea-tions of J. K. Rowling. A registered nonprofit, The Protego Foundation (n.d.) "fights to end the abuse of the animals in the Muggle world through our inspiration from the magical creatures in the wizarding world [...] empowering all magical persons to get active for animals" (no page). Likewise, Gregory Maguire's (1995) retelling of the "Wicked" witch of Oz sees her (Elphaba Thropp) as a social justice activist who advocates for Nonhuman Animals and the environment. Vegan feminist scholar Christopher Sebastian (2020) suggests that her skin is green as a symbolic reference to her advocacy for nature and other animals, but also to mark her as a monstrous other in protesting the violent social stratification of Oz, where the oppression of humans and other animals are explicitly entangled.

Conclusion

Modern witchcraft can be understood as a lifestyle, a secular practice, a spiri-tuality, or a religion. It can also be understood, in some contexts, as a social movement. It is certainly political in recognizing the individual's innate wisdom, capacity for learning and developing skills, and ability to change their circumstances rather than passively subject themselves to societal pressures and patriarchal caprices. Witchcraft is also political given its feminist prioritization of self-care in a society that has traditionally shamed women who were seen to put their needs above others. Of course, it is also political in resurrecting ancient pagan connections to the natural world, connections that most institu-tionalized religions have worked for centuries to eradicate. This chapter has demonstrated that witchcraft characteristically advocates eco-pride over eco-cide, and adherents are encouraged to take responsibility for healing nature. It has also shown that witches of color, who are burdened by systems of colonialism, racism, ethnocentrism, and classism in addition to sexism and religious marginalization, may be more prone to recognizing the inherent activism to their practice (Monteagut 2021). However, the most central aspect of witchcraft—the belief in practitioners' ability—as individuals or collectives—to create change through intention and spellwork—makes it an activist-oriented practice, even if witches do not identify as activists. The idea that one can resist and recalibrate authority, the status quo, and hegemony is profoundly radical, especially if the aim is to challenge inequality. Indeed, an imagination for change is itself fundamentally political.

Greenwood insists the purpose of witchcraft is to resist "social alienation and fragmentation from the self" (2000). Yet, if women and other marginalized groups remain alienated from Nonhuman Animals and their own animality, surely they will reproduce this fragmentation. Although stigma and persecution have ensured that many modern witches work in secret and hide their identity, witchcraft is experiencing a cultural renaissance largely in part to its alignment with middle-class white womanhood. The persecution and mass murder of white women during the burning times is abhorrent and worthy of contemporary efforts to remember and reclaim, but there has been a tendency to deprioritize the comparable persecution of other marginalized groups. People of color, non-binary and trans people, and Nonhuman Animals, I have evidenced, find a precarious solidarity despite having experienced comparable exclusions and persecutions. Not unlike white-identified cis-gender women accused of witchcraft, their oppression is premised on a presumed lack of humanity and their perceived threat to society. The heavy debate over the inclusion of homosexual people in the 20th century witchcraft discourse is an important caution that radical inclusivity is not guaranteed in the craft; Nonhuman Animals may continue to wait in the margins for some time to come. Some 21st-century witchcraft communities are coming to recognize intersections of race, class, gender, and sexuality, but the attention granted to other animals remains wanting.

Vegan witchcraft, I have suggested, might be better positioned to negotiate this troubled inclusiveness by encouraging a structural analysis of otherization that compels witches to reconsider the exclusion of others based on cultural constructs, particularly those associated with animality. The vegan witch path is a feminist one that requires individual responsibility as well as collective consciousness. It necessitates a careful overriding of anthroparchy's normalized domination over the natural world and an embracing of the deep empathy that resides within the human species. The hierarchies, binaries, and categories that have been introduced and maintained by this system of domination, particularly under colonialism, invite magical confrontation. Some of these confrontations have been summarized here, including the efforts of anti-speciesist pioneers such as Anna Kingsford, Lind-af-Hageby, and Witches for Animal Rights. Feminist and environmental contributions from Susan B. Anthony Coven No. 1, The Reclaiming, and W.I.T.C.H. Witches of color, too, have introduced pivotal theories and strategies for magical activism that might inform a vegan witchcraft grimoire. Strength is more readily found in diversity and informed magical thinking, it has been argued, than exclusivity, individualism, and consumerism.

Notes

1 By 1990, The Reclaiming began moving toward nonprofitization, which it achieved in 1994, creating a hub for its dispersed community and requiring a reorganization of its agenda (Eller 1995). Following this shift, it began to center fundraising, upgraded its newsletter to a magazine, and lessened its focus on San Francisco. In its informal years, the reliance on friendships and networks to bind the group left many in the margins; as an official charity, however, The Reclaiming became more inclusive.
2 As this book was originally published in the 1990s, this is likely a response to the anti-pornography campaigning of second wave feminism.
3 Some witchcraft texts do include spells for dealing with the loss of a companion animal. Grimassi (2021) offers a ritual for the death of a familiar.

References

Adams, C. 1993. *Ecofeminism and the Sacred*. New York: Continuum.
Adler, M. 2006. *Drawing Down the Moon*. London: Penguin.
Andrews, T. 1993. *Animal Speak*. Woodbury: Llewellyn.
Behringer, W. 2002. "Weather, Hunger and Fear." pp. 69–86, in *The Witchcraft Reader*, D. Oldridge (Ed.). London: Routledge.
Berger, H. and D. Ezzy. 2007. *Teenage Witches*. New Brunswick: Rutgers University Press.
Blake, D. 2015. *Everyday Witchcraft*. Woodbury: Llewellyn.
Budapest, Z. 1976. *The Feminist Book of Lights and Shadows*. Venice:The Feminist Wicca.
Budapest, Z. 1986. *The Holy Book of Women's Mysteries*. Oakland: Consolidated Printers.
Clifton, C. 2006. *Her Hidden Children*. Oxford: AltaMira Press.
Coombes, M. 2004. "A Queer Situation: Queering the Craft the Wiccan Way." pp. 239–241, in *Pop! Goes the Witch*, F. Horne (Ed.). New York: The Disinformation Company.
Cunningham, S. 1995. *Wicca: A Guide for the Solitary Practitioner*. St. Paul: Llewellyn.
Davies, O. 2021. "The Rise of Modern Magic." pp. 195–226, in *The Oxford Illustrated History of Witchcraft and Magic*, O. Davies (Ed.). Oxford: Oxford University Press.
Davis, K. and W. Moore. 1945. "Some Principles of Stratification." *American Sociological Review* 10: 242–249.
Diani, M. 1992. "The Concept of Social Movement." *The Sociological Review* 40 (1): 1–25.
DW Documentary. 2023. "The Dirty Business of Beauty." Retrieved May 15, 2024, from: https://www.youtube.com/watch?v=eAIKvD_gLJo&ab_channel=DWDocumentary.
Eller, C. 1995. *Living in the Lap of the Goddess*. Boston: Beacon Press.
Eller, C. 2000. "The Roots of Feminist Spirituality." pp. 25–41, in *Daughters of the Goddess*. W. Griffin (Ed.). Oxford: AltaMira Press.
Evans, A. 1978. *Witchcraft and the Gay Counterculture*. Boston: Fag Rag Books.

Feminists for Animal Rights. 1994. "Resources." *Feminists for Animal Rights Newsletter* 8 (1–2): 16.

Ferguson, C. 2022. "Anna Kingsford and the Intuitive Science of Occultism." *Aries* 22: 114–135.

Finney, C. 2014. *Black Faces, White Spaces*. Chapel Hill: The University of North Carolina Press.

Forte, S. 1989. "Guerilla Space: A Few Many Things about ABC No Rio." *X-posure* Summer.

Fox, S. 2019. "Selena Fox, W&M Class of 1971." Retrieved April 20, 2025, from: https://oh.libraries.wm.edu/index.php/collection/william-%26-mary-women/item/selena-fox-w%26m-class-of-1971.

Gallagher, A. 2000. "Woven Apart and Weaving Together: Conflict and Mutuality in Feminist and Pagan Communities in Britain." pp. 42–58, in *Daughters of the Goddess*. W. Griffin (Ed.). Oxford: AltaMira Press.

Greenwood, S. 2000. *Magic, Witchcraft and the Otherworld*. Oxford: Berg.

Griffin, W. 2000. *Daughters of the Goddess*. Oxford: AltaMira Press.

Grimassi, R. 2021. *The Witch's Familiar*. Woodbury:Llewellyn.

Grimassi, R. 2001. *The Wiccan Mysteries*. St. Paul: Llewellyn.

HearthWitch. 2024. "Occult Supplies and Witchy Books." Retrieved June 9, 2024, from: https://www.youtube.com/watch?v=nj9AgT5Jk38&ab_channel=HearthWitch.

Jackson, Z. 2020. *Becoming Human*. New York: NYU Press.

Jasper, J., M. Tramontano, and A. McGarry. 2015. "Scholarly Research on Collective Identities." pp. 18–41, in *The Identity Dilemma*, A. McGarry and J. Jasper (Eds). Philadelphia: Temple University Press.

Jencson, L. 1998. "In Whose Image? Misogynist Trends in the Construction of Goddess and Woman." pp. 247–267, in *Spellbound*, E. Reis (Ed.). Wilmington: Scholarly Resources.

Johns, J. 1969. *King of the Witches*. London: Peter Davies.

Jones, P. and C. Matthews. 1990. "Introduction." pp. 13–40, in *Voices from the Circle*, P. Jones and C. Matthews (Eds.). Wellingborough: Aquarian Press.

Karade, I. T. A. 2004. "Voodoo Queens and Goddesses: Feminine Healers of the African Diaspora." pp. 216–217, in *Pop! Goes the Witch*, F. Horne (Ed.). New York: The Disinformation Company.

Kheel, M. 1985. "Speaking the Unspeakable." *Feminists for Animal Rights Newsletter* 2 (1): 1–6.

Kheel, M. 2007. *Nature Ethics*. Lanham: Rowman & Littlefield.

Kingsford, A. 1889. *Dreams and Dream-Stories*. New York: Scribner & Welford.

Ko, A. 2019. *Racism as Zoological Witchcraft*. New York: Lantern Books.

Lady Sabrina. 2001. *The Beliefs, Rites, and Rituals of the Wiccan Religion*. Franklin Lakes: New Page Books.

Leek, S. 1973. *The Complete Art of Witchcraft*. New York: New American Library.

Leek, S. 1975. *The Complete Art of Witchcraft*. London: Leslie Frewin.

Lind-af-Hageby, L. 1917. *Mountain Meditations*. London: George Allen & Unwin.

Lind-af-Hageby, L. and L. Schartau. 1904. *Shambles of Science*. Self-published.

Lobbedez, E. and L. Buchter. 2023. "The Strength of Pushback Collective Identity in a Fragmented Mass Movement." *Mobilization* 28 (1): 61–88.

Lorde, A. 2017. *The Master's Tools Will Never Dismantle the Master's House*. London: Penguin Books.

Lyons, S. 2019. *Revolutionary Witchcraft*. New York: Running Press.

MacCormack, P. 2020. *The Ahuman Manifesto*. London: Bloomsbury.

Maguire, G. 1995. *Wicked*. New York: HarperCollins.

Marcuse, H. 1972. *One Dimensional Man*. London: Sphere Books.

Markowski, K. and S. Roxburgh. 2019. "'If I Became a Vegan, My Family and Friends Would Hate Me': Anticipating Vegan Stigma as a Barrier to Plant-Based Diets." *Appetite* 135: 1–9.

McGarry, A. and J. Jasper. 2015. *The Identity Dilemma*. Philadelphia: Temple University Press.

Miernowska, M. 2020. *The Witch's Herbal Apothecary*. Beverly: Quarto.

Monteagut, L. 2021. *Brujas*. Chicago: Chicago Review Press.

Moore, A. and S. Stathi. 2020. "The Impact of Feminist Stereotypes and Sexual Identity on Feminist Self-Identification and Collective Action." *Journal of Social Psychology* 160 (3): 267–281.

Morningstar, S. 2005. *The Art of Wiccan Healing*. London: Hay House.

Penczak, C. 2004. "Coming Out of Two Closets: The Path of the Gay Witch." pp. 234–238, in *Pop! Goes the Witch: The Disinformation Guide to 21st Century Witchcraft*, F. Horne (Ed.). New York: The Disinformation Company.

Phillimore, M. 1964. "Emilie Augusta Louise Lind-af-Hageby Obituary." *Light* LXXXIV (3.456): 40.

Riley, S. 1993. "Ecology is a Sistah's Issue Too: The Politics of Emergent Afrocentric Ecowomanism." pp. 191–204, in *Ecofeminism and the Sacred*, C. Adams (Ed.). New York: Continuum.

Russell, J. 1985. *A History of Witchcraft*. London: Thames and Hudson.

Salisbury, D. 2019. *Witchcraft Activism*. Newburyport: Weiser Books.

Salomonsen, J. 2002. *Enchanted Feminism*. London: Routledge.

Sanders, M. 2017. "Museum of Witchcraft's Simon Costin Interviews Maxine Sanders." YouTube video. Retrieved August 21, 2023, from: https://www.youtube.com/watch?v=3hWiBSjcvFM&ab_channel=AlexandrianWitchcraft.

Sebastian, C. 2020. "Adaptation: No One Mourns the Wicked, But We Should." pp. 212–221, in *The Edinburgh Companion to Vegan Literary Studies*, L. Wright and E. Quinn (Eds.). Edinburgh: Edinburgh University Press.

Sexton, A., T. Garnett, and J. Lorimer. 2022. "Vegan Food Geographies and the Rise of Big Veganism." *Progress in Human Geography* 46 (2): 605–628.

Smith, E. 1997. "Food Not Bombs Builds Community." *The Reclaiming* 66 (Spring): 8–9.

Sollée, K. 2017. *Witches, Sluts, Feminists*. Berkeley: ThreeL Media.

Sophia, E. 1986. "Seven Sibylline Sayings." p. 118, in *The Holy Book of Women's Mysteries*, Z. Budapest (Ed.). Oakland: Consolidated Printers.

Springman, M., M. Clark, M. Rayner, P. Scarborough, and P. Webb. 2021. "The Global and Regional Costs of Healthy and Sustainable Dietary Patterns: A Modeling Study." *The Lancelet: Planetary Health* 5 (11): e797–e807.

Starhawk. 1987. *Truth or Dare*. New York: HarperCollins.

Starhawk. 1997. *Dreaming the Dark*. Boston: Beacon Press.

Starhawk. 1999. *The Spiral Dance*. Third edition. New York: HarperOne.

Starhawk. 2005. *The Earth Path*. New York: HarperCollins.

Taylor, V. and N. Raeburn. 1995. "Identity Politics as High-Risk Activism." *Social Problems* 42 (2): 252–273.

The Protego Foundation. n.d. "Who We Are." Retrieved April 15, 2024, from: https://www.protegofoundation.org/who-we-are.html.

United Nations. 2020. "Concept Note on the Elimination of Harmful Practices Related to Witchcraft Accusations and Ritual Killings." Retrieved May 6, 2024, from: https://www.ohchr.org/en/documents/tools-and-resources/concept-note-elimination-harmful-practices-related-witchcraft.

Valiente, D. 1978. *Witchcraft for Tomorrow*. London: Robert Hale.

Vanderbeck, P. 2020. *Green Witchcraft*. Emeryville: Rockridge Press.

Vaudoise, M. 2020. *Honoring your Ancestors*. Woodbury: Llewellyn.

Weinstein, M. 1991. *Earth Magic*. Custer: Phoenix Publishing.

What Witches Do. 2021. "Rare Wicca / Witchcraft Documentary Featuring Doreen Valiente & Alex Sanders." Youtube video. Retrieved August 21, 2023, from: https://www.youtube.com/watch?v=0VZpJZ6OVUo&ab_channel=WhatWitchesDo.

Wicca Magazine. n.d. "Witches of History: Doreen Valiente." Retrieved May 18, 2024, from: https://www.wiccamagazine.com/blog/witches-of-history-doreen-valiente.

Whitehurst, T. 2015. *Holistic Energy Magic*. Woodbury: Llewellyn.

Wisconsin Historical Society. n.d. "Juliet Severance, Radical Victorian." Retrieved May 8, 2024, from: https://www.wisconsinhistory.org/Records/Article/CS259.

Witches for Animal Rights. 1994. "Save the World with Your Fork!" *Feminists for Animal Rights Newsletter* 8 (1–2): 15.

Wrenn, C. L. 2019. *Piecemeal Protest*. Ann Arbor: University of Michigan Press.

Wrenn, C. L. 2020. "Free-Riders in the Nonprofit Industrial Complex: The Problem of Flexitarianism." *Society & Animals* 26 (4): 567–591.

Wrenn, C. L. 2024. "Selling Veganism in the Age of COVID: Vegan Representation in British Newspapers in 2020." pp. 104–118, in *Human-Animal Relationships in Times of Pandemic and Climate Crises*, J. Browne and Z. Sutton (Eds.). London: Routledge.

Zeisler, A. 2016. *We Were Feminists Once*. New York: PublicAffairs.

7

CONCLUSION

Introduction

This book has reasoned that both witchcraft and veganism seek to consciously engage with the natural world for the purposes of personal, communal, and even global betterment. Witchcraft has been flagged as an important nature-based spiritual practice that challenges the predominance of patriarchal mainstream religions in vegan studies. It draws on many elements of ecofeminism popularized in the latter half of the 20th century but modernized with renewed 21st-century mainstream feminist interest in the occult. I have positioned witchcraft and veganism as movements born of Western modernity that exhibit several areas of overlap including a radical reinterpretation of humanity's relationship to nature and other animals, a blurring of the human/nonhuman binary, and individual and collective resistance to violence against women and other marginalized human groups, Nonhuman Animals, and the environment. Witchcraft and veganism consciously align with the natural world to manifest positive change, but witchcraft stops short of true allyship with nature in its inconsistent relationship with other animals. To this end, I have advanced a theory of vegan witchcraft, one that is rooted in vegan feminist theory; it interrogates the entangled oppression of Nonhuman Animals and other feminized groups, contests anthroparchal determinations of appropriate social relations, and undermines human supremacist hierarchical organization. Vegan witchcraft advances communal and democratic care-based collaboration and finds symbiotic, life-affirming possibilities in a multispecies society. It argues that witchcraft has much to gain as a spiritual and social justice endeavor by extending solidarity to other animals.

The status of Nonhuman Animals, as vegan feminism understands it, has implications for the status of marginalized humans, given the historical entanglement of their oppression. Markers of animality—lack of rationality,

DOI: 10.4324/9781032649801-7

cognitive inferiority, evolutionary stuntedness, brutishness, consumability, and overall lowly social status—have been applied to Nonhuman Animals as well as all manner of vulnerable human groups and used as justification for differential treatment and systematic violence. Indeed, animality (particularly women's own animal status and their entanglement with both domesticated and free-living Nonhuman Animals) was a key reason for the persecution and mass killing of those accused of witchcraft. Modern witchcraft is informed by its solemn recognition of this institutionalized violence, but it also aims to reclaim the villainized wisdom, connectedness, and independence that undergirded it. Only by recognizing the personhood of Nonhuman Animals, however, will witchcraft be able to unlock the liberatory power of lost magical practices. Both veganism and witchcraft recognize that humanity's present relationship to nature is overwhelmingly toxic and oppressive but also that a reconnection with nature has the capacity to heal and liberate. For these reasons, I have presented vegan witchcraft not simply as another individualistic or stylistic path that inclined witches might choose. Instead, I have positioned veganism as a central, if overlooked tenet of Western witchcraft in all its manifestations.

Starhawk warns that stuntedness befalls spiritual paths that fail to prioritize the minimization of suffering: "We cannot grow in strength through being parasites" (1987: 136). Sjöö and Mor (1991) emphasize that religious systems that "support any kind of dominance-submission social structures" must be "utterly repudiated" as they are "vampire machineries" that "obstruct and deform our evolution" and rationalize status quo inequalities and suffering (421). Yet, these same parasitic, vampiric, counter-evolutionary tendencies remain rampant in modern witchcraft, even goddess traditions. This chapter concludes by identifying veganism's ability to counter such harmful and addictive behaviors, encourage solidarity over individualism, champion ethical living, and reclaim the power of the oppressed to transform culture and social structures. This chapter also summarizes many challenges that remain. Witchcraft's anti-authoritarianism, for instance, makes the creation of a universal ethic difficult. The blatant speciesism that persists in conventional witchcraft, furthermore, suggests that the desire to make space for vegan ethics cannot be assumed. Yet, the most fundamental of witch ethics, the principle of no harm, offers hope for a more inclusive and liberatory witchcraft.

Speciesism and Witchcraft

The Enlightenment introduced rationality and hierarchy into Western ideology and social organization, a process that, for all its attempts to advance and develop society, nonetheless created considerable vulnerabilities for certain groups who were considered unredeemable, inimical to the new value system, and either unvaluable or valuable to the point of exploitability. The Enlightenment moved faith in the supernatural to the realm of reason. This process may have reduced the perceived threat of witchcraft to the anthroparchal state, but the considerable social, political, and economic shifts it introduced would continue to jeopardize the wellbeing of marginal groups such as women and other animals. The shift to modernity, for that matter, was fueled by the exploitation of natural systems, women's labor, and the bodies of Nonhuman Animals, further depreciating their status. Postmodernism of the mid-20th century challenged these newly introduced knowledge and belief systems, troubling the idea of absolute truths and recognizing their tendency to conflate the interests of the white male colonial dominant class with that of everyone else. Postmodernism also confronted the concept of "progress," casting a critical eye upon the environmental devastation that modernity and "enlightened" ideas had wreaked. Feminism, veganism, environmentalism, witchcraft, and so many other countercultural efforts found considerable momentum in the post-war years as Western populaces sought a return to simpler, more interconnected times. Typical of postmodern thought (Strauss 1966), this was not a simple replication of the past but rather a bricolage of ideas and desires new and old, a reclaiming and a re-creating.

Identity, recall, also transformed during the late 20th century into the 21st, an era in which consumerism, hobbies, and social networks began to shape the sense of self, resisting clear categorization and rendering collective solidarity difficult. Witchcraft of this postmodern era thus encompasses numerous variations and affiliations, making a comprehensive definition and coherent analysis somewhat of a challenge. Witchcraft might be religious or non-religious, but it is most characteristically attuned to nature, glorifies femininity, and ascribes to humanism in its belief in the capacity of humans to create change for the better of themselves and society more broadly. In many ways, it is a form of feminist resistance, creating voice and stirring power in the very shadow of one of womankind's most terrible eras of persecution. The historic persecution of witches was based to an extent on the misogynistic belief that women were both deviant and dangerous, especially in their capacity for radical, power-disrupting discourse. Indeed, Reis (1998) has suggested that the burning times were a means of punishing the "crime" of female speech. All women, whether arrested or absconded, were subject to the chilling effect of this misogynistic ideology and social system. Chiding and punishing women for scolding, gossip, and tongue-wagging were further patriarchal effort to silence women and undermine feminist protest. As such, women's words today act as a potent form of resistance. Indeed, witches often describe women's words of resistance as word-weaving, a powerful practice employed by individuals, consciousness-raising groups, and feminist theories to undermine androcentric realities and construct egalitarian alternatives.

Politicizing language is only one aspect of this magical work. The more fundamental measures of thinking radically, collaborating, and demanding justice are magical acts as well. For Greenwood, this feminist witchcraft "offers a practical, political model for women's empowerment in the socio-economic world—a vision for transformation of the world's reality" (2000a: 177). Subsequently, witchcraft is entangled with morality, rooted as it is in the anthroparchal state's regulation of societal norms as well as modern witchcraft's efforts to reclaim women's autonomy and dignity. Witchcraft makes the personal political: it demands a recognition of how one's individual actions are linked to the wider wellbeing of the world. Writes Starhawk: "Magic is the art of turning negatives into positives, of spinning straw into gold" (1997: 99). Making space for the voices of those historically silenced is key to societal transformation. Today's witchcraft centers this reasoning, encouraging free thought, open discussion, and a radical imagination for alternative societal possibilities. "Perhaps the greatest harm patriarchy has done to us is to stifle, coopt, and deform our powers of imagination," Sjöö and Mor opine (1991: 421).

In *practice*, however, I have argued that witchcraft systematically fails to realize this responsibility to the self, society, and even nature. The modern witchcraft discourse examined herein has created a mythological past based on the needs and norms of the present, creating awkward thealogical and philosophical inconsistencies, replicating patriarchal Western categories, and otherizing Nonhuman Animals. The romanticization of "the hunt" and the interplay between the goddess and "the horned one," for example, have affirmed modern humanity's speciesist penchant for killing and eating others as a ritual means of demonstrating power and status. Nature, being positioned as the arbiter of morality, has been interpreted by many witches in such a way as to equate the behaviors of obligate predators as ethically equivalent to the cultural behaviors of human primates. This manipulation of reality, backed by appeals to divinity and intended to support existing oppressive hierarchies, erodes witchcraft's distinctiveness. Patriarchy entertains a superstitious belief that its adherents gain power through the consumption of others, the bodies and labor of women and other animals in particular. Institutionalized religions extend this domination to include their souls as well, damning and sometimes exterminating those who resist. Should witchcraft align with this expectation of gaining power from the suppression of others, it will find that it only replicates what it has sought to overturn.

Witches, too, appeal to lineage and tradition as evidence of righteousness. Anthropology, archaeology, and history are weaponized against other animals to justify their oppression, not unlike the weaponization of tradition, ancestry, and science against women. This socially constructed speciesist past lacks the critical reclaiming that women's history has enjoyed. If a feminist reclaiming were applied to multispecies history, the focus on domination could be eclipsed by a focus on shared sentience. The capacity for suffering and pain that both humans and other animals embody might motivate contemporary witches to reduce suffering wherever possible rather than excuse anthroparchal violence. Dismissing humanity's speciesism as part of the "spiral dance," as does Starhawk (1999), ignores the widespread symbiotic and prosocial behavior that many species extend to one another, both within *and* without their own species. This has included caring for the young, ill, or disabled, defending one another from predation, and sharing food, water, and shelter. Strangely, the mutual care system that dominates in the natural world is seen as more sentimental than scientifically accurate and often fails to resonate even with feminist witches.

Furthermore, comparing humans with nonhuman predators to deflect criticisms of human supremacist violence against other animals is false equivalency. Humans are in a category of their own making, a "super predator" species that attacks at least *one third of the species on planet Earth*. This is a cultural practice unmatched among other animals (Darimont et al. 2023).[1] Indeed, nonhuman predators are facing extinction as humans encroach on them as well. Unseen, of course, are the trillions of animals who perish each year as humans destroy ecosystems with Nonhuman Animal-based agriculture, oil production, pollution, and other fixtures of Western "development." Witchcraft, in avoiding appeals to god, appeals to nature instead, but in doing so obscures real power relations that shape humanity's interactions with other humans, Nonhuman Animals, and the environment. For those who appeal to a goddess, this too remains vaguely human supremacist. Historically, she tended to take nonhuman form and blurred the boundary between humans and other animals, but in almost all contemporary depictions of "the goddess" she is anthropomorphized and identified as distinct from other animals.

Witchcraft of the secular and religious variety may pay lip service to the special connection humans share with other animals, but the very animality of humans as *apes* goes unacknowledged. Human distinctiveness and supremacy remain the norm. Although the regular work with physical and metaphysical familiars suggests an interest in a multispecies craft and the traditional expectation of working in the nude indicates an attuning to the witch's own animality, it is evident that humans are seen as distinct and superior. In Wiccan thealogy, recall, the belief in reincarnation pulls humans from a position above nature to a more interconnected position: all humans must eventually die, like anything else in nature, and be "reborn" as that energy later rematerializes in another form. But many witches do not even include Nonhuman Animals as participants in reincarnation, and for those who do include them, the emphasis on individual responsibility for one's social position in this life and the next suggests that Nonhuman Animals, who have next to no agency in a deeply speciesist society, are somehow culpable for their present condition of suffering. These ideologies do little to advance the status of nonhumans. This book's analysis of foundational and popular texts in modern witchcraft presents a rather conflicting spiritual and practical expectation for human relations with other animals. Many authors take a decidedly feminist approach, even advocating for the acknowledgment of Nonhuman Animals as persons, helpers, and subjects of life. Yet, just as many, if not more, however, see the harming and consumption of other animals as morally legitimate, as justified by tradition, the capitalization of available resources, and even a desire to temper the psychic affect that vegetarianism and veganism can have. Nonhuman Animals, by and large, remain objectified as resources, consumables, and magical servants.

As explored in an earlier chapter, one of the theological barriers to veganism in the pagan tradition is the acceptance of death as both natural and necessary in life. As Moura (2020) explains: "Death is a natural passage to new life and is not feared or labelled evil" (41). This reconfiguring of death is, of course, helpful, as modern life has obscured death from ordinary society, hiding it in hospitals and hospices or denying it with lifesaving or preserving technologies and medicines. Increasing secularism, too, may be leaving many spiritually or psychologically unprepared for coping with their death or the death of others. But what of other animals? With the standardization of Nonhuman Animal-based agriculture, vivisection, and "euthanasia" or "culling" in supposedly "overpopulated" so-called "shelters," "zoos," and wild spaces, the routinized deaths of Nonhuman Animals have been all but removed from everyday awareness. With few practitioners having any first-hand knowledge (or second-hand, for that matter) of Nonhuman Animal experiences, the popular "circle of life" reasoning provides an easily accessible refrain that maintains cognitive dissonance. To die in order to provide life, in the case of other animals, has different meaning for nonhumans in an anthroparchal human society. Humans do not need to kill and eat other animals to live. Their death is not a passage to a new life; it is a means for human ends. Notably, there is little Wiccan myth-making about fishes, pigs, cows, chickens, sheeps, and other animals who are sacrificed. Once killed, packaged, sold, bought, and eaten, their personhood is largely forgotten. In fact, it may have never been recognized in the first place. The "natural passage" that Moura romanticizes for fellow humans differs considerably from that facing Nonhuman Animals. Their postmortem journey begins through decomposition in the bowels of humanity before being flushed to their "next life" in a sewage treatment plant.

Acquiescence and Resistance

Thus, witchcraft today is marked by a very particular paradox. On one hand, it seeks to legitimate nature-based spirituality and the divine feminine. Seasonal and weather changes, moon phases, water patterns, Nonhuman Animals, and even unseen mythological creatures of the wild such as faeries are recognized and revered. Adherents (most of whom are women) are encouraged to acknowledge the power within themselves as an extension of these natural forces, a power long denied by institutions of patriarchy. On the other hand, the sentient inhabitants of witchcraft's sanctified nature are often objectified or even harmed and killed in ritual practice. Many tools and rituals call for bones, feathers, bees' wax, or flesh procured from grocery shopping, "hunting," or scavenging "roadkill." And, while ritual sacrifice is a stereotype increasingly relegated to the past, major holiday observances and recipes regularly advise the use of animals' "meat," breastmilk, birds' eggs, and bees' honey. Witchcraft may celebrate feminine power, care, and connection, but it also makes space for patriarchal power with its frequently oppressive, nonvegan relationships with other animals.

Valiente has indicated that male priests of old engaged in Nonhuman Animal sacrifice as they had no other means of raising power (What Witches Do 2021). But women, who have now come to dominate leadership roles in modern witchcraft, have no need for blood sacrifice, as they have other means for summoning power, including, for many, a highly empathetic or spiritual connection with nature and other animals, sisterhood or comradery with other witches, sex magic, and, for some, a capacity to menstruate and bear children. The inclusion of *living* animals as persons and comrades in rituals for manifesting power is perhaps the least understood aspect of the craft, as witches vacillate between admiring other animals as totems, colonizing them with shapeshifting rituals, and killing them ritualistically in speciesist mythmaking or non-vegan crafting. The etymology of the Anglo-Saxon term "witch" is relevant here. It is a cognate of the German word *weihen*, meaning holy and sacred chosen person, and the Latin word for victim, *victima* (Weekley 1921). The sacredness of witches, in other words, is bound to their victimhood, with the very concept of witchcraft exhibiting the historic tension between the inherent divinity claimed by pagan practitioners and the Roman church's systematic eradication of competing sources of power and knowledge. Witchcraft today complicates this tensioned meaning even further by acknowledging the sacredness of other animals as early pagans might have while also reproducing their anthroparchal domination. Yet, the original Anglo-Saxon meaning of the term "witch," *wice*, referred to flexibility (Weekley 1921). Just as nature and the cosmos are ever changing and ever bending, so must witchcraft flex in confronting its allegiance with systemic violence and its own subjection to colonization. To be fit for purpose, witchcraft must embrace its wicker roots and be ready to adapt.

Vegan religious scholars have advocated the recognition of nonhuman personhood and their capacity to enhance human spirituality (even suggesting that Nonhuman Animals exhibit their *own* spirituality). They also observe many areas of overlap between human and nonhuman spiritualities within a religious naturalism. Looking to other animals "can inspire awe, wonder, and profound respect for the multitude of beings with whom we share this planet, and it can bring us closer to the deep mysteries of existence that inspire religion" (Smuts et al. 2024: 277–278). Witchcraft, be it religious or secular, embraces this spiritually infused naturalism in its focus on finding magic (whether perceived as real or metaphorical) in the natural world, but much more might be gained by consciously including other animals. Exhibiting such a diversity of life experiences, other animals can offer insight into symbiotic and cooperative living and other strategic adaptations. Taking seriously their experiences will also unveil the full spectrum of social and environmental inequality, including harmful processes of otherization and hierarchical organization based on perceived physical and cognitive difference. This broader understanding will contribute to more comprehensive, accurate, and presumably effective social justice campaigning. Honoring animality could fundamentally disrupt the persecutions that have aggrieved women, older persons, persons with disabilities, queer persons, and nonhuman persons. Witchcraft has embraced death so that life can spring anew, but humans are not obligate carnivores. Killing Nonhuman Animals for anthropocentric wants or conveniences need not be a part of the Wiccan cyclical thealogy: *it is human privilege that must be sacrificed so that others can thrive.* A multispecies society that prioritizes the reduction of suffering and the maximization of pleasure and potential for as many as possible regardless of species identity is the ultimate goal for a *vegan* witchcraft.

The failure of Western witchcraft to implement its doctrines consistently, fairly, and inclusive of Nonhuman Animals is a reflection of strained intersectionality in feminism, anti-speciesism, and environmentalism. These movements have overlapped in space and time such that their failure to collaborate must surely be intentional. In the United Kingdom, where witchcraft rekindled following its decriminalization in the 1950s, new Wiccans who followed the back to the land naturist movements coincided with the burgeoning vegan community, and yet two divergent paths were taken. British Wiccans celebrated hedonistic indulgence after the scarcities of war and persecution, feasting on animal corpses roasted over fire pits on sabbat evenings and re-creating old Celtic myths of horned gods and the sacred hunt. British *vegans*, meanwhile, increasingly relied on Judeo-Christian appeals, abandoning the secular and even atheistic approach, which had been favored up to that point. Achieving harmony with nature and other animals meant eating them for some and liberating them for others, and increasingly from dramatically different spiritual standpoints. In the United States, feminist witches and feminist vegans worked alongside one another in exploring women's connection to the nature and homosexuality as a source of empowerment[2] but apparently not together. These American collectives may have been more aligned in vision than their British counterparts, but rarely the two did meet. Green witchcraft, which sprouted from these ecofeminist roots, furthermore, has also overwhelmingly ignored the plight of Nonhuman Animals, especially domesticated ones categorized as food. Indeed, as was explored in a previous chapter, green witchcraft celebrates ancient traditions of "hunting" and Nonhuman Animal sacrifice, with little regard for veganism or vegetarianism.

The aversion to dogma in the witchcraft community has precluded a strong ethical stance against speciesism (as well as environmental destruction, feminism, racism, heterosexism, and other systems of inequality). However, an adamant rejection of dogma becomes a dogma in of itself, particularly if it goes so far as to eschew basic ethical principles. Most of the leading thinkers covered in this analysis have failed to extend their principle of anti-authoritarianism to Nonhuman Animals. The domination of humans is discouraged, but the domination of other animals remains normalized. Indeed, most renounce vegetarianism or veganism for trivial, self-centered, or scientifically dubious reasons. Cunningham (2007) rejected vegetarianism as he believed it rendered him psychically vulnerable. Starhawk (2005) claims to crave flesh, rejecting vegetarianism for fear it would physically weaken her, conflating her "power-over" other animals with the "power-within" that she believes their consumption nutritionally provides. She also reasons that vegetarianism is inferior as it is unobtainable by impoverished people living in deserted regions (although her own

San Francisco region is one of the most vegan accommodating in the world, and plant-based eating was historically quite common in desert regions including the Mediterranean, Middle East, and much of Africa). Gardner (1959) enjoyed the primitive aesthetics of corpses roasting on open fires. Leek (1975) was suspicious of "restrictive diets," while Budapest (1976) tried vegetarianism for a time to manage her weight, quickly dropping it when that goal was satisfied. Whitehurst missed pizza topped with curdled bovine breastmilk (Levinger and Whitehurst 2019). Crowley appealed to hedonism, prioritizing personal pleasure, sexual gratification, and magical extraction from the bodies of Nonhuman Animals killed for mealtimes (Tillie 2023). Rarely are the interests of Nonhuman Animals themselves examined, despite witchcraft's supposed connection with nature and other animals and ample incorporation of Nonhuman Animals as familiars, power animals, totems, and spirit guides. Indeed, as explored in an earlier chapter, familiar work, centered as it is on serving human interests, almost always obscures the voices of other animals. Were witches to truly listen to their messages, they would undoubtedly sense a plea for deliverance and a call to action.

McColman (2002) summarizes that witchcraft is rooted in "love, trust, freedom, and healing" (37). "For this reason," they continue, it is practiced so that witches can grow "more kind, more loving, [and] more compassionate" (38). As this book has identified, witchcraft struggles to achieve these aims. McColman concedes that cognitive dissonance binds it to some extent:

> Some people who practice Wicca[3] may behave in harmful or destructive ways. [...] Any group of people will have a few problems in the ranks. But taken as a whole, Wicca stands for positive qualities such as love, happiness, and joy.
>
> *(2002: 38)*

From a vegan feminist perspective, however, this harm and destruction reaches beyond "a few problems." Recall that witchcraft has promulgated harmful essentialist ideas about gender, and some have also promulgated heterosexism. There has also been a history of appropriating Indigenous traditions. Starhawk, in emphasizing the mythical creation of modern witchcraft, embraces the multicultural elements of this bricolage practice but clarifies that,

> any real power we gain from any tradition carries with it a responsibility. If we learn from African drum rhythms or the Lakota sweat lodge, we have incurred an obligation to not romanticize the people we have learned from but to participate in the very real struggles being waged for liberation, land, and cultural survival.
>
> *(1999: 232)*

The traditions, labor, and very lives of Nonhuman Animals have perhaps lent the most to the making of witchcraft today. It would seem only fitting that witches acknowledge the responsibility to other animals thus incurred. This political consciousness, she adds, develops the witch's capacity for empathy and inclusion. It seems, then, that 21st-century vegan discourses may have a role in modern witchcraft, if seeing through the eyes of others "can be tremendously enriching" (1999: 19) as Starhawk supposes.

Accommodating Addiction

Despite these shortcomings, Western witchcraft has demonstrated a capacity to relinquish entrenched, ethnocentric, and excluding practices. The pleasurable and plentiful benefits of human privilege, however, render species inclusivity significantly more difficult. The mass slaughter of Nonhuman Animals in agricultural, scientific, fashion, and other speciesist industries should be reason enough for witches to consider veganism, but perhaps it will be the spread of increasingly dangerous zoonotic pandemics and the devastation of climate change that will finally flag the nonhuman experience as relevant. Some witches have acknowledged how ethnocentrism and consumerism have posed similar reluctancies to embrace environmentalism in witchcraft. In her 10th anniversary introduction to *The Spiral Dance*, Starhawk suggests that individual exploitation of the environment is an "addiction" that might call for a twelve-step program to "counter our collective addiction to ecological destruction" (1999: 22) that witchcraft could successfully supplement. This is not simply an addiction indulging the bounties of the Earth but also an addiction to the power and privilege that provide it. The anti-hierarchical, circular organizational style of witchcraft and its belief in the power of personal transformation lends a curative element. Others have also highlighted the importance of witchcraft in disrupting addictive patterns. Foltz (2000), for instance, points to goddess spirituality as a means of breaking through substance abuse. This theme is not restricted to Dianic denominations, however, as it also surfaced in the Alexandrian tradition, understandably so given its intense prioritization of community healing (Deutch 1977).

If, as Starhawk (1997) herself admits, eating other animals results from a "craving," perhaps witchcraft may be useful for breaking the addiction of speciesism, too. Indeed, ritual, which is prioritized in witchcraft practice, can serve as a powerful antidote to harmful, destructive behaviors and is thought to manifest real and lasting change. It does this, Starhawk notes, through the psychological effort involved in the ritual, including the preparation involved and the accountability offered by an audience of community members (2005). Initiation is one such ritual, considered a sacred foundation to witchcraft. In the 20th century, initiation would have entailed many years of training, mentorship, and engagement with the witches' community, although self-initiation rituals are more commonplace today given the rise of solitary practice. In any case, as examined in a previous chapter, ritual is vital for building solidarity, fortitude, and resilience. Breaking the "addiction" of speciesism might benefit from ritual and community witness, perhaps offering an initiation ceremony for new vegans to highlight the joy in multispecies living and reinforce group solidarity. As with witches, vegans have been stigmatized and marginalized for their politics, such that ritual offers resilience.

Addiction framework individualizes toxic behaviors and may obfuscate the noxious social structures that create them, but given its ubiquitousness in the witchcraft discourse, it may resonate for those who are reluctant to relinquish anthropocentrism and human supremacy. Starhawk (1987) muses of addiction that they are "very hard to break because we identify them with being bad, rebellious, disobedient, unenslaved," though they may kill the user, "quickly or slowly" (83), but "accepting responsibility generates hope" (167). The incorporation of addiction treatment in modern witchcraft is, of course, an extension of its emphasis on personal agency and potential for transformation. It is also, however, a reflection of a presumed responsibility to the community; witches do not simply engage the craft for personal healing but for the wellbeing of all who have been manipulated into an unhealthy state of dependency on capitalism and its deleterious effects. For Starhawk, violence and fear enforce this dependency and cannot be incorporated consistently into a sustainable witchcraft practice. "We are called to take a radical leap of faith," Starhawk charges, "to believe that people, given the opening to dream of new possibilities, with tools and visions will create a living future" (1999: 23). To this point, a vegan feminist perspective encourages a break from the addiction of speciesism, confronting the spellbinding influence of capitalism that renders sentient beings into consumables, sickens humans, and decimates ecosystems.

A hardened social justice activist, Starhawk is sympathetic to the frustration witches may experience due to the slowness of social change and the imperfection of available solutions: "To *will* does not mean that the world will conform to our desires—it means that *we* will: We will make our own choices and act so as to bring them about, even knowing we may fail" (1999: 224). While guiding principles sometimes leave loose ends, contradictions, and inconsistencies, she concedes that "only when we are ready to confront the muddiness and unclarity of reality can we hope to transform it" (1999: 223). Surely one of witchcraft's muddiest of contradictions is its radical reconnection to nature and other animals and romantic fascination with patriarchal oppressions like "hunting" and domestication. For Starhawk, a confrontation with inconsistencies cannot simply be a theoretical matter; it must be integrated into daily practice. Witches, in other words, must endeavor to "walk the walk." "Unless I have enough personal power to keep commitments in my daily life, I will be unable to wield magical power," Starhawk notices (1999: 138). Extending Starhawk's advice, vegan witchcraft understands a vegan multispecies comradery as the most fundamental commitment needed to wield this magical power. This can only be the case, as Starhawk's utopian ecofeminist future explicitly aims to dismantle patriarchal death cults and replace them with a "culture of life" (1999: 215). Vegan witchcraft calls for a shift in consciousness, one that radically embraces multispecies experiences and entanglements, rejecting the occulture of death for an occulture of life. In line with Starhawk's vision, it insists on seeing good, hope, and promise in a world that systematically obscures that vision and the possibility of achieving any alternative.

Greenwood (2000b) describes feminist witchcraft as emerging from a legacy of women's rebellion informed by second wave consciousness-raising and practical acknowledgment of how the political aligns with the personal. Changes, she notes, emerge from within, and this process is reflexive. Just as one's outside environment shapes individuals, individuals in making inner change can reflect that change back into their environment: "Healing involves coming to understand the way that domination has been internalized" (145). Veganism, I suggest, can be a powerful means of making internal change that resists the internalized domination of speciesism. Recall that witchcraft, in response to institutionalized patriarchal religion, rejects the need for sacrifice but does valorize sacrificing "*to* nature" (Starhawk 1999: 54). Realizing this selflessness in vegan witchcraft will necessarily entail "sacrificing" human privilege and anthropocentric entitlement to the bodies of others, but compassionate living with other animals also presents considerable joy (as does the bounty of plant-based foods and cuisines). Indeed, with the positive health outcomes associated with vegan diets, this shift will be a welcome boost both psychologically and physically. Budapest's *Feminist Book of Lights and Shadows* (1976) begins with a reminder to readers that replenishing one's energy for revolution work is key for a sustained and successful challenge to patriarchy. Witchcraft may provide a sacred strength complemented by the physical benefits of veganism.

The Witches' Rede

In the 1970s, with witchcraft firmly in resurgence, a council of American witches convened to delineate the "Principles of Wiccan Belief" (Buckland 2002). These early principles aligned Wicca with natural rhythms, environmental stewardship, and the rejection of authoritarian hierarchies. As a nature religion, Wicca was distinctive in honoring nature as a space of healing and health. In lieu of divine authority that typified other religions, the council appealed to evolution as spiritual guide, identifying humans themselves as divine creators. Indeed, humans are not just positioned as part of nature but, to an extent, superior to it. As Buckland chronicles, "We recognize that our intelligence gives us a unique responsibility toward our environment" (2002: 9).

This perspective can prove both helpful and troublesome from a vegan perspective. Although appeals to nature may be interpreted as a means of decentering the human and resituating them as part of the ecosystem, relying on evolution for moral guidance can just as easily reinforce an ideology of human supremacy. Evolutionary science has historically placed humans as "naturally" dominant above other species, as either paternalistic caretakers or entitled exploiters. This creates a serious vulnerability for Nonhuman Animals, given that humans—depending on their beliefs and cultural background—will frequently align with anthroparchal ideations of a predatory nature to justify all manner of culturally constructed violence. This vulnerability is further aggravated by Wicca's expectation that adherents "seek within Nature that which is contributory to our health and well-being" (Buckland 2002: 10). If Nonhuman Animals are constructed as natural resources who are necessary to that health and wellbeing for humans, they have little hope of achieving Wiccan solidarity in practice.

The self-directedness emphasized in witchcraft makes it unique among religions, as morality is not strictly ordered or prescribed. Buckland (2002) insists, "There is no one denomination of witchcraft that is right for all witches. And that is as it should be. We are all different. Our backgrounds—both ethnic and social—vary greatly" (xi). Recall that, as a political movement, this individualism also poses a challenge for inclusivity and solidarity (Greenwood 2000b). Feminist witchcraft tends to reject dogma while tolerating disagreement and diversity (Eller 1995), but this respect for difference rarely includes other animals. Without an awareness of capitalism's influence, nature and other animals remain commodities, and social movements that resist injustice are vulnerable to conflating social progress with the freedom to participate in capitalism's marketplace. If morality is solely a matter of personal choice, then collective solidarity is lost. Witchcraft ardently defends individualism and openly pursues pleasure to resist women's historic exclusion from the public sphere as well as expectations of self-denial and self-sacrifice that continue to unfairly burden them. This sentiment undergirds Leek's appeal to radical indulgence: "We never believe that anything enjoyable or harmonious can be sinful and for this reason alone, most witches lead a full life in which they can enjoy earthly things such as eating, drinking, and making love" (1975: 195). While embracing pleasure and freedom is indeed an important marker of liberation, it is easily co-opted by consumerism. In these conditions, the witchcraft community is transformed from a movement of resilience and resistance to a malleable and exploitable market demographic, while Nonhuman Animals, once comrades, languish as commodities.

Despite its libertarian claims, modern witchcraft does not shirk morality completely. Fundamental to almost all variants of modern witchcraft is the creed: "Do no harm." This principle is outlined in numerous texts on Wicca and witchcraft, including Farrar and Farrar's (1999) *Witches' Bible*, a seminal text that sought to codify early Gardnerian and Alexandrian tenets. Some variations of "do no harm" include a repercussive element. The Rule of Three, for instance, also known as the Law of Threefold Return, warns practitioners that any energy manifested will return to them three times over, whether benevolent or malevolent. Gardner's disciple Doreen Valiente (1978) echoes this in her recording of early Wiccan scripts:

> Eight words the Wiccan Creed fulfil—
> And it harms none, do what ye will.

(41)

This rede is widely reproduced in key witchcraft texts, often described as simple and straightforward: "Do what you will ... but don't do anything that will harm another. It's as simple as that" (Buckland 2002: 9). Marion Weinstein (1991) agrees: "The only law of witchcraft is The Threefold Law: Everything you do comes back to you three times" (1). Cunningham, too, advises that "the wiccan ideal of morality is simple: do what you want, as long as you harm none" (1995: 5).

The witches' rede suggests that the agency and independence that witchcraft encourages should always be moderated by a social responsibility, and it is perhaps the most foundational of all ethics in modern witchcraft. Yet, ethics are rarely interpreted so simply and straightforwardly in a deeply unequal society. As was examined in the previous chapter, witchcraft's aim to transform the world (an aim that frequently includes undermining patriarchy and other systems of oppression) sometimes runs afoul of this creed. The fight for social justice necessarily entails interference, defiance, resistance, and even harm to those protecting the system in contest. Indeed, it is unclear just who should be protected from harm. Nor is it clear what motivates witches to "do no harm." The rede sometimes seems to be based on a system of karmic punishment rather than ethical obligation. That is, witches may avoid harming others not out of ethical obligation and moral concern but to avoid retribution. For instance, Cunningham warns that engaging in any rites that involve "blood or death or living sacrifices" will invoke a dangerous deity (1995: 109). Witchcraft's prioritization of personal healing and self-improvement in tandem with its resistance to institutionalization and outside authority further inhibits a sense of responsibility to others (Greenwood 2000b). Wisdom is instead embodied in the practitioner; the individual is the expert. Raven Grimassi summarizes that "Wiccans basically believe in 'live and let live,' non-violent philosophy, and tend to be tolerant of the beliefs and lifestyles of others" (2001: 35). They are "striving toward peace coexistence," not policing one another, as they "focus on themselves and their personal needs" (2001: 35).

Despite these challenges, even Grimassi admits that witches adhere to a "basic sense of right and wrong" and accepts that self-defense is admissible in the face of injustice (2001: 35), principles that diverge from traditional Christian expectations of deference and subservience. Morality and willpower, in fact, are thought key to this rede, since witchcraft devalues validation through personal gain. For Greenwood, this right and wrong is more than an internal moral code; it is understood through "harmony with natural 'cosmic truths'" (2000a: 3). Appealing to universal truths, of course, risks replicating the same hegemonic ideologies promulgated by mainstream religions, potentially masking ethics that cause harm to some, especially Nonhuman Animals, who have been just as harmed by the "common sense" of speciesism as they have been by institutionalized religions.

Given their political engagement, feminist witches are strong proponents of moral guidelines. *The Holy Book of Women's Mysteries* advises, "All living beings must be considered in this 'harm none' clause" (Budapest 1986: 116). Cunningham also notes that the rule of harming none also extends to oneself: "If you as a Wicca abuse your body, deny it the necessities of life or otherwise harm yourself, you're in violation of this principle" (1995: 5).

Violence is believed to beget violence. Psychological research supports this assumption, finding strong correlations between the abuse of Nonhuman Animals and the abuse of other vulnerable groups such as women and children (Ascione and Arkow 1999). Psychological research also finds the connection between dominant attitudes regarding minoritized groups and diminishment of other animals (Stone 2022). Furthermore, it is worth considering that the "law of return" is not restricted to the individual practitioner, nor is it evenly distributed. Exploiting Nonhuman Animals directly impacts the wellbeing of Nonhuman Animals, of course, but nonvegan consumption is also a leading contributor to climate change. This environmental crisis reduces quality of life for *everyone*, especially free-living Nonhuman Animals and people of the Global South (Gaard 2017). Vegan witchcraft thus adapts the witches' rede to include other animals and, in doing so, encourages positive returns in physical, emotional, social, and global health.

Toward a Multispecies Witchcraft

As a subset of vegan feminist thought, vegan witchcraft recognizes three important components in the reproduction of shared oppression between feminized human groups and other animals. First, the boundary driven between women and other animals is a permeable one, and this permeability invites policing. The reliance on familiars in the Western anti-witchcraft discourse illustrates this, whereby women were regularly depicted in unholy collaboration with other animals, sometimes even transfiguring into another species. This boundary crossing threatened the distinctiveness (and superiority) of humans, but it may also have threatened the sharpening divide between women and men, such that animalizing women naturalized men's superiority. Animalizing women (and feminizing animals) remains a potent tactic in the modern anthroparchal state today (Adams 2000), where it is no less useful in its ability to uphold culturally constructed binaries in a modern "enlightened" society. Second, the oppression of women and other animals has been rationalized by rendering them evil, literally the antithesis of god's will, and thus in need of severe control. Third, institutionalized religion, as an extension of the anthroparchal state, characteristically supports the manufacture and maintenance of sexism, speciesism, racism, heterosexism, and other identity-based systems of oppression for the benefit of the dominant class.

Vegan feminist thought has acknowledged these connections for some time, but an explicit exploration of witchcraft—as an historical phenomenon and as a modern reclaiming—is a necessary theoretical supplement, highlighting the spiritual and metaphysical mechanisms of anthroparchy. Vegan witchcraft finds the maintenance of multispecies intersections in churches, sacrificial altars, execution pyres, bibles, and edicts. These intersections also spin through cultural traditions, ancestral fantasies, evolution stories, karmic beliefs, tales of gods and goddesses, notions of nature and the cosmos, and meanings attributed to life and death. Vegan witchcraft accounts for these politics of existentialism for they are not evenly commanded and are too often weaponized against society's most vulnerable. Matters of the spirit do not only inform a system of violence, of course. As a vegan feminist practice, vegan witchcraft also envisions these inter-species oppressions informing an interspecies *resistance*. Vegan witchcraft is a critique of inequality *as well as* a theory of change. Modern witches are well versed in reclaiming women's knowledge and power expunged by patriarchy's long rule, everyday forging new mythologies for resilience and flourishment. What might vegan feminism reclaim from the ashes of anthroparchy?

This book has also encouraged witches and Wiccans to consider wicking from veganism. Sollée (2017) cautions that witches must remain vigilant and flexible to stay abreast of oppression as it persists into the 21st century: "although the witch-hunting era did officially end, it did not end all witch hunts, nor did it end the practice of women being scapegoated for society's ills" (145). Sollée and other witches might consider the scapegoating of goats them-selves, for it is the persecution and degradation of *animality* that lies at the root of woman-hating, witchcraft persecution, and all manner of other societal oppressions. Indeed, Starhawk has emphasized that witches are at their most powerful in resisting false binaries and hierarchies, but the human/nonhuman binary and human supremacist hierarchy has yet to be seriously disrupted. Starhawk has critically observed that even women can find shelter and privilege within the hierarchy of patriarchy, themselves dominating over those more precariously situated (1999: 122). I have suggested that witches, once persecuted as other-than-human, now shelter themselves within human supremacy.

Here veganism provides an invaluable critique that has the potential to realign witchcraft with its commitment to the natural world and those, both human and nonhuman, who call it home. Witches must break the spell of anthroparchy and capitalism and embrace veganism as a potent magic of symbiotic, multispecies, care-based life on Earth. Lyons (2019) presents witchcraft as a means to combat the disenchanted world with all its tendencies to separate and commodify, but vegan witchcraft can go further to reinvigorate a domesticated world, inviting opportunities to reconnect and rewild. "The Disenchanted World is a desecrated one" (2019: 107), Lyons observes, adding that witches must "listen to the land" (2019: 110). But what could witches learn from listening to Nonhuman Animals as well? Starhawk, despite her support for speciesist foodways, has described witch-craft as rooted in a community that "includes not just the human but the inter-dependent plant, animal, and elemental communities of the natural world," as this would model "what we can become" as a society (1987: 22). Witchcraft today centers healing as a sacred personal and social act. This is approached by embodying natural rhythms. As Salomonsen explains, "the relationship between humanity and divinity" is a never-ending, cyclical process, gradually manifesting to "sanctify the world as it is: natural cycles and seasons, mind, body, spirit, and emotions" (2002: 287). I suggest that plant-based eating and cooperative living with other animals, being fundamental to human life before anthroparchy, indicates that veganism might aid in this manifestation. What if human beings, as "great" apes, stepped up as familiars themselves and offered aid to other species? Might they use stereotypical human traits—including technological capacity and advanced rational thought—to create a more peaceable world for all species?

As a malleable practice, then, witchcraft might be further reconstructed to accommodate marginalized groups, be they human or nonhuman. In restricting its attention to humans, today's witchcraft continues a legacy of persecuting difference. Community, Starhawk notes (1999), reaches beyond those physically close to us to also include all those inhabiting Earth, as violence is today a very global and interconnected phenomenon. For logical consistency, this must reach beyond the species barrier. Persistent stigmatization of modern-day witchcraft may be a continuation of this pursuit of control and obedience to authority. To be fit for purpose, witchcraft's respect for autonomy and individualism must be balanced with solidarity and community responsibility. Self-interested indulgence will otherwise prove an exercise in privilege at the expense of others.

Vegan feminism looks to anthroparchal culture, not nature, as the source of oppression and society. Society, being pliable, is identified as a site for feminist transformation. Vegan feminism is also a vehicle for self-care in that it encourages the avoidance of toxic animal ingredients. It also reduces the cognitive strain that many experience in purporting to care about other animals while simultaneously eating them. Likewise, it is a form of community care in advocating healthy, sustainable foodways, particularly for groups whose diets have been colonized, leading to disproportionate rates of diet-related chronic illnesses for racialized and lower-income groups. It is a form of *global* care, for that matter, in reducing the unnecessary violence inflicted on Nonhuman Animals in speciesist economies and unnecessary violence inflicted on free-living animals and ecosystems straining under climate change.

Starhawk is clear that magic must be grounded with real-world action: "Integrity means consistency; we act in accordance with our thoughts, our images, our speeches: we keep our commitments" (1997: 35). Elsewhere, she has noted that "a change in consciousness changes our actions or it is not true change" (1987: 24). Eller (1995) agrees: "All the candle wax in the world cannot convince men that there is something wrong with rape, or the government that there is something right about economic parity between the sexes" (197). Tactics and intentions must align. Intention cannot be manifested without some effort on our part, and this effort must extend beyond the individual to also challenge human supremacy, patriarchy, colonialism, and, perhaps most importantly in the 21st century, capitalism. As a manufacturer of ideologies that have historically supported institutionalized oppression, religion, too, must also be interrogated—feminist, nature-based religions included. We cannot consume our way to social justice, nor can we pray our way to total liberation.

Veganism and witchcraft, respectively, demonstrate the importance of ethical consumption and intentionality, but they must put pressure on educational institutions, local and national governments, charities and nongovernmental organizations, and other agents of social change in support of just transitions away from systems that harm, especially speciesism, but also sexism, cis-sexism, heterosexism, ableism, ageism, sizeism, ethnocentrism, and anti-environmentalism. As feminist witchcraft has advised, anti-hierarchical, circular types of social organization that live in harmony with the Earth's rhythms are most appropriate in resisting oppression and ensuring true sustainability. Reminds Starhawk, "A Witch is a 'shaper,' a creator who bends the unseen into form" (1999: 32). What might the vegan witch deliver into creation?

Veganism is a means of ethical, political, psychological, and even spiritual resistance to humanity's violence against Nonhuman Animals, other humans, and the environment more broadly. By living vegan, witches can invoke power from their community, Nonhuman Animals, elemental forces, and effective strategies for social change. It is also important to be intentional in wielding veganism to manifest a multispecies society that is as equitable as it can be. This is a collective effort, but it also requires personal responsibility. Vegans, conversely, might also learn from the centuries-old legacy of witchcraft persecution and resistance, to consider how archetypes of female power and resilience might be adopted for everyday advocacy. Witchcraft's ritualism and the consistent, grounding attention it pays to nature can provide further emotional support for vegan activity. One of the most fundamental aspects of witchcraft is the simple act of spending time outdoors, observing and noting natural processes. Selena Fox emphasizes this time spent in nature as vital for stepping out of human-dominated spaces, acknowledging other ways of being and knowing to increase understanding of the world as well as the self (Puca 2023). Subsequently, while connecting with nature is the base requirement for doing witchcraft, a vegan practice might also include solidarity with other animals and a radical acknowledgment of the witch's own animality.

Witchcraft asks for both reclamation and creation; it does not seek to return to the past necessarily but instead draws upon bygone wisdoms and pieced-together traditions to generate something radically new and better suited to supporting a sustainable quality of life for all (Eller 1995). Indeed, it is this very fluidity, Lady Sabrina contends, that has allowed witchcraft to "adapt, change, and contribute to the social structure of its time" (2001: 10). The social structure of *this* time, arguably, is anthroparchy. The global atrocities enacted upon other animals and the associated crises of climate change and zoonotic pandemics, all of which are direct consequences of anthroparchy, must be incorporated into the witch's ethical scope. Vegan witchcraft thus calls on ecofeminism, paganism, and witchcraft more broadly to relinquish the immutability of tradition to best support the needs of the present. Horne (2019) agrees, wary of protecting outdated practices in the craft to maintain a superficial sense of historical accuracy, ancestral connection, and spiritual legitimacy. "If we look closely to the witch-lore, we find a world that is diverse, complex, and pluralistic," they caution (Horne 2019: 193). Witchcraft today must therefore determine what aspects of the practice to call into focus and refine them within the context of contemporary norms and values. "This discernment," Horne adds, will be "conducted under the guidance of familiar spirits" to root out and reject the racist, sexist, and heterosexist "baggage we have inherited" (193).

Greenwood (2000a) notes the importance of developing an imagination for these possible futures, what she refers to as an "otherworld" (26). This other-world is metaphysically envisioned, being both internal to the self and external in an alternate dimension. Knowledge and transformation, she advises, are found in regularly communicating with it. Alterity already exists, in other words, and need only be mobilized to activate it. Reminds Leek, "we do not think in terms of a future Utopia, but of means to make life, here, *now*, more attractive and harmonious" (1975: 196). Veganism is a line of communication to this otherworld, offering a means to reclaim humanity's connection to nature, its inherent animality, and its birthright to peace and conviviality as inhabitants in this universe. We can start this journey by embracing our shared animality and offering solidarity to other animals. In doing so, we must see them as cap-able and worthy in their own right and resist the anthroparchal temptation to reduce them to totems, symbols, messengers, servants, ritual tools, food or ingredients, and sacrifices. If we intend it, a vegan otherworld is already here.

And so it is.

Notes

1 This number is 300 times that of any other predator on Earth, with at least 1,300 times the ecological impact (Darimont et al. 2023).
2 Starhawk's The Reclaiming, Budapest's Coven No. 1, and Kheel's Feminists for Animal Rights were all lesbian centric.
3 McColman uses Wicca and witchcraft interchangeably (2002: 36–37).

References

Adams, C. 2000. *The Sexual Politics of Meat*. London: Continuum.
Ascione, F. and P. Arkow. 1999. *Child Abuse, Domestic Violence, and Animal Abuse*. West Lafayette: Purdue University Press.
Buckland, R. 2002. *Complete Book of Witchcraft*. Woodbury: Llewellyn.
Budapest, Z. 1986. *The Holy Book of Women's Mysteries*. Oakland: Susan B. Anthony Coven No. 1.
Cunningham, S. 1995. *Wicca*. St. Paul: Llewellyn.
Cunningham, S. 2007. *Encyclopaedia of Wicca in the Kitchen*. Woodbury: Llewellyn.
Darimont, C., R. Cooke, M. Bourbonnais, H. Bryan, S. Carlson, J. Estes, M. Galetti, T. Levi, J. MacLean, I. McKechnie, P. Paquet, and B. Worm. 2023. "Humanity's Diverse Predatory Niche and Its Ecological Consequences." *Communications Biology* 6, article 609.
Deutch, R. 1977. *The Ecstatic Mother*. London: Bachman & Turner.
Eller, C. 1995. *Living in the Lap of the Goddess*. Boston: Beacon Press.
Farrar, J. and S. Farrar. 1999. *A Witches' Bible*. RBJT6.

Foltz, T. 2000. "Thriving, Not Simply Surviving: Goddess Spirituality and Women's Recovery from Alcoholism." pp. 119–136, in *Daughters of the Goddess*, W. Griffin (Ed.). Oxford: AltaMira Press.

Gaard, G. 2017. "Feminism and Environmental Justice." pp. 74–88, in *The Routledge Handbook of Environmental Justice*, R. Holifield, J. Chakraborty, and G. Walker (Eds.). London: Routledge.

Gardner, G. 1959. *The Meaning of Witchcraft*. New York: Magickal Childe.

Greenwood, S. 2000a. *Magic, Witchcraft and the Otherworld*. Oxford: Berg.

Greenwood, S. 2000b. "Feminist Witchcraft: A Transformatory Politics." pp. 136–150, in *Daughters of the Goddess*, W. Griffin (Ed.). Oxford: AltaMira Press.

Grimassi, R. 2001. *The Wiccan Mysteries*. St. Paul: Llewellyn.

Horne, R. 2019. *Folk Witchcraft*. Moon Over the Mountain Press.

Lady Sabrina. 2001. *The Beliefs, Rites, and Rituals of the Wiccan Religion*. Franklin Lakes: New Page Books.

Leek, S. 1975. *The Complete Art of Witchcraft*. London: Leslie Frewin.

Levinger, N. and T. Whitehurst. 2019. "Episode 1: Intro, Healing Your Inner Child & Communing with Flowers." *Magical Mondays*. Podcast.

Lyons, S. 2019. *Revolutionary Witchcraft*. New York: Running Press.

McColman, C. 2002. *The Well-Read Witch*. Franklin Lakes: New Page Books.

Moura, A. 2020. *Green Witchcraft*. Woodbury: Llewellyn.

Puca, A. 2023. "Nature Spirituality & Paganism with Selena Fox." Retrieved May 16, 2024, from: https://www.youtube.com/watch?v=Dw2FlyWVVqM&ab_channel=Angela%27sSymposium.

Reis, E. 1998. "Female Speech and Other Demons." pp. 25–51, in *Spellbound Women and Witchcraft in America*, E. Reis (Ed.). Wilmington: Scholarly Resources.

Salomonsen, J. 2002. *Enchanted Feminism*. London: Routledge.

Sjöö, M. and B. Mor. 1991. *The Great Cosmic Mother*. San Francisco: HarperSanFrancisco.

Smuts, B., B. Franks, M. Gagliano, and C. Webb. 2024. "The Connection We Share: Animal Spirituality and the Science of Sacred Encounters." pp. 277–288, in *Animals and Religion*, D. Aftandilian, B. Ambros, and A. Gross (Eds.). London: Routledge.

Sollée, K. 2017. *Witches, Sluts, Feminists*. Berkeley: ThreeL Media.

Starhawk. 1987. *Truth or Dare*. New York: HarperCollins.

Starhawk. 1997. *Dreaming the Dark*. Boston: Beacon Press.

Starhawk. 1999. *The Spiral Dance*. New York: HarperOne.

Starhawk. 2005. *The Earth Path*. New York: HarperCollins.

Stone, A. 2022. "The Relationship Between Attitudes to Human Rights and to Animal Rights is Partially Mediated by Empathy." *The Journal of Social Psychology* 163 (3): 367–380.

Strauss, L. 1966. *The Savage Mind*. Chicago: University of Chicago Press.

Tillie, C. 2023. "The Decadent Diet of Aleister Crowley." Retrieved December 12, 2023, from: https://www.atlasobscura.com/articles/aleister-crowley-diet.

Valiente, D. 1978. *Witchcraft for Tomorrow*. London: Robert Hale.

Weekley, E. 1921. *An Etymological Dictionary of Modern English*. London: John Murray.

Weinstein, M. 1991. *Earth Magic*. Custer: Phoenix Publishing.

What Witches Do. 2021. "What Witches Do." Youtube video. Retrieved August 21, 2023, from: https://www.youtube.com/watch?v=0VZpJZ6OVUo&ab_channel=WhatWitchesDo.

FURTHER READING

Adams, C. 1993. *Ecofeminism and the Sacred*. New York: Continuum.

Adams, C. 2025. *The Sexual Politics of Meat*. New York: Continuum.

Adams, C. and L. Gruen. 2014. *Ecofeminism*. London: Bloomsbury.

Adler, M. 2006. *Drawing Down the Moon*. London: Penguin.

Conway, D. 2013. *Animal Magick*. Woodbury: Llewellyn.

Gaard, G. 1993. *Ecofeminism*. Philadelphia: Temple University Press.

Kheel, M. 2007. *Nature Ethics*. Landham: Rowman & Littlefield.

Ko, A. 2019. *Racism as Zoological Witchcraft*. New York: Lantern.

Luke, B. 2007. *Brutal: Manhood and the Exploitation of Animals*. Champaign: University of Illinois Press.

Lyons, S. 2019. *Revolutionary Witchcraft*. New York: Running Press.

MacCormack, P. 2020. *The Ahuman Manifesto*. London: Bloomsbury.

Mason, J. 1993. *An Unnatural Order*. New York: Simon & Schuster.

Morningstar, S. 2005. *The Art of Wiccan Healing*. London: Hay House.

Nibert, D. 2013. *Animal Oppression and Human Violence*. New York: Columbia University Press.

Salisbury, D. 2019. *Witchcraft Activism*. Newburyport: Weiser Books.

Sebastian, C. 2022. "Adaptation: No One Mourns the *Wicked*, But We Should." pp. 212–221, in *The Edinburgh Companion to Vegan Literary Studies*, L. Wright and E. Quinn (Eds.). Edinburgh: Edinburgh University Press.

Starhawk. 1999. *The Spiral Dance*. New York: HarperOne.

Weinstein, M. 1991. *Earth Magic*. Custer: Phoenix Publishing.

Whitehurst, T. 2015. *Holistic Energy Magic*. Woodbury: Llewellyn.

INDEX

Adams, Carol 9, 16, 21–2, 24, 62, 73, 83, 86, 90, 106, 145, 156
Africa 15, 39, 88, 112, 167–8, 188
age: aging, ageism 12, 30, 32, 65–6, 81, 133, 158, 164, 169, 183, 186, 197
agriculture 9–10, 12, 123, 129–33, 135, 137, 185; *see also* animals: agricultural use
alliance-building 3–4, 154, 180, 197
ancestors 53, 60, 77–8, 84, 88, 96–7, 100–1, 102–5, 114, 119, 123, 133–4, 165, 173, 187, 197–8
Andrews, Ted 34, 36, 39, 42, 44, 48–9, 55, 83, 106, 143, 144, 155
animals: agricultural use 12–13, 19–20, 23, 29, 38, 44, 49, 69–71, 80–1, 90, 97, 104–5, 106, 107–8, 110, 111–13, 114, 119–20, 125–6, 127, 129, 132–3, 134–5, 137, 184–5; oppression of 4, 12, 35, 41–2, 46, 51, 60, 67–71, 79, 97, 108, 113, 118, 125–6, 141, 175, 186, 189, 191–2, 194; religious use 8, 35–7, 60, 77–80, 83–6, 90, 101, 146, 186; societal function 8–10, 30, 48 ; *see also* anthroparchy; familiars; sacrifice; speciesism; totems; veganism
animism 54–5, *see also* animality; totems
animality 7, 30, 32, 42, 52–4, 136–7, 168, 175, 180–81, 194, 195, 198
anthroparchy 17, 51, 54, 60–1, 67–8, 71, 76–7, 88–90, 97, 110, 112, 115–16, 124, 126, 132–3, 137, 152, 158, 160, 175, 181, 183, 185, 194–8; *see also* animals, oppression of; domestication; speciesism

apes 42, 51, 102, 127, 184, 196
Asia 7, 14, 50, 52, 74, 88, 125; *see also* South Asia
atheism 3, 6, 23, 138; *see also* secularism; rationalism
Australia 169

bears 12, 39, 42, 48, 86–7
bees 81, 113–14, 143, 146; *see also* honey
birds 29, 40, 42, 45–7, 48, 62, 78–9, 83, 111–12, 123, 127, 144, 185; *see also* animals; chickens; geese; owls; ravens; turkeys
Blake, Deborah 17, 36, 38, 40, 45, 108–9, 155–6
Bloodroot Collective 75
bones 44, 76, 78, 79–81, 90, 102, 106, 109–10, 115–16, 127, 143, 145
boundaries 21, 28, 29–30, 31–2, 42–5, 50–1, 53, 61–4, 72, 82, 144, 146, 164–6, 169, 180, 194, 195
Budapest, Z. 22, 62, 74, 81, 102, 106, 133, 135–6, 160–2, 165, 169, 173, 176, 191, 193–4, 198
Buckland, Raymond 15, 23, 50, 84, 98, 101, 133, 191–3
burn-out *see* compassion fatigue

Canada 132
capitalism 10, 12, 16, 20–1, 54, 60–1, 63, 70–1, 76, 79–80, 84–6, 89, 97, 109, 119, 133, 152, 154–5, 162, 164, 169–71, 190, 192, 196; *see also* consumption

cattle 39, 40, 47–9, 51, 56, 81, 103–4, 107–112, 114–15, 124–27, 129, 131, 133, 135, 146, 185; *see also* dairy
cats 28, 31–3, 36–7, 39–40, 46, 68, 102
Celtic witchcraft *see* Ireland
Chamberlain, Lisa 96, 97, 99–100, 104–5, 107–8, 110–11
chickens 47–50, 51, 72, 81, 102–3, 108–9, 112, 119–120, 126–29, 135, 185
children 47, 49, 56, 60, 79, 81, 84, 90, 104–6, 110–12, 114–16, 125–27, 131, 147, 161, 169–70
Christianity 3, 4, 6–7, 11, 16, 30, 54, 84, 126, 134, 157, 161–2, 186–7, 193
colonialism 11, 19, 39–41, 43–5, 54–5, 60, 71, 84, 85–8, 89, 97, 103–4, 106–7, 109, 117–18, 131, 164, 167, 169, 170, 175, 186, 196; *see also* Indigeneity
compassion fatigue 3, 17–18
consumption 21, 63, 75, 97, 117, 145, 155, 169–71, 176, 182, 189, 192
Conway, D. J. 33, 34, 37–9, 43, 47
Cunningham, Scott 23, 96, 98–9, 100–1, 104, 107, 109–16, 125, 127, 130, 132–3, 143, 153, 155, 165, 187, 193, 194
critical animal studies 9, 22
Crowley, Aleister 16–17, 23, 158–9, 188

dairy 13, 35, 40, 46, 49, 56, 68, 72, 81, 96–7, 100, 103–6, 109–16, 118–19, 120, 125–27, 141, 145– 46, 185; *see also* eggs
deer 42, 44, 143
disability 12, 33, 66, 67, 106, 110, 133, 183, 186, 197
divination *see* psychic powers
dogs 31, 37, 46, 48
domestication 10, 19–20, 34, 47–8, 53, 68–9, 77, 88, 103, 108, 114, 124–25, 126–7, 137, 190, 195
dualism *see* boundaries

ecofeminism 4, 5, 6, 8–10, 15, 16, 21–2, 59, 61–6, 70–6, 84, 87, 89–90, 106, 127, 130, 156, 168, 190
Ecofeminist Voices Rising 74–5
eggs 49, 80, 104–5, 108, 111, 112–13, 116, 118–19, 120, 123, 127–29, 145, 185; *see also* chickens
emotions 3, 47, 55, 136, 142, 144, 162, 164, 172–6, 189
empathy *see also* emotions; psychic communication
environmentalism 3, 4, 15, 60–1, 63–4, 70–5, 81, 84–5, 87–90, 108, 114, 117, 130, 139, 147, 152–3, 155–7, 162, 167, 175, 182, 184, 186, 189, 197

familiars 16, 69, 101, 137, 176, 184, 188, 198; *see also* animism; animals; animality; totems
feathers 49–50, 79, 144, 146–7; *see also* birds; chickens; geese
feminism 14–15, 43, 45, 60–2, 67, 69, 76–7, 84, 89, 90, 107, 127, 135–9, 154–5, 157, 160–2, 173, 175–6, 180, 182, 184, 187, 191–4, 197; choice 152, 154–55, 161–63, 165, 168, 170, 173–4; *see also* ecofeminism; vegan feminism
Feminists for Animal Rights 73, 74, 90, 158, 174, 198
fish 37, 43, 46, 47, 84, 185, 101–2, 105, 107, 118, 124, 133, 136, 145, 185
food 1, 5, 10, 12, 18, 31, 38, 43, 45, 49, 67, 69–71, 78, 84–6, 88–90, 125–28, 130–4, 137–9, 142–5, 159–60, 166, 198; food justice 6, 96, 127, 167, 187, 196; *see also* dairy; eggs; meat; veganism; vegetarianism
Fox, Selena 64, 74, 166, 197
Franklin, Anna 32, 35–6, 45, 48, 50
fur 40, 46, 84, 143

Gardner, Gerald 14, 23, 43, 76–9, 81, 83, 159, 192; *see also* Wicca
gays, lesbians and bisexuals 16, 67, 73, 75, 133, 140–41, 154, 158, 160, 162–6, 175, 186–8, 194, 197–8; *see also* transgender identity
geese 42, 48–9, 103, 123, 131–2, 144
ghosts 46
goats 16, 23–4, 48–9, 83, 104–5, 131, 195
Green, Marian 18
Grimassi, Raven 34–6, 48, 53, 77, 81, 84, 90, 100, 165, 193

healing 1, 5, 8, 11, 18, 21, 31, 34–5, 38, 60, 64–5, 74, 89, 90, 95–6, 111–12, 115, 117, 127, 135, 137–8, 141, 157, 159, 167, 173, 189, 190–2, 195; *see also* herbs
herbs and herbalism 59, 64–5, 74, 82, 88–9, 95, 100, 106, 111, 113, 115–16, 117, 118, 126, 129, 130, 137, 140, 141, 142, 143, 145, 147, 167, 173; *see also* healing
holidays *see* sabbats
honey 81, 104–5, 107, 110–1, 113–14, 116, 118, 129, 141, 185; *see also* bees
horses 23, 46

hunting or The Hunt 9–10, 36, 46, 50, 60, 77, 79, 81, 83–90, 97, 102, 106, 124, 165, 183, 185, 187, 190

India *see* South Asia
individualism 1, 15, 17, 21, 39, 41, 51, 67, 69, 75, 80, 98–9, 110, 152, 153–5, 164, 166, 169–71, 176, 181, 192–3, 196
Indigeneity 11, 14, 15, 16, 39–40, 41, 43–5, 54, 86–7, 89, 103–4, 132, 134, 140, 144, 147, 154, 165, 167–8, 188
insects 37–8, 40, 37, 51, 79; *see also* bees
intersectionality 10, 12, 16–21, 30–2, 54, 61–2,73–5, 79, 87–8, 106–7, 118–19, 136, 158–9, 161– 63, 167–68, 170, 174, 180–1, 186–8, 192, 194, 196–7
Ireland 23, 33, 35, 39, 55, 105, 125, 127, 129–31, 132, 134–5, 137, 147, 187

Jainism 6–7
Judaism 3–4, 6, 7, 15–16, 30, 119, 157, 161–2, 187

Kheel, Marti 9, 66, 68, 73–4, 84, 90, 117, 124, 158, 198
Kingsford, Anna 159–60, 175–6
Ko, Aph 32, 44, 49, 87, 168

language 3, 34, 40, 41, 74, 78–9, 81–5, 182, 186
leather 46, 84, 143
Leek, Sybil 7, 15, 35, 50–2, 60, 66–7, 72, 98, 139, 15–57, 164–65, 192, 198
Lind-af-Hageby, Lizzy 160
Lyons, Sarah 41, 151–2, 154, 169, 172, 195

MacCormack, Patricia 18–19, 154–5
Mason, Jim 19–20
meat 56, 69, 71–2, 75, 78–9, 80, 88, 97, 101–3, 105–13, 116, 118–119, 123–24, 126–27, 132–33, 137; *see also* food
media 33, 41, 65, 69, 74, 83, 141, 159, 164–5, 170
men 23, 50, 71, 75, 85, 158, 161, 164, 196
modernity 4–5, 10, 13–14, 16, 21, 47, 59, 65, 80, 105, 118, 159, 169, 180, 182
monkeys 28
moon 44, 76, 81, 104, 123, 136–7, 146–7, 185
Morningstar, Sally 34, 38–9, 46, 48, 72, 138, 155
Moura, Ann 40, 59, 184–5
Murphy-Hiscock, Arin 35, 36–7, 48, 69, 109–11, 115–16, 127, 141

Native Americans *see* Indigeneity
Nibert, David 9, 19, 21, 75, 82, 84
nutrition 5

owls 33, 40, 42

patriarchy 9–10, 11, 15–17, 20, 23–4, 30–1, 47–8, 51, 60–1, 63, 65–6, 68–9, 71, 73–4, 77, 85–6, 88–9, 106, 111, 119, 124, 133, 136, 139–41, 154, 157–58, 160–61, 163–6, 172, 175, 180, 183, 185, 190–1, 195– 6; *see also* anthroparchy
Patterson, Rachel 33, 34, 36, 40, 42, 48–9, 73, 79, 81–2, 101, 108, 137, 143, 146
pet-keeping 17, 31–2, 34–5, 37–8, 46, 185
pigs 41, 46–9, 103, 107, 110, 119, 124, 129, 131, 133, 185
predation 7, 12, 42–3, 68, 104, 184, 191–92, 198
Protego Foundation 174
psychic powers 1, 3, 29, 30–1, 33–6, 41, 45–7, 55–6, 72–3, 101–2, 106, 110, 116, 134, 140, 159–61, 163, 172, 184

rabbits 42, 44–6, 131
racial minorities 15, 16, 44, 76, 86–8, 103, 109, 116, 118, 127, 154, 167–9, 175, 194, 196–7; *see also* Indigeneity
rationalism 3, 5–6, 10, 13–14, 20–1, 60–1, 63–4, 70, 84–5, 136–37, 159, 172, 180–81, 196
ravens 36, 39
reincarnation 29, 46, 50–2, 67–8, 83, 90, 123–4, 138, 146, 184, 195
reclaiming 1, 5, 17, 19–20, 28, 53–5, 77, 89, 124, 132, 146, 161, 164, 173, 175, 181, 195, 197; *see also* The Reclaiming; vegan witchcraft: possibilities of
religion 3, 5–8, 11, 16, 23, 30, 32, 38–9, 44–5, 55, 59, 66, 74, 78–9, 88, 112, 117, 119, 124, 138–40, 157–58, 169, 171, 174–75, 180–3, 186, 191–95
reptiles 37, 42; *see also* snakes
Robinson, Sarah 82, 97, 103, 106, 115–16, 127, 134–5, 138
Roderick, Timothy 33, 36, 43, 47, 48, 142

sabbats 49, 59, 80, 90, 105, 110, 116, 173
Sabrina, Lady 59, 123, 136, 137, 170, 197
sacrifice 1, 16, 31, 33, 39, 49, 59, 75–9, 82–3, 88–90, 97, 102–4, 109–11, 115, 127, 131, 134–5, 143, 146, 185–7, 191, 193–4, 198
Salisbury, David 154

Sanders, Alexander 14, 65, 76, 158–9, 165, 189, 192
Sanders, Maxine 14, 156, 159
science 5–6, 13–14, 61, 65–6, 74, 78, 112, 116–17, 118, 120, 159, 160, 183; *see also* rationalism; vivisection
Scotland 135; *see also* Ireland
secularism 3–4, 5–6, 13, 23, 142, 184
self-care 109, 174, 181, 189; *see also* healing
Severance, Juliet 159
sex 52, 127, 147, 192; sex magic 49–50, 53, 62, 77, 88, 107, 129, 130, 136, 139–41, 186; sexualization 16, 158, 165; sexual violence 16, 23, 68, 77, 85, 106, 139, 147, 158–59, 161, 164, 165, 173, 188, 196
Sheba, Lady 76, 84, 90
sheep 12, 40, 48, 78, 106, 125–27, 129, 131, 146, 185; *see also* wool
skyclad 52–3, 56, 159
snakes 35, 81
sociology 6, 13, 17, 19, 21, 32, 41, 47–8, 64, 71, 109, 113, 138–39, 146, 155, 157, 166
South Asia 6, 7, 14, 39, 50, 52, 56, 74, 99, 112, 120, 168; *see also* Jainism
speciesism 1, 19, 41, 43–4, 46, 49–52, 55, 71–3, 80, 82, 95, 97, 109, 113–14, 123, 131, 163, 166, 172, 184, 186, 189, 191, 193, 196, 197; *see also* animals; anthroparchy; veganism
spirit animals *see* totems
Starhawk 1, 15, 20, 34, 36, 43, 53, 61–2, 63–5, 67–72, 73–4, 75–7, 79–80, 85, 89–90, 97, 101, 103, 106, 111–12, 115–16, 123–24, 133, 139–140, 144–5, 151, 156–7, 162–3, 165, 166–9, 172–3, 181, 183, 187–9, 190–1, 195–8; *see also* The Reclaiming

tarot 33, 136, 170
taxidermy 44–5, 49
telepathy *see* psychic powers
Telesco, Patricia 101, 103
The Reclaiming 72, 97–8, 102, 162–3, 165, 176, 198
totems 39–44, 48–9, 137, 143, 186, 188, 198; *see also* familiars
transgender identity 9, 62, 73, 154, 165–6, 175; *see also* gays, lesbians, and bisexuals
turkeys 49, 106–7, 123, 132

Valiente, Doreen 23, 50–1, 53, 76–8, 84, 137, 143, 147, 158, 164, 185, 192

veganism 69–72, 89, 99, 101–2, 115–18, 124, 130, 134, 141–2, 147, 170, 173, 180–2, 187, 190– 1; definition of 2, 21, 95, 197–8; history of 4–5, 187, motivation for 2; philosophy 5–6, 8, 20– 1, 42, 46, 67–8, 171; prevalence of 2, 38, 98, 130–1, 141, 145; resistance to 60, 63, 72, 75, 85, 88–90, 98–9, 105–6, 112, 115, 140–1, 187–8; strategy 3, 5–6, 144–5, 187, 197; studies 7, 23, 186
vegan feminism 4, 8–10, 12, 22, 28, 32, 37, 46–7, 54, 60, 66–7, 71, 73–76, 78, 89, 99, 104, 107, 118–19, 123, 126, 139–141, 145–7, 151, 159–60, 173, 180, 188, 190, 194–6
vegan witchcraft: aims of 17–18, 22–3, 55, 119, 133, 141, 152, 175, 190–1, 197; definition of 1–2, 9, 16, 18, 22, 88, 95, 99, 146, 151, 175, 180, 181, 190, 194–5, possibilities 38, 47, 53, 55, 70, 75, 81, 83, 85, 88–90, 113, 116–18, 127–28, 130, 132–42, 145–6, 152, 171–4, 186, 189–91, 195–7; *see also* The Reclaiming; prevalence of 2, 17, 46, 100, 111, 114–15, 142, 176
vegetarianism 7, 22, 42, 60, 63, 70–4, 78, 90, 98–9, 100, 108–12, 114–15, 137, 159–60, 163, 166, 187–88; history of 5; *see also* veganism
vivisection 6, 46, 51, 66, 78, 117, 142, 160, 185

Weinstein, Marion 17, 33–5, 50–1, 67–8, 133, 139, 143, 151, 153, 193
West, Kate 96–8, 107, 115, 129, 131–3
Whitehurst, Tess 34, 37–8, 46, 48, 59, 72, 81, 100, 142, 172
Wicca 7, 14, 17, 23, 38–9, 48, 53, 62–3, 67, 69, 74, 76, 78, 90, 98, 114–15, 135–36, 138–39, 144, 153, 155, 170, 184–8, 191–5; *see also* Cunningham, Scott; Gardner, Gerald; Sanders, Alexander; Valiente, Doreen
W.I.T.C.H. 163, 173, 176
witchcraft: American 5, 11–13, 61–5, 72, 74, 84, 155, 157–8, 161, 166, 169–70; British 5, 11–12, 29–31, 33, 44, 48, 63, 65, 84, 156–9, 161, 169, 187; definition of 1–4, 14–15, 21, 23, 28, 88, 151–3, 156, 174, 180, 183, 198; early modern 11–13, 20, 29–30, 54, 65, 89, 133, 140, 152, 163, 174–5, 181–2, 195; *see also* ancestors; ethics of 2, 17, 19, 41–3, 51, 59, 62, 69, 72, 75–6, 79–81, 83–5, 88, 98–9, 105, 109–12, 116, 118, 138, 146,

153, 157, 170, 181, 191–4; *see also* healing; reclaiming; reincarnation; emergence of 4–6; organizational style 15, 52, 59–60, 62, 64–6, 123, 162, 164, 166–67, 169, 181, 189, 197; *see also* individualism; sabbats; skyclad; Wicca; goddess tradition 61–6, 67–8, 74, 77, 84, 117, 139, 158, 174, 183–4, 189; prevalence of 2; as social movement 17, 18–19, 63–4, 67, 133, 190, 192, 196–7

Witches for Animal Rights 174
wolves 12, 33, 39, 40, 42, 48, 100, 136
women 9–10, 11, 16, 20–1, 23, 30–1, 37, 44, 54–6, 61, 68, 70, 75, 77, 79, 84, 88, 106, 118–19, 137, 139, 140, 147, 154, 157–58, 160–2, 165, 166, 173, 175, 180–3, 187, 194
wool 12, 54, 125

zoos 36, 46, 144, 185